STANLEY COMPLETE

BATHS

Meredith® Books
Des Moines, Iowa

Stanley Complete Baths
Editor: Ken Sidey
Copy Chief: Terri Fredrickson
Publishing Operations Manager: Karen Schirm
Senior Editor, Asset and Information Manager: Phillip Morgan
Edit and Design Production Coordinator: Mary Lee Gavin
Editorial and Design Assistant: Renee E. McAtee
Book Production Managers: Pam Kvitne,
    Marjorie J. Schenkelberg, Rick von Holdt, Mark Weaver
Contributing Copy Editor: Amy Spence
Contributing Editorial Assistant: Janet Anderson
Contributing Proofreaders: David Craft, Sara Henderson,
    David Krause, Cheri Madison
Indexer: Donald Glassman
Cover Photographer: Blaine Moats

**Additional Editorial Contributions from
    Abramowitz Design**
Publishing Director/Designer: Tim Abramowitz
Writer: Martin Miller
Designer: Joel Wires
Photography: Image Studios
    Account Executive: Lisa Egan
    Project Coordinators: Deb Jack, Karla Kaphaem,
        Vicki Sumwalt
    Director of Photography: Bill Rein
    Photographers: Will Croft, Dave Classon, Scott Ehlers,
        Glen Hartjes, Shane Van Boxel, John von Dorn
    Assistants: Mike Clines, Mike Croatt, Max Hermans,
        Bill Kapinski, Roger Wilmers
Contributing Photographer: Doug Hetherington
Illustration: Art Rep Services, Inc.
    Director: Chip Nadeau
    Illustrator: Dave Brandon

Meredith® Books
Executive Director, Editorial: Gregory H. Kayko
Executive Director, Design: Matt Strelecki
Executive Editor/Group Manager: Larry Erickson
Senior Associate Design Director: Tom Wegner
Marketing Product Manager: Isaac Petersen

Publisher and Editor in Chief: James D. Blume
Editorial Director: Linda Raglan Cunningham
Executive Director, New Business Development: Todd M. Davis
Executive Director, Sales: Ken Zagor
Director, Operations: George A. Susral
Director, Production: Douglas M. Johnston
Director, Marketing: Amy Nichols
Business Director: Jim Leonard

Vice President and General Manager: Douglas J. Guendel

Meredith Publishing Group
President: Jack Griffin
Executive Vice President: Bob Mate

Meredith Corporation
Chairman and Chief Executive Officer: William T. Kerr
President and Chief Operating Officer: Stephen M. Lacy

In Memoriam: E.T. Meredith III (1933-2003)

Thanks to
Home Valu Interiors, Urbandale, Iowa

All of us at Meredith® Books are dedicated to providing you
with the information and ideas you need to enhance your home
and garden. We welcome your comments and suggestions
about this book. Write to us at:
    Meredith Corporation
    Meredith Books
    1716 Locust St.
    Des Moines, IA 50309–3023

If you would like more information on other Stanley products,
call 1-800-STANLEY or visit us at: www.stanleyworks.com
Stanley® and the notched rectangle around the Stanley name
are registered trademarks of The Stanley Works and
subsidiaries.

If you would like to purchase any of our home improvement,
cooking, crafts, gardening, or home decorating and design
books, check wherever quality books are sold. Or visit us at:
meredithbooks.com

Note to the Readers: Due to differing conditions, tools,
and individual skills, Meredith Corporation assumes no
responsibility for any damages, injuries suffered, or losses
incurred as a result of following the information published in
this book. Before beginning any project, review the instructions
carefully, and if any doubts or questions remain, consult local
experts or authorities. Because codes and regulations vary
greatly, you always should check with authorities to ensure
that your project complies with all applicable local codes and
regulations. Always read and observe all of the safety
precautions provided by manufacturers of any tools, equipment,
or supplies, and follow all accepted safety procedures.

CONTENTS

CONTENTS *(continued)*

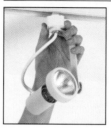

HOW TO USE THIS BOOK

If remodeling your bathroom is high on your list of home improvement priorities, and if buying this book is the first step you've taken, you're off to a great start.

Stanley Complete Bathrooms contains all the information you'll need to plan, design, and build the bath you've been dreaming of. Even quickly flipping through its pages will likely bring you ideas you've never considered. But this book is not just a large

wish list. It's practical. We'll show you how to turn your dreams into plans and your plans into plumbing, new lighting, sinks, and fixtures—all in a striking, unified design that increases the comfort and enjoyment of your home within the limits of your budget.

No other room in a house packs as much complexity in as small a space as a bathroom. There are wires and pipes that come and go through the walls—some with no apparent beginning or destination. Sinks, toilets, and tubs might seem to have been bolted there forever, with the rest of the bath built around them—so how do you get them out, how do you change them? Even the faucets hide small parts that work together to mysteriously control the flow of water. And somehow, all these complicated systems work together. So how can we change them?

That's where this book comes in. Although it might seem you should start by turning off the water, bathroom remodeling begins

before that with research, dreams, lists, and planning. Then you need an understanding of each of the systems and how they work together. Once you've got that down, then you can turn off the water (and the power) and grab your hammer and other tools.

Chapter One helps you plan and design your bathroom according to the needs of your family and your personality. Page through—or read it closely—and you'll find how to discover those needs and organize them into priorities. We take a look at the latest trends in bathroom design—from tubs to toilets, floors to ceilings—and how to choose fixtures that integrate the look you want with what you can spend. Even if you've already decided what your bathroom should look like, you might encounter design ideas you want to incorporate. And we've included a host of photos to get your creativity flowing in case you're having a little trouble making up your mind about which stylistic elements you want to employ.

An inventory of tools comes next, in Chapter Two, just so you can make sure your toolbox is complete, and if it's not, you'll know what you need to purchase or rent.

The remaining chapters take each bathroom system and remodeling task in logical order. Step-by-step instructions and photos will show you how to prepare the room by removing fixtures, walls, and wall coverings. Then rebuilding begins, and each of the following chapters illustrates how to

frame and finish walls; put down new flooring; renovate plumbing in your new design; rewire the room for electrical upgrades; install tubs, showers, and other fixtures; build vanities and cabinets; and install lights and fans.

What if. . .?

Since no two projects are alike, you may encounter conditions that depart from the norm. So if the steps shown for any task don't conform to your situation, check the lower half of the page for boxes that provide additional information.

Those labeled "What if… ?" help you apply techniques to specific needs. You'll also find "Stanley Pro Tips," "Refresher Courses," and "Safety First" boxes. These items contain tricks of the trade, quick reviews of methods found elsewhere in the book, and information you need to keep in mind so that your work proceeds safely.

Know your limits

Understanding your limits and time constraints will go a long way toward making your work enjoyable and safe.

Plan your time carefully—make a list of the stages of your work. Check the "Prestart Checklist" at the beginning of each project to get an idea of how much time it will take, and allow a little extra if you're new to the business of home improvement.

SAFETY FIRST
Keeping the work site safe

All remodeling projects come with potential safety hazards. Stay safe with these steps:
■ Set goals, allow time to complete them, and take breaks. Nothing makes you more accident prone than fatigue and frustration.
■ Keep tools spread out but close at hand. Invest in a tool belt or bucket belt, and put each tool back in the same place after using it. Knowing where a tool is saves time.
■ Wear a respirator when sawing, sanding, or doing anything that produces dust.

■ Eye protection is a must when sawing or chiseling any material. Get the kind of safety glasses with protection on the sides.
■ Knee pads and work gloves will save your knees and hands.
■ Have all materials and tools on hand before starting a project. Running to the home center robs your work time.
■ Above all, turn off the water when working on plumbing and turn off the power when doing any electrical work.

DESIGNING YOUR NEW BATHROOM

Like most rooms in the contemporary home, bathrooms have evolved over the years—in both their style and function. But unlike the evolution of other rooms, the transformation of the bath has occurred in leaps and bounds. The plain space that once defined itself in strictly functional terms with white toilets, sinks, and tubs now features sunlight coming from above; whirlpools; not one, but two (or more) sinks; lots of storage; and not just showers, but luxurious showers.

Market forces have certainly influenced trends in today's bathrooms. But many of the changes are because lifestyles are different from those in the past. We've revved up the pace considerably in the last few decades. We now have deadlines that push us out of the house "on time." That makes personal comfort and pacing more difficult. A renovated bathroom can take those few moments we grab for ourselves and make them just a little more enjoyable. It can ease the transitions at both ends of the day.

So what does "renovated" mean, exactly? Well, it can take many forms. At its simplest level, it's a transformation you can bring about with nothing more than paint and a brush. At the other end of the scale, it can mean knocking out walls, adding new ones, doubling or tripling the size of the bathroom, and installing custom showers, whirlpool tubs, color-coordinated toilets, and lots of cabinetry. In between you'll find many options. A small wall creates two spaces out of one. A well-placed mirror makes the room look larger. So do track lights and new fixtures.

A bathroom is a personal room—your room. Its design can evade all the subtle necessities required for the more public rooms in your house, such as the living or dining room. That gives you the freedom of expression to make your bath a place you want to be. And while a renovation can return some of its cost if you sell your home, the *ongoing* return on your investment is the comfort it brings each day. Besides, doing the work yourself leaves you with a sense of accomplishment. When you and your family members open the door, you can say, "We made this."

CHAPTER PREVIEW

Planning a new bath
page 8

Tubs and whirlpools
page 16

Saunas and steam rooms
page 18

Showers
page 20

Sinks
page 22

Faucets and showerheads
page 24

Toilets
page 26

**Vanities, cabinets,
and countertops**
page 28

Lighting
page 32

**Walls, floors,
and ceilings**
page 34

Universal design
page 36

**Building codes
and drawing plans**
page 40

PLANNING A NEW BATH

Many bathroom remodeling projects begin with a trip to the home center to gather ideas or just to see what's out there. There's nothing wrong with that, but don't start bringing new fixtures home just yet. You'll create a much more functional and useful space by making specific plans.

Planning is a process, and it begins with lists. The first list is a wish list—a written collection of everything in your existing bathroom that everyone in the family wants changed. That's probably easy, but you can use the questions in the chart below to make sure you haven't left anything out.

After you've got everything down on paper, it's time to pare it back to a list of what you need—with an eye toward practicality and your hand on your pocketbook. Maybe a new whirlpool tub would be nice, but it also might mean beefed-up flooring, new wiring, an additional circuit, and more floor space. A shower tower might be an effective compromise, and it could also open up space for more storage or a larger vanity.

How much space?

Practical planning will be affected by the available space in your bathroom. Sometimes an existing bath might seem too big, especially in rural homes. Most often though, the bathroom will be small, especially in urban homes built in the first half of the last century, when the bath was stuck in space left over or borrowed from bedrooms.

In an overly large room, you may have trouble coordinating the space and keeping it from feeling cavernous. Here's where short walls can come to the rescue, dividing up the space into areas that create privacy and spatial balance. By comparison, a tiny bathroom can present you with different design opportunities. You can make it larger by invading bedroom closet space. You can make it *look* larger with mirrors, lights, and accents. Or you can surrender, change its use, and turn it into a guest bathroom (a decision that requires a new bath somewhere else for the family, of course).

Priority needs

Once you establish the must-have elements of your new bathroom, put them in some kind of priority order. Then group them into categories—architectural alterations, major fixtures, floor and wall surfaces, and cabinetry. This is the order of things as they drive your budget. Installing a skylight, tearing out a wall and building a new one, installing a new tub, sink, or toilet, perhaps running new lines for them, and replacing windows are items that will consume the greatest portion of your budget. You need to account for them first before you attend to details such as faucet style and color.

Planning help

Even if you plan to do the construction work yourself, you may find that engaging the services of a professional planner can save you time and money in the long run. Rather than waste time trying to make tough planning decisions, why not let someone else help you make them? Once the

Making a wish list

Get the family together for a freewheeling discussion. Make a list of changes everyone wants, using the questions below to prompt the conversation.

■ Does the amount of space in the bathroom allow for convenient use by everyone who uses it at the same time, or do you have to schedule your use of the space?
■ Do you need a shower or a tub? Or both?
■ Do the children need a bath of their own to free up space for the master or family bath? What changes need to be made to make it safe?
■ Is the location of the bathroom convenient to the bedrooms? Does the bath have its own clear access from different areas of the house, or does bathroom access require passage through other rooms?

■ Does the door hinge conveniently to the hallway and the bathroom? Would changing its hinges improve convenience, safety, or access by handicapped individuals?
■ Are there sufficient electrical outlets and are they easy to get to? Are they located on one or both sides of the sink or in an over-the-sink light fixture? Are they GFCI protected?
■ Does the bathroom have enough towel bars for family members and guests? Are they located near the tub and sink? Does anyone want towel warming racks?
■ Is there a place for everything associated with bathroom use—towels, laundry, bathrobes, cleaning supplies?
■ Do you need more sinks? Or a larger one? More counter space?

The glass shower doors and the half-wall make this small bathroom appear much larger and more open than its actual size. The skylights allow for daylight and proper ventilation.

planning decisions are made, construction decisions become minimal. You can get three levels of help from different pros.

An **architect** can help plan your bath, draw the plans for all the systems—structural, plumbing, electrical, and heating and cooling—and turn them over to you for implementation. An architect can also supervise the work of any contractors.

An **interior designer** whose specialty is bathroom work won't be able to address structural or engineering details, but can bail you out when you're having trouble with the layout, materials choices, and the overall style of your bath. Look for the professional seal of approval—certification by the National Kitchen and Bath Association (NKBA). A designer receives that designation only after completing instruction and mastering the requirements of a rigorous training program.

A **design/build firm** will both design your project and build it for you. If you're intent on building the project yourself, you may find such a firm reluctant to be engaged for just the design services.

The separate soaking tub and shower allows for greater flexibility with different family members' needs and schedules, and the green tile bordering the floor grounds the space and adds visual interest.

This bathroom has it all: dual sinks for multiuse, plenty of counterspace and storage, and a window strategically placed to let light in. The mirrors can adjust to an individual's desired angle.

PLANNING A NEW BATH (continued)

The rich wood of the built-in and the elaborate mirror give this bathroom a grown-up feel. The display shelves, which add balance, may be used for storing items as well.

The dark wood is balanced by the natural light let in by the shower windows and glass doors. The half-wall between the toilet and the sink provides needed privacy. Towel racks and outlets are plentiful and placed for convenient use.

This serene space is created with a simple design. The fireplace adds warmth and the curtains provide additional privacy. Convenient cubbies flank the fireplace for storing towels, and the chair is strategically placed for sitting or laying out robes or clothing.

This custom sauna features a state-of-the-art heater that stores thermal energy and as a result can begin heating the sauna as soon as it's needed. A cedar door with etched glass separates the sauna from the shower, which is just a convenient step away.

This nontraditional bathroom is highly functional because of its separate pieces, which add both warmth and interest to the space. The side table allows a place for storing towels and bath items and displaying flowers and pictures.

STANLEY PRO TIP: Solve problems before they happen

Remodeling a bathroom can disrupt daily home life and requires hard work and money. It's well worth your while to plan the project thoroughly before you begin. A good plan will reveal problems before they occur and will suggest solutions you might not think of in the middle of the construction process.

The first part of developing a remodeling plan is to put together a program. A program is a list of the results you would like to accomplish by remodeling. Be as objective as you can when working on the program. Abstractions can actually help you in this process. For example, if you start out listing "more closet space," you are likely to be locked into developing a plan for closets in your bathroom. That can lead you to a dead end if there is simply no room for closets. If, however, you list "more storage space," you may discover better, more workable solutions—built-in shelving, overhead cabinets, or a larger vanity, for example.

Once you have your program, draw a floor plan of the existing space and copy it on tracing paper overlays. Sketch in ideas that accomplish the goals defined in your program. Draw each idea on a different copy of the floor plan to compare or combine them.

The smooth and clean lines of the oval pedestal sink are complemented by the square lines of the wood-framed mirror. The wall sconces flanking the mirror enhance the calming blue color of the walls. Towel racks are conveniently placed on each side of the sink.

MASTER, HALF, OR FAMILY BATH?

The results of all your list-making will lead you to the second phase of the planning process—establishing the size of the bathroom so it will comfortably meet your needs. Bathrooms fall into three general categories—master baths, half baths, and family baths.

Master baths

Large, luxurious, and often designed as a "home" within the home, a master bathroom creates a sanctuary for the owners of the house—usually right next to the master bedroom. Its design doesn't absolutely convey that it's off-limits to other family members, but it comes close. Because it's an upscale version of a full bath, it houses a sink, tub, and toilet, but doesn't stop there. In top-of-the-line master baths, you'll find everything designed for two. An oversize tub and generous walk-in shower, one or both equipped with massaging water jets or steam; two sinks in a large double vanity—or even two vanities—dressing rooms, and lavish surfaces such as stone and decorator tile, are features considered "normal" for a high-end master bath.

Not all master baths need to be created equal, however. For example, if no one uses a tub these days, put an angled shower in a corner or slip one into an alcove. That will open up space you can use for a double vanity and increased storage. If two sinks aren't in the budget, install a large unit with double faucets. Don't scrimp on counterspace, however—you'll need plenty of surface area for toothbrushes, hairbrushes, dryers, and cosmetics. You can forego the steam room, of course, but think twice about scratching the whirlpool off your list. The current demand for whirlpool tubs has driven the price down—a number of models are quite affordable. Dispense with marble tile and opt for colorful laminates and ceramic tile, adding tile borders and strategically placed accents, and you can create a luxurious master bath on budget.

Half baths

At the other end of the scale is the half bath, so named because it contains only a toilet and sink. "Powder room" is another name for it. Usually located on the first floor (with doors that open to a hallway and not the dining room or living room), it is often intended for visitors and used to eliminate traffic jams at the main bath.

You don't need any more than a 4×5-foot area for a half bath. Even 3×6 will do. That makes it a practical conversion for unused space tucked under a stairwell or into a large half-filled closet. And even though it's the abridged version of a full bath, it can still pack a design wallop. This is the place to let your creativity loose. It's perfect for offbeat design schemes, brash colors, and eclectic accents. Because the space is small, you can splurge a little on fancy faucets and surfaces. If your guest bedroom needs a separate bath, add a shower stall to create a three-quarter bath.

Family baths

This is the one-size-fits-all version of the bathroom, and it often comes (or has to fit) in a small package. Many family baths perform perfectly well in a 5×7 space.

The light blue of this half bath is calming and the checkerboard design welcomes you in. The skylight provides needed light opening up the small space. The wicker table adds a place to display a plant or candle, plus adds storage for additional rolls of toilet paper.

This master suite bathroom has room to roam. High ceilings enhance its spacious interior. Dual sinks give each person ample space, and a vanity and mirror provides a comfortable spot for applying makeup or sipping morning coffee.

Located near the bedrooms of the family members who will use it, it may have to accommodate more than one person at the same time. Dividing the space into zones of use with short walls will allow you to get the most out of the space. What matters is what the walls are made of. Solid partitions will block the light and make the room feel cramped. Using glass block or translucent materials like frosted glass will separate the zones and still leave the room feeling open. Enhance this effect by adding a skylight or new track lights and wall sconces on either side of the mirror.

A change in lighting, a refinished tub, and new color-coordinated fixtures can make over a family bath with very little cost. There's no reason to go to the expense of altering the plumbing if it's in good shape. Where you might want to spend a little more for looks is on the faucets. Even such a small detail as a fancy faucet can brighten up the whole room. Besides, cheap faucets don't last and will cost more to repair in the long run.

The windows above the soaking tub were added to push out the room and provide necessary air circulation. This bath is ideal with its dual sinks, separate tub and shower, and sufficient counter and storage room. The border tiles give a sense of playfulness to the space.

This family bath is bright and cheery, and the dual mirrors and pedestal sinks encourage camaraderie when more than one family member is in the bathroom at a time. The shelf on the wall makes up for lost counter space.

Kid proof the family bath

At a certain age, kids grow up and will use the bathroom without needing supervision of a parent. Plan now for their increased independence and safety.

Single-handled faucets are easier to reach and require less leverage to turn on and off. They will minimize dangerous overreaching by young children, and the fixtures will still look good years from now.

Antiscald guards will protect them from hot water surges when someone turns the water on in another room. An adjustable showerhead can help prevent falls. So can friction strips on the bottom of the shower or tub.

Grab bars will make the space safer not only for the kids, but for mom and dad, too.

Lowered sinks or a split-level vanity might be a luxury, but you can employ solid, rubber-tipped one-level step stools or a vanity with a pullout step that makes washing up safer.

STANLEY PRO TIP

Avoid the bath in a box

A bathroom is a box, but that doesn't mean its shape has to limit its styling. Don't just "think outside the box," open it up.

A bathroom has six sides—start with the ceiling. Incorporating a skylight not only breaks up the empty space above, the light that floods in can effectively double the apparent size of the room. You can open up the walls, too. Add a deck on the bathroom side and a door to the deck to create a solitary getaway for morning coffee. Replace an old window with a greenhouse kit—with a few container plants, you've got a second-story garden. You'll also be amazed at how much light this small change will bring in. Or add a new exterior door to a first-floor bathroom and it can spill out to your private morning patio.

FACELIFT, RENOVATE, OR EXPAND?

When you've decided whether you need a master bath, a half bath, or something in between, the next step is to figure out how much change you need to get the bath you want. Levels of remodeling fall into a number of categories. Choose the one that best meets your needs and budget.

Facelift

If your bathroom looks dull, but for all practical purposes performs conveniently, maybe all you need is a facelift. This means making only cosmetic changes to the surfaces of the room. You can repaint, add wallpaper, install beadboard, tile the tub and shower surround, change the flooring, and revamp the lamps, and for not much cash going out the door, you won't recognize your old bathroom.

Attack dark surfaces first—they create gloom. Lighten up the space with a coat of bright paint or hang wallpaper with a two-tone or simple pattern. What you want to do is create surfaces that reflect the natural and electric light around the room.

Next look at your lighting. Many old baths were lit with a single incandescent bulb and (maybe) an ornate globe. You might like the old globe, but you'll like the light from a track system even more. Tracked canisters let you put light where you want it. You can wall-wash one surface with one light, brighten the tub with another, and task-light the vanity with what's left over. Change the door on your old medicine chest or put in a new one—replacements install easily. While you're at it, those old fluorescents next to the cabinet ought to go. Hang new sconces where the old "cool" lights were.

Then tackle the furniture, even if it's only a vanity. They're almost always stained in a dark wood tone. That's OK for some design schemes, but you can brighten them up with a neutral-tone paint. Installing new doors can give them some originality.

Next look inside. Would your storage needs be better served by removing or adding a shelf? Fasten 1× strips to the sides to support a new shelf for towels or supplies.

Renovate

A renovation is one step up from a facelift, but it's a big one. It can mean replacing fixtures, changing the layout, and putting in new windows as well as altering the surfaces and lighting. A renovation will cost more than a facelift, but it's what you need if "inconvenient" tops your planning lists.

Some bathrooms can be made more efficient just by adding a sink. Others will work better if you add short walls to define individual areas. An additional sink might require a larger vanity, but even if the sinks are freestanding, the plumbing changes will be minimal. At this stage, consider a matching toilet too. It won't increase the usefulness of the bathroom, but the unity of style will make its appearance more pleasant.

If you're planning a major change, consider gutting the room and starting

This unique shower and bath design takes full advantage of the shower window that lets in a strong stream of morning. Additional window coverings could be added for desired privacy. The wide ledge in the shower is nice for placing candles and bath products.

The wall of mirrors extends to the sliding glass doors, giving a sense that the bathroom continues on. Dual sinks and a separate soaking tub accommodate more than one person and the rug adds needed warmth.

over—but try to keep fixtures on a wall with existing plumbing. That will allow you to change the location of the toilet, tub, and sink, making the layout more useful without making major changes to the plumbing. If you keep the fixtures on the "wet" walls (those that house the supply and drain pipes), you may only have to extend the piping to the new fixtures. Adding plumbing to a "dry" wall increases costs substantially.

When you actually start drawing plans (page 42), place the toilet first because it requires the most clearance around it. Then decide where you want the vanity, tub, and shower stall—in that order.

Expand the bath

Expanding your bathroom is a major undertaking, but still within the reach of most do-it-yourself homeowners. If the bath is just too small—for example, if you want to convert the old 5×7 family bath into a master bath—then you'll have to find the additional space. The primary source for more space

is hall or bedroom closets. Other spaces qualify too. If the kids have already left the nest and you have guest accommodations, the unused bedroom might be perfect.

In almost all cases, an expanded bathroom means one wall is coming down and another is going up. It also might mean cantilevering new floor space out through an existing exterior wall—a major structural change that ties into the existing floor. It's a job best left to a pro.

What if your expansion is not an expansion at all, but the conversion of a large second-story bedroom? This is one installation that might not require new wall framing, but choose a room that's above one with existing plumbing—a kitchen, laundry room, or bathroom. It's a lot easier and less expensive to extend plumbing up into the new bath than to run the pipes across other rooms to their final location.

This modern design features a vessel sink with sufficient storage provided underneath. The warm glow of the wall sconces provides task lighting and adds to the aesthetics of the room.

Rules for renovation

If you're changing the location of fixtures in your new bathroom, a few guidelines will help keep the layout convenient and comfortable.
■ Set the vanity closer to the door than other fixtures. It's usually the last stop on the way out of the bathroom.
■ Enclose the toilet, tub, and shower in a separate compartment for increased privacy. Close space off with pocket doors—they don't take up much extra space. Glass block obscures the view without shutting off the light to an enclosed area.
■ Observe the clearances required for all fixtures (page 41). This will keep the space comfortable while helping you avoid code violations.
■ Insulate new walls—this adds a large measure of soundproofing. Nothing feels more private than quiet space.

Guidelines for style

Once you have established the size and layout of your new bath, it's time to turn to style. A complete discussion of all the variables in good bathroom design would fill a book (or several). There are, however, a few guidelines you'll find useful.

■ Use color carefully. It's the most powerful element and can quickly overpower a room. Reds and oranges convey cheer. So do yellows. They will also make your walls seem closer. Blues and greens feel calm and will make their surfaces recede.
■ Textures affect mood too. Rough textures, like tumbled stone, feel casual or classic. Smooth and polished surfaces look modern.
■ Patterns in floor and wallcoverings affect the perception of space. Diagonal floor tiles can hide an out-of-square room. Squares will call attention to it. Vertical stripes make a room feel taller. Horizontal lines "shorten" the space.
■ Details can make or break a good design.

Think of vanity and closet pulls. There are a lot of them, offering a chance for unity and contrast.
■ A floor or wall can function as a background for the rest of the design or as the predominant feature of the room. Neutral colors and muted tones will push other design elements to the forefront. Strong colors and textures and bold patterns on walls and floors will attract attention. Make sure you don't start a visual war between the surfaces.
■ Scale your furnishings to the size of your room. Leave the ottoman in the bedroom if it won't fit in front of the bathroom corner chair. By itself, the ottoman would make an interesting accent.
■ Furnishings don't need to be bolted to the wall. If you have the room, incorporate freestanding cupboards and soft chairs.
■ A single bathroom floor level is not a mandate. Tubs and pedestal sinks on raised platforms make the floor more interesting.

TUBS AND WHIRLPOOLS

Modern tub designs are so varied and their accessories so numerous that about the only thing you can't get with a new tub these days is a steering wheel. You'll find corner tubs, freestanding tubs, tubs with TVs, armrests and neck rests, claw-foot tubs, tubs for a dais, contours, ovals, squares, and tubs in the round. Before you put your plans on paper, it's a good idea to take a couple of shopping tours through your bathroom centers and the Internet. You may find something that fits your design you didn't know was out there.

When designing your tub space, you have two options—either find something that fits your space or design the space to house the tub. Even if you have a basic alcove in which your existing tub fits, you may want to change the layout and the style or shape of the tub to make more effective use of the available space.

In addition to cost, four factors will influence your tub choice—style, shape, size, and material. However, after all is said and done, the most important consideration is the comfort of the user.

Style

Tub styles fall into four categories.

Alcove or **recessed tubs** are made with three open sides and one side finished with an apron. They are designed for three-walled alcoves, and they come with the drain at either end to match your plumbing.

Corner tubs, a variation of the alcove tub, also come with an apron on the exposed side and drains to fit your layout. They snug into corners, some occupying far less space than rectangular models. A further variation is the corner tub with both a finished side and end apron, usually rounded.

Freestanding tubs have four finished sides so you can put them anywhere. Claw-foot styles mimic the turn-of-the century classic, and so do pedestal styles (which don't require cleaning under them). For the contemporary bathroom, sleek linear styles make a stunning fit.

Deck-mounted tubs don't have aprons. They are designed to be supported on the floor and by a raised deck surround. Like freestanding models, they can go anywhere in the room.

Shape

Rectangular tubs are the most popular and are easily combined with a shower in a shower surround. In cramped quarters a space-saving square or triangular tub will open up floor space for other uses. Oval, round, hourglass, and other shapes take up more space but make a good choice for a master bath.

Size

Standard alcove tubs are sized at 32×60 inches, but 24- and 42-inch widths are also available. A whirlpool model can run up to 84 inches long. Most corner tubs are 48 inches on the sides that fit against the walls. Some are 5 or 6 feet long.

Material

Enameled cast-iron tubs are heavy, durable, thick, and hold heat better than any other style. They may require reinforced flooring.

Enameled steel tubs are made by spraying enamel on a molded steel base and baking it. They chip more readily than cast-iron tubs and tend to be noisy. Look for an

This private sanctuary features a deck-mounted, rectangular tub with privacy glass on three sides, a surrounding ledge space for candles, plants, and towels, and a convenient step for getting in and out of the tub with ease. The tub surround blends with the color of the walls to create a seamless transition.

The playful and bright design of this bathroom is enhanced by a unique corner tub and shower combination. The privacy curtains can be closed while showering or easily left open if soaking in the tub. This type of design makes the most of what space is available.

undercoat, which muffles the sound.

Acrylic tubs, made from heated acrylic sheets formed in a press, are reinforced with fiberglass, wood, or metal. They're light and come in a myriad of colors. They cost more than fiberglass models and are prone to scratches, but they offer better heat retention.

Fiberglass tubs have a polyester layer on a fiberglass base with wood or metal reinforcements. Reasonably priced, these tubs are not as durable as acrylic models and don't hold heat well.

Cast polymer tubs can mimic the appearance of granite or marble. They're thicker than acrylic tubs so they hold the heat better, but are not as durable as acrylic or cast-iron models.

Whirlpools

Whirlpools have been around for more than 30 years, and over their lifetime, they've gone from "novelty" to "luxury" to "affordable."

Most models are made of acrylic that allows for almost endless choices of shapes and sizes. Price is governed by size and the number of water jets in the unit. Costs range from a few hundred dollars to several thousand.

The chief attraction of whirlpools is the therapeutic massage created by the force of water coming from the jets. The water is forced through by air pressure—as much as 50 gallons of water per minute. All this aquatic activity requires a pump, of course, as well as new wiring, a dedicated circuit, and filters. Certain models feature timers, variable-speed pumps, heaters, mood lights, and mirrors. As the number of accessories goes up, costs and maintenance increase, of course. So when you purchase a whirlpool, you should know that you're in for a long-term relationship.

Installing a whirlpool *(pages 206–209)* is within the reach of most homeowners with even moderate skills. The easiest installation is one with a unit small enough to fit the standard tub-size alcove, but even a small whirlpool may call for beefed-up floor framing to carry the extra weight. Generally the most convenient whirlpools will be housed in a deck or tiled surround.

This oval tub features whirlpool jets to maximize the experience. The window makes the most of the natural light and takes full advantage of the view of the gardens—a great place to relax any time of the day. The tub is flanked by plants and candles that add to the overall theme of the space.

Great planning went into designing this tiled surround soaking tub. Its contoured seats allow for comfortable sitting and are made up of small mosaic tiles. There's enough room for some accessories and a window to take advantage of the view and curtains for additional privacy.

Sizing up your tub

When you shop for a new bathtub, take along the measurements of the space in which you plan to install it. The size of the space, however, is only one of the criteria you should use in choosing a tub. Factor in your height and how much comfort you want. Get into the tub to see how it feels. Longer tubs may feel just right for tall people, but too large a tub can feel as uncomfortable as one that's too small. Pay attention to the fit of any headrests and armrests. If you are not sure whether a particular model feels comfortable, then it doesn't. Choose another model. When you find the right one, you'll know immediately.

SAUNAS AND STEAM ROOMS

Health professionals have been extolling the benefits of steam for decades. Steam helps the body expel toxins, many of which are generated by the stress and pace of modern living. Steam rooms and saunas have long been a fixture of health clubs and spas, of course, but they have recently become a popular addition to the home bathroom, especially in luxury-bath or master-bath settings.

If you want a sauna in your new bathroom, don't be deterred by what you might think are their extravagant space requirements. Saunas don't need much room—some prefab units are made to fit a floor space of only 4×4. That's about the size of a small closet, and saunas can be custom-made to almost any size and shape.

Ready-to-install sauna kits are a do-it-yourselfer's dream. They come either prefabricated or as custom-cut kits. Both include everything you need, except the framing—a prehung door that seals tight to keep the steam in, benches, electric heaters, and other accessories. You'll get insulated panels with the prefab models, which speeds up your installation.

Installing a custom kit

Prefab kits limit your sauna to the size, shape, and design of the manufacturer. Custom kits allow you to build the sauna of your own design. You supply the manufacturer with the dimensions and shape of the space, and you get back all the parts cut to fit your design. You don't have to worry about picking the best pieces of cedar, redwood, or spruce for the sauna walls or the aspen or hemlock for the benches. You do have to frame the space, however, a job that requires details not needed in other framing projects.

This prefabricated kit sauna has elegant wood features and trim. There is plenty of bench seating and the shelves and towel rack on the outside of the unit provide a perfect place for storing accessories for the sauna.

Sauna walls and ceilings require insulation, so when you get the walls framed and drywalled on the outside, you'll have to install two 3-inch layers of unfaced fiberglass insulation, one on top of the ceiling joists and perpendicular to them, and one between the joists and studs. After that you staple the vapor barrier and nail the precut facing.

When you design your sauna, plan on a water-resistant floor—a concrete slab or ceramic tile is best, but resilient sheet flooring is acceptable. Also, even if you are an experienced DIY electrician, you may need to contract the wiring to a licensed pro to avoid voiding the manufacturer's warranty or running afoul of local building codes.

Steam showers and steam rooms

As an alternative to a sauna, consider a steam shower or steam room. Smaller than a sauna, they can be tucked easily into the corner of a bathroom or even a bedroom. Acrylic steam-shower units come with built-in steam heaters. Steam rooms require an independent steam generator. Both units call for additional plumbing and wiring.

Your DIY options include installing a steam-room kit or building your own from the ground up. Kits are the easier of the two options, but also the more costly. Installing one yourself is neither difficult nor complicated. You can purchase the components separately, including the prehung doors that seal tightly on all sides. Be sure to match the output of the steam generator to the size of the steam room. An overpowered installation will make it difficult to control the temperature. An underpowered unit can take forever to generate enough steam. As a guideline you can figure you'll need five kilowatts of power for every 100 cubic feet.

Not taking up much room, this sauna room was easily fit into the design of this master bathroom. You have the option of building your own or installing a prefabricated kit.

This steam shower features a water-resistant ceramic tile floor, and while it's tucked away in the corner, the glass panes and door give a sense of openness. The heated towel racks are conveniently placed just outside for easy accessibility.

This steam room is conveniently located just off the shower area.

SHOWERS

A separate shower, once a fixture reserved for the luxury master bath, is more and more becoming a standard feature, even in modest family baths. If your budget and floor space will allow it, a separate shower will prove a good investment, allowing two family members to share the bath at the same time.

Even if your installation can't handle a separate unit, you can add a shower to an existing tub. Installing a showerhead will require the addition of a diverter valve to direct water to either the shower or the tub. You'll have to waterproof the walls with ceramic tile, acrylic or solid-surface panels, or tile board. For new installations you might want to get a one-piece fiberglass or acrylic tub-and-shower combination. They're made to fit standard-size tub alcoves. And if nothing else will do, you can easily install a handheld showerhead *(page 189)*.

Shower stalls

Seamless one-piece shower stalls are made for renovation projects. Most common are the fiberglass models with an acrylic or plastic finish coat. Like other molded products, they come in a wide variety of styles, shapes, and colors, some with tempered glass doors. One of the newer options is the neo-angle stall, which is made to fit corners and is fastened to the wall studs on two sides.

Because they're one-piece and seamless, these prefab stalls are a breeze to clean, but that asset can also prove to be a drawback. A one-piece unit might not fit through the doorway of your bathroom. If your doorway won't accommodate a one-piece stall, see if a two- or three-piece version will fit. You can also purchase barrier-free units with either a low curb or no curb at all, providing easy access for persons with special needs.

Prefabricated shower pans

If you're looking for a little more than plastic on your shower walls, start with a prefabricated shower pan. Once you've put the pan in place and framed the stall *(pages 192–194)*, you can finish the walls with any material you choose. You can get pans in a variety of materials, even stone. Their primary drawback is that they limit you to manufactured sizes.

Custom shower pans

"Custom shower pan" is actually a misnomer—custom pans don't actually exist independently of the whole shower installation.

Building a custom shower starts with framing the installation and laying a mortared floor. An integral part of the mortared floor—and the key to the success of this installation—is the heavy-duty plastic

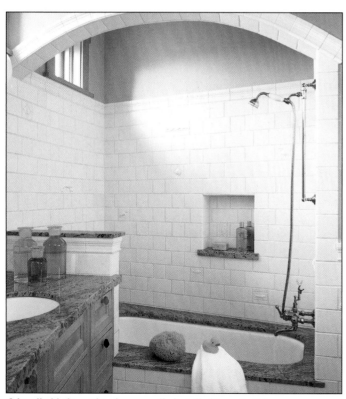

A handheld showerhead was easily installed to make this space more usable. It's great for taking showers and bathing children. A window was added for ventilation and to let in some natural light into an otherwise dark room.

This shower room is ideal for anyone with disabilities as it is easily accessible with no ledges. It also has dual showerheads and a bench was added that can be used as either a place to sit or store shower items. The privacy glass still allows natural light to stream through.

membrane that waterproofs the shower. Once the floor is in place, you can tile the walls, hang solid-surface panels, or build them from glass block. You can include seats, benches, and soap dishes as an integral part of the unit.

Shower towers

Shower towers are a relatively recent addition to bathroom accessories. Multiple showerheads deliver hydro-massage sprays under pressure. You won't need but one water line for most models, but the volume of water they put out usually requires a ¾-inch supply line that feeds only the shower and not other fixtures in the bathroom. You also may need to install a larger water heater or add a backup to your existing heater. Shower towers use a lot of hot water.

This modern design utilizes a glass privacy wall to give a bit more intimacy to this open space. The separate shower and soaking tub is a great feature.

An arched entryway complements the rounded walls of this open yet private shower. The cutout in the wall allows for storing needed items in the shower.

The strategic placement of tiles brings a bold look to the simple design of this bathroom. The glass shower leaves the room open and makes the most of the windows in the shower area. The shower has dual showerheads, and towel knobs are conveniently placed within reach.

SAFETY FIRST
Safe showers

In many bathrooms the shower and tub area is woefully underlit. Brighten up the area with canister lights or track lighting aimed at the shower (but don't install track lights directly over the shower—they're not waterproof). Any light directly overhead must be housed in a waterproof fixture.

SINKS

Sink styling has really taken off in the last few years, so much so that you should reserve several trips in your planning schedule just to go sink shopping. You'll find round sinks, oval sinks, square sinks, and "bowls" that sit on top of the vanity. Colors abound, but white is still the primary choice of home remodelers. Even with this almost endless parade of styles, all sinks fall into one of just a few categories.

Wall-mounted sinks

Wall-mounted sinks are fastened to the wall on a bracket, which is secured to the studs or blocking between them. Wall-mounted sinks leave the plumbing exposed, which makes it easier to repair, but may not suit your design. This style fits well in small spaces such as half baths and is the sink of choice for universal design. You can mount them at any height, and the clear space underneath provides easy access. And for those who don't like exposed plumbing, some models feature chrome or brass legs. The legs don't really hide the plumbing, but they offer a bit of visual distraction. Wall-mounted sinks don't provide counter space, but you can make up for that even in a half bath with narrow shelving close to the sink.

Pedestal sinks

Like wall-mounted models, pedestal sinks also get their support from a bracket attached to the wall. Underneath, however, lies a column or pedestal that partially conceals the plumbing and functions as a part of the overall sink style. Pedestal sinks are made in traditional and contemporary styles. Some have a wide surrounding lip, which can make up a little for the otherwise absent counter space.

Countertop sinks

This category further subdivides according to how the sink is mounted.

Self-rimming or **drop-in sinks** feature a wide lip that supports the sink on the counter. The bowl fits down through a hole cut in the surface. They're easy to install—the hole doesn't have to be cut precisely. Small deviations from the outline of the sink will be covered by the rim.

Integral sinks are molded of the same material as the countertop so counter and sink are one unit. Because there's no joint between the sink and counter, cleaning is easy. So is installation—all you must do to mount the sink is fasten the countertop to the vanity frame.

Undermounted sinks are fastened to the counter with clips under the edge of the cutout. This leaves the edge of the cutout exposed, so undermount models are usually found in solid-surface or stone countertops.

Flush-mounted sinks sit slightly above the countertop on a plane flush with the countertop material—usually tile. This calls for precise—and difficult—installation, and the resulting gap between the sink and counter can prove difficult to clean.

Vessel sinks are the latest innovation in sink design. They look like large bowls resting on the counter (but most often are recessed slightly into a cutout). Some translucent models can be lit from below to add a soft glow to the bathroom ambience. Others look like handwrought pottery.

Dual wall-mounted sinks made of a combination of stainless steel and white porcelain give this bathroom a sleek look. The towel bars on the sinks add functionality without taking up wall space.

Shopping for materials

When you shop for sinks, here are the most common materials you'll find.

■ Enameled cast-iron—Extremely durable and easy to clean, the porcelain finish resists chipping but its weight requires a reinforced countertop.

■ Vitreous china—Solid all the way through and finished with a highly polished surface, it resists staining and is not as heavy as cast iron.

■ Solid-surface—Made from acrylic resins and natural coloring agents, solid-surface materials often resemble stone or marble. The color and pattern go clear through, making scratches and minor damage easy to sand out. This is the most common material for integral sinks.

■ Stainless steel—In a mirror or satin finish, stainless steel is lightweight and often found in self-rimming sinks. It tends to show water stains and is noisy. Get 18-gauge steel with an undercoat to reduce the noise.

■ Cultured marble—Not marble at all, but marble dust and cast polymers, it is found in inexpensive integral vanity sinks.

■ Tempered glass—One of the mainstays of the new vessel sinks, it comes in a variety of colors and shapes.

Side-by-side pedestal sinks are ideal for multi-use bathrooms. In this bathroom, side carts flank the sinks to make up for the lack of countertop space.

These self-rimming, stainless-steel countertop sinks were easy to install. When cleaned properly they have a sophisticated look.

The handmade pottery look of this vessel sink gives a softer look to a modern design. The brushed stainless-steel faucet valves complement the design and are easy for people of all ages to handle.

Dual white porcelain vessel sinks keep this bathroom functional and stay true to its modern design. The shelves underneath can act as storage or a place to display a favorite picture or plant.

Traditional pedestal sinks make the most of the layout of this bathroom space. Towel racks are conveniently located next to the sinks, and the bench can act as a place to sit or store extra items.

FAUCETS AND SHOWERHEADS

Modern faucet designs are so plentiful that they almost defy categorization. Even showerhead design has branched out into a number of different styles.

Faucets may be grouped according to their configuration—their "setup."

Single-handled faucets are the mainstay of modern faucet design, and they offer a measure of convenience that two-handled models do not. You can control both the temperature and water flow at the same time. You can also turn them on with your elbow or arm if your hands are dirty or greasy. And if your model can be equipped with a memory-setting accessory (which consistently stops the handle in the same place), you'll get water at the same temperature every time you turn it on.

Center-set faucets are a style you'll recognize as having been around for a long time. Cast in a one-piece unit to be mounted in three holes, with the valve holes at a maximum 4-inch spread, most center-set faucets have two handles. Lever-style handles are easier to operate, especially for elderly persons and children. Cross-style

handles go well with traditional bathroom styles, but can be more difficult to grip and turn.

In a **spread-fit faucet,** handles and spout are independent of each other. Spread-fit faucets offer greater design flexibility—you can adjust them to fit mounting holes in the sink up to 16 inches apart. With some models mounted on the deck, you can set the valves on one side and the spout on the other.

Wall-mounted faucets are made for tubs and specialty sinks. They come in plain, inexpensive styles and top-of-the-line models, which make a noticeable design statement.

What's inside?
Although much of the price of a faucet will depend on its style and finish, even the most stunning faucet isn't worth its price if it requires constant repairs. Look for precisely machined brass fittings or ceramic valve components. Avoid faucets with plastic shells, seals, and handles.

Showerheads
Once upon a time, a showerhead was a permanent item affixed to the wall. It may or may not have been adjustable. Design experts will tell you that the single showerhead is a remnant of the past—though it's still available.

A standard **wall-mounted showerhead** is the least expensive and its neck is adjustable to change the angle of the spray. All but the bargain-basement variety offer adjustable spray patterns.

A low ceiling can reduce the height of the showerhead to an impractical level. To remedy this shortcoming, install a **top-mounted showerhead.**

The combination of a mounting clip and gooseneck hose makes a **handheld showerhead** a versatile and more efficient source of water than most other styles. That's because you can direct the water where you need it. If you're tempted to think "Special TV offer only," take a look at today's styles. Brass and chrome-plated models can hold their own with any style.

SAFETY FIRST
Install anti-scald valves

Anti-scald valves keep the hot water at a safe, pre-set temperature. Some faucets come with built-in anti-scald devices, but you can purchase and install them separately.

This sink features a spread-fit faucet; the valves can be closer or more widespread to fit pre-drilled openings. The valves control the hot and cold temperatures separately.

Nothing beats a **sliding bar showerhead** for families with children. This showerhead slides up and down on a bar fastened to the wall, and you can lock the showerhead at various heights to accommodate kids and parents with equal ease.

Something like a vertical whirlpool, **shower panels,** mounted on one or more walls, push water through jets to give you a whole-body massage.

Showerheads carry a flow rating that specifies how many gallons of water they spray per minute. Low-flow models are equipped with a restricting device that limits the flow to 2.5 gallons per minute.

Choosing your faucet

Faucet style makes a major contribution to the overall appearance of your bathroom, so it's not a choice you should take lightly. Obviously the quality of the unit will figure in your choice, but so should the compatibility of its style with the overall decorating theme you've chosen. Make sure the mounting holes on your sink match the configuration of the faucet.

These single-handled faucets are easy to handle, and the sinks were installed at varying heights to accommodate the needs of all members of the house.

This faucet combines the modern convenience of a single-handled faucet with a style that has more traditional lines. The stainless steel complements the granite countertops.

Offering the best of both worlds, this wall-mounted showerhead is paired with a sliding bar showerhead to accommodate family members of all sizes.

This soaking tub features a brass waterfall faucet that enhances the modern and relaxing feel of the space.

This wall-mounted faucet is operated by dual valves. Its design adds to the old-world feel of the sink and vanity.

TOILETS

Toilets make as much of a stylistic contribution to a new bathroom as any other design element. They may come in fewer sizes and shapes than sinks, tubs, and showers, but they still need to function as an integral part of your overall design.

All toilets are made in basically the same shape, but there are some variations in their appearance—as well as how they work.

Two-piece toilets are the standard configuration. They've been around since the invention of the fixture. They're made (and most often shipped) as individual pieces—the water tank and the bowl—that you assemble on site.

Just because this style has a long history doesn't mean it won't look at home in a variety of bathroom styles. You'll find polished stainless-steel units with hard-edged geometric tank designs, others with a wood-finished tank, sleek porcelain

models with contemporary lines, as well as many variations of Victorian styles, including a model whose tank fastens to the wall high above the bowl. All of the porcelain units come in a wide variety of blues, greens, blacks, off-whites, and other colors. In addition to the design variations available, you can dress up your toilet even further with custom handles and hinges.

One-piece toilets, a newer item on the market, come with tank and bowl cast in a single seamless unit. They have a lower profile than two-piece units and you'll find them somewhat easier to clean. The catalogue of their styles is no slimmer than that of other toilets. One Internet supplier features an on-line catalogue of more than 50 models, and that doesn't account for the various colors in which a number of styles can be ordered.

Elongated toilets, a variation of both

styles, feature a bowl about 2 inches longer than the standard bowl. They are more comfortable for tall people, as are **elevated toilets,** whose seats rise 18 inches above the floor, not the standard 15. Elevated toilets are also more convenient for household members with disabilities.

Two-piece and one-piece toilets are mounted to the floor. **Wall-mounted toilets** employ a tank hidden in the wall. They discharge wastewater to the rear rather than through plumbing in the floor. Their construction makes them quieter and their sleek lines make an excellent addition to contemporary themes.

Engineering

Just as the styling of toilet units has improved over the years, so has their engineering. **Gravity-assisted toilets** rely on a siphoning principle to flush. When a large

This toilet and bidet are separated from the rest of the bath by a door of privacy glass that provides seclusion and still maintains the theme of the bathroom.

This toilet and bowl are cast in a single seamless unit. It allows for easy cleaning and similar one-piece toilets are available in a variety of colors and styles.

volume of water (limited to 1.6 gallons since 1996) rushes from the tank into the bowl, it fills a siphon tube at the rear of the unit. This siphon tube empties, and that lowers the water pressure in the bowl, causing the water in the bowl to follow the siphoned water down the drainpipe.

Pressure-assisted toilets enhance the siphoning effect and use pressurized air to flush the toilet. More flushing power means fewer clogs and more complete cleansing.

Pump-assisted toilets rely on a pump below the tank to propel water into the bowl and down the drain. They're especially useful in basement bathrooms because you don't have to cut into the concrete slab to tie the toilet drain into the main waste line.

Pressure-assisted toilets make more noise than a gravity-assisted unit and cost more than the standard porcelain toilet. Pump-assisted toilets are quieter, but costly.

The eclectic charm of this bathroom is balanced by the contemporary lines of the single seamless toilet unit.

This wall-mounted toilet's tank is hidden in the wall, enhancing the design of this contemporary bathroom. This type of construction also means a quieter toilet.

This bathroom uses glass to separate the shower and bath and leaves the toilet and bidet open to the rest of the room, but the identical lines of the toilet and bidet seamlessly integrate into the space.

Bidets

Bidets have long been a standard fixture in many European households and are becoming more popular in the United States.

If your plans include a bidet in your new bath, purchase it paired with the toilet. That way you'll get consistent styling.

A bidet will require the addition of its own hot and cold water supply lines and a separate drain.

VANITIES AND CABINETS

The best way to plan for vanities and cabinets in your new bathroom is to forget for a moment that they're vanities and cabinets. That's because your first impulse when visualizing these furnishings is to think about how they look rather than what you need them to do. Think "storage" instead—that opens up a whole new world of design and functional options.

Storage space is woefully deficient in almost all existing bathrooms. Most notable is the absence of sufficient space for toiletry items and grooming supplies. At best, these are stuffed together in a drawer, lumped in plastic baskets, or tossed loosely on shelves somewhere across the room.

Your first design task is to make sure you have enough storage for these items and that what you use at the sink is near the sink and what you need for bathing is convenient to the tub or shower.

Furnishing the sink area

The vanity and medicine cabinet are the primary storage facilities near the sink in most bathrooms. Make a list of of what you need your vanity to do. Store toothbrushes and shaving gear? Hairbrushes and dryers? Cosmetics? Soaps and towels? All of the above? Once you know what this piece of furniture is supposed to do, you know what kinds of storage space it has to contain—drawers, shelves, hooks, or racks. Already you can begin to redefine your notion of "vanity" as something other than a nesting place for the sink.

To start with, the two-doored vanity without shelves or drawers probably won't do. Look for units that resemble dressers or at least include drawer and shelf space. You can even retrofit your existing vanity if you need to keep it. Tack wire racks on the inside of the doors. Install pullout or even stationary shelves supported by glides or 1× rails. Fasten towel hooks or racks to the sides. Even at discount department stores you'll find inexpensive fixtures in durable, tasteful styles.

When you get to the medicine cabinet, look for adjustable shelves that will accommodate items of different heights. Use organizers to keep small things readily available—and no more than two layers of "stuff" in each bin.

The bathing area

First you'll need spaces for shampoos, bath oils, soaps, conditioners, and perhaps shaving lotion and a razor. This space isn't really storage as such (although it's sometimes called "open" storage), just a place to keep things out of the way but still in plain sight and within reach—inside the tub or shower. Built-in niches in prefab shower and tub surrounds can keep things handy. In a tiled enclosure, mount porcelain shelving as you tile the wall (page 199), or build in a wide bench at the rear of the shower—large enough to let you sit without being disturbed by all the bottles lined up against the back wall. The back wall is also a great place to mount towel bars. They're out of the shower spray and easy to grab so you can dry off before opening the shower doors. If interior shower locations won't

This built-in cabinetry is strategically placed to be easily accessible from both sink areas. It is practical and offers adequate storage for two with a nice combination of drawers and cubbies.

Sufficient storage and well positioned fixtures are important to the functionality of a bathroom. Here the built-ins provide ample storage, towel racks are within easy reach of the sinks, and the freestanding lamp adds character to the design.

work in your design, try to locate towel storage close to the shower door.

Toilet area

The wall above the toilet presents you with a wide-open area for a cabinet—either a wall-mounted unit or shelving on legs that straddle the tank. Enclosed wall-hung cabinets are shallow, and you might not get your towels in them, but they are just right for backup toiletries, cleaning supplies, and paper goods.

Stock and custom cabinetry

Once you've developed a storage strategy, you can turn your attention to style.

Stock cabinets, mass produced and available at home centers, offer a surprising variety of well-appointed styles.

Custom cabinets are built to order by a cabinet shop. They permit more design flexibility and generally are produced with a higher quality workmanship, but come at a higher price.

For a distinctive style, furnish your bathroom with as much freestanding furniture as the design and space will allow.

Your vanity, for example, doesn't have to come from a home center or custom shop. The bottom section of an antique cabinet will make a turn-of-the-century vanity with a sink cutout and some retrofit storage added behind its doors. Paint an old glass-front hutch to keep things organized and show them off attractively—mix accents with towels and supplies. A modern dresser can complete a contemporary design and bring a large amount of storage space to your new bath.

Don't overlook the space between studs for storage and bathroom display. If you're installing major fixtures, you're going to have to remove the wall covering anyway. Design framing for recessed cabinets (pages 238–239) for storage and display. A cabinet also helps break up empty wall space while putting it to good use.

This mirrored vanity opens up to show adjustable shelves and a unique chalkboard for writing a daily reminder or a message to a loved one. Installing it above the pedestal sink keeps the area around the sink free of clutter.

This sink area has adequate storage underneath, and the shelf cutouts in the wall above the tub provide additional storage for towels and other items. The decorative mirror above the sink could be replaced by a mirrored vanity for additional storage above the sink.

This built-in vanity maximizes wall space with cabinetry that supplies plenty of open and closed storage, a large mirror, and a comfortable place to sit.

COUNTERTOPS

Although they don't have to take the abuse doled out to a kitchen countertop, bathroom counters have to stand up to water, soap, solvent-based liquids (like nail-polish remover), toothpaste, cosmetics, cleaners, and the occasional dropped razor or water glass. Fortunately you have many materials to choose from that will do the job.

Laminates

Laminates are plastic—hard, thin sheets bonded solidly to a particleboard substrate. An extremely popular material because of its low cost and wide selection of colors, laminates clean up easily and are resistant to most stains.

Once available only in solid colors, today's laminates come in a variety of patterns, some with a stone look-alike finish. You'll find a variety of finishes also, from smooth to tiny embedded squares (a nice effect, but a little more difficult to keep clean). When you shop for laminates, ask for a sample board. A large sample will give you a better idea of how the color and pattern will look. Small color chips can mislead you.

Laminates are tough, but not indestructible. They will scratch and gradually lose their luster. They are also subject to chipping when struck with a sharp object—something not likely in a bathroom. Unfortunately you can't repair chipped laminate. Hair dyes will stain a laminate surface permanently, and abrasive cleaners will quickly destroy its luster.

Solid-surface material

Solid-surface materials are also plastic—sheets molded (often with an integral sink) from acrylic resins and natural coloring agents. Solid-surface material has become very popular, largely because of the variety of styles and colors. It is almost completely impervious to stains and it won't mildew. You should avoid abrasive cleaners on this product, but if it gets nicked or scratched, you can polish out the damage with fine sandpaper or a polishing agent made by the manufacturer.

Ceramic tile

Tile is a long-standing favorite for countertops. No other material offers as many colors, patterns, finishes, and shapes

Now available in a variety of colors and textures, and fairly durable, laminate is a popular choice for bathroom countertops. This bold red countertop adds playfulness to the already cheery bathroom.

Impervious to stains, solid-surface material is increasingly popular. This bath combines the practicality of the vibrant green solid surface with the accent of a ceramic tile backsplash.

as tile. Their hard surface makes them stain- and wear-resistant, and you can't damage them with the heat from your hair dryer. Your chief concern with ceramic tile will be the grout lines. Grout is not impervious and needs to be sealed to keep it from staining. You'll have to keep the grout scrubbed clean to maintain its initial appearance, and periodically reseal the joints.

Cultured marble

Cultured marble is an inexpensive alternative to stone made from marble dust and resins covered with a wear coat. Most often you'll find it in your home center with an integral sink. It's easy to install but difficult to maintain. The gel coat can develop spider-web crazing and it scratches easily. It's probably not the best choice for a children's bath, but is better placed in a guest bath where it won't see as much use.

Stone

There's probably no material that can equal stone for its beauty and durability. Granite is the most popular for countertops because it is the hardest and most stain-resistant. Marble runs a close second and offers a larger variety of colors and patterns. Marble, however, can be soft—much softer than granite—and even sealing it provides no guarantee against stains. Slate, bluestone, and sandstone offer additional choices for bathroom countertops.

Making a solid base

Ceramic tile and stone countertops require a sound, smooth base so the surface material won't crack. The best substrate for these materials is a combination of plywood topped with cement backerboard. Such an installation requires only basic skills and a few tools. For information about building a solid base for tile and stone, see *pages 222–223*.

You may choose between stone slabs or tiles for your countertop. Leave slab installation to the pros. A stone-tiled countertop is an easy do-it-yourself project.

Concrete, glass, and wood

These materials are increasingly finding their way into bathroom design as consumers and designers look for new ways to beautify a bathroom. Concrete is durable, heavy, but not completely stain resistant. Glass adds interest and can make a small space seem larger. Get frosted glass to hide scratches and think about this material for a bathroom that doesn't get much use. Wood brings a touch of elegance to a bathroom, but is extremely prone to all of the damages associated with bath use. If you're considering these materials, be sure to research their limitations as well as their maintenance requirements.

With proper care this neutral ceramic tile will withstand the test of time. Tile grout lines must be periodically cleaned and resealed.

This granite countertop becomes the focal point of this otherwise neutral bathroom. The cut of the granite complements the lines of the space and its classic look will stand the test of time.

LIGHTING

Lighting is critical to both the aesthetic appearance of your bathroom and its safety and convenience. Once you have the layout of your bathroom complete, develop a lighting plan. Good lighting means more than sticking canisters in the ceiling and sconces on the wall. It means lighting the room without creating shadows or glare. You can achieve the effect you want by combining two or three kinds of lighting using a mixture of fixtures.

General lighting

General lighting casts light evenly across the entire room, usually from one or two ceiling fixtures, depending on the size of the bathroom. For most baths you can light up to about 35 square feet with one fixture. More floor space will require additional fixtures. General lighting provides the base lighting to which you'll need to add task and accent lighting.

Task lighting

Task lighting focuses on a specific area where you'll be engaged in activities such as applying makeup, shaving, or bathing. The goal of task lighting is to illuminate the area without casting shadows. Wall sconces are perfect for the bathroom mirror because they don't cast shadows. You may also want to light the shower and tub area, especially if your plan calls for half-walls to separate them from the rest of the space.

Check your building codes before installing tub and shower lighting. Most codes specify vapor-proof downlights. Place them so they light up the area but don't shine in your eyes when you're relaxing in the tub. Install the switch at least 6 feet from the tub or shower.

Accent lighting

Accent lighting is a little like theatrical spotlighting, only on a smaller scale. Its purpose is to call attention to an architectural detail, a work of art, or other object whose function is strictly aesthetic. Soft light that washes over the surface of the object creates a better effect than glaring light.

Fixtures

No single fixture can do all your lighting jobs, even in a small bathroom. You'll need a combination of styles.

Canister lights are made to be recessed in the ceiling and provide downlight. They are an excellent source of general and task lighting. To get even, uninterrupted coverage, set them so their light patterns overlap. You can get this information from the canister packaging or from your retail staff.

Recessed lighting fixtures are spread evenly throughout this bathroom space, working to provide both general and task lighting.

This light fixture adds to the aesthetic qualities of the space as well as to the general lighting of the room by providing lighting for a specific task.

Pendant lighting is hung by a chain or wire from the ceiling and can provide both general and task lighting. Pendant lights tend to attract attention, especially in a small bathroom, so if you don't want your light to be the main attraction, choose a different fixture.

Surface-mounted lights, made generally for wall mounting, are available in many styles for both incandescent and fluorescent bulbs. Wall sconces are an example of a surface-mounted fixture. So are track lights, which let you aim the light from separate bulbs at different areas. Surface-mounted fixtures are much easier to mount than canister lights—you don't have to cut into the ceiling to install them.

Bulbs

There's a tremendous difference in the kind of light coming from different bulbs.

Incandescent bulbs, the most common and the style that has been around since the bulb was invented, cast light in different color ranges depending on their wattage and the kind of internal frosting or coating. Once voluminous energy eaters, incandescents are now longer lasting and more energy efficient.

Fluorescent lights use a gas in the bulb that emits light when fired by filaments at both ends. They are more energy efficient and longer lasting than incandescents. In their early days, they produced only a cool blue-white light, but now offer a wider spectrum of colors. Subcompact models are made to fit standard incandescent sockets.

Halogen bulbs are filled with a gas that emits a powerful, bright white light. They can make excellent accent lights, but they produce a tremendous amount of heat. Make sure you mount them in a fixture designed for halogen bulbs.

Halogen bulbs lining the edge of the mirror fulfill the need for adequate task lighting and act as a focal point—adding to the overall design of the bathroom.

The recessed light above the sink sends off a soft light that is both general and task oriented. The light bounces off the soft color of the walls and creates a warm visual effect.

This bathroom houses a combination of recessed lighting, track lighting, and wall sconces that can be used in combination for maximum light or separately for specific activities.

Lighting the bathroom mirror

Lighting the bathroom mirror might qualify as the most important lighting task you accomplish in your bathroom. This is the primary grooming center, and you need to light it evenly, without shadows. Those movie-star lights that surround a mirror completely are there for a reason: they eliminate shadows. This may not be what you're looking for in your bathroom design, however.

To get the same even lighting, you'll need one or two fixtures above the mirror placed so their light falls over the front edge of the sink and countertop. Two lights centered on each side of the mirror will provide enough cross-lit illumination.

Be sure to use bulbs made especially for vanity-mirror use. They produce light in the daylight range.

WALLS, FLOORS, AND CEILINGS

All materials used on bathroom surfaces have to meet three standards: They must be durable, resistant to water and humidity, and easy to clean. To choose the material that's right for your bathroom, consider how much wear and tear it will have to endure, how the pattern and color match your design, and how much you can afford to spend on it.

Drywall
Drywall is the most widely used wall covering because it's inexpensive, easy to install, and functions as a substrate for many wall coverings. It's fine for bathroom use except in tub and shower areas. **Greenboard** is a moisture-resistant variety of drywall.

Paint and wallpaper
You can use paint to dress up the appearance of your bathroom walls, ceilings, furnishings, and trim. Flat or matte surfaces create a more subtle effect than gloss paints, but glossy surfaces are easier to clean. Wallpaper for a bathroom must be either a textured-vinyl product or vinyl coated. Even the more expensive brands tend to lift at the corners and edges.

Ceramic tile
No material does a better job of meeting the demands of a bathroom floor than ceramic tile. Carefully chosen, tile will unify the design of the entire room.

If you're planning tile for your bathroom, think of the tub, vanity, sink, walls, floor, and fixtures as an ensemble, and experiment with designs for the entire room. Take tile samples home so you can judge their appearance, and don't focus too much on single-color themes. A little variety can improve your design. Use accents sparingly—they'll overwhelm a small space.

As you shop for ceramic tile for your bath, think small, at least at first. Tiles four inches or less fit more easily around sinks, tubs, and toilets, and require less cutting. Choose vitreous tile, either glazed or unglazed. Glazed tiles on the walls are much easier to clean than those with a matte finish.

Be wary of glazed tiles on floors—they're slippery. Use tiles with a matte finish and seal them with enough sealer that water beads on the surface. Mosaic tiles are great for the floors. Their abundance of grouted joints makes the floor virtually slip-free.

Stone
Stone tiles make a beautiful, classic, and durable floor or wallcovering, but in addition to their cost, they come with certain drawbacks, depending on the kind of stone and where you use it.

Polished stone is not a good choice for floors—it's too slippery when wet and can cause dangerous falls. Tumbled stone surfaces like marble have a warm soft texture, but won't wear as well as some materials. Both polished and matte-finished stone work fine on bathroom walls.

Laminate flooring
Laminate flooring should not be confused with its countertop counterpart. This flooring

This bathroom has a Victorian theme with matching chintz wallpaper and privacy curtain around the claw-foot tub. Bathroom wallpaper should be vinyl coated or made of a textured vinyl.

The dark wood floors give this bathroom a timeless look and are complemented by the stone tile wall that transitions into the shower area.

is made in many layers—a high-density fiberboard core covered with a bonding layer, a print layer (which is actually a photograph of the pattern you've chosen), and a hard, clear melamine wearcoat.

Laminate offers many choices of colors and patterns, and its hard surface resists damage from dents and furniture. It is, however, prone to scratches and can't be refinished or repaired. Not all laminates will work on bathroom floors, so check the manufacturer's warranty. Even snap-together planks, which are very easy to install, require glue in their joints to seal them against water damage.

Resilient flooring

Resilient sheet and tile flooring combines appearance, durability, and various colors and patterns with ease of installation. No flooring is completely dent proof, but resilients come close. Their surface is made to "bounce back" when whatever is causing the compressive pressure is removed. This is an excellent flooring choice for a children's bathroom or family bath. It has a soft "walk," resists stains, and is easy to keep clean.

Wood

Wood can add a feeling of quality, permanence, and elegance to a bathroom, whether installed as a floor or wallcovering. Beadboard paneling can turn a bathroom style into country or Victorian, and today's products go up quickly *(pages 102–103)*. Tongue-and-groove panels and milled planks also make a good wainscoting. Hardwood flooring, though stately, is not the best choice for bathroom floors—especially in bathrooms used by children—because of its susceptibility to water damage. In any case, woods used in a bathroom must be sealed with a high-quality polyurethane varnish.

Solid-surface panels

The same solid-surface materials found in countertops are also available in sheets for covering walls. They are too soft and damage-prone to be suitable for floors, but they make a good wallcovering, even in showers and tub surrounds. Most of these materials are hung on the wall with adhesives designed specifically for this purpose. Joining two sheets is usually accomplished by slipping them into "tracks," which are also designed for this material.

Plaster

Thin-coat earthen plasters are rapidly moving into the realm of wallcoverings. You can use them to create textures and colors reminiscent of the work of Venetian craftsmen. They are remarkably easy to apply and are compatible with all existing wall surfaces. These plasters won't stand up to direct and constant water sprays, so don't use them on shower walls. They are fine for other bathroom walls, though some manufacturers recommend that they be sealed. Search the Internet for "earthen plasters."

Cement backerboard

Made in sheets of cement-based fibrous compound, backerboard resists water and provides a stable and strong base for ceramic tile.

White beadboard paneling is used on the walls to add a Victorian flair and the mosaic tile floor offers a practical surface.

This modern bathroom's uniformity is primarily created through the installation of the same stone for both the walls and the floors. The glass shower leaves the space open and allows the natural light of the window to illuminate the whole space.

UNIVERSAL DESIGN—DIMENSIONS FOR ACCESSIBILITY

In the past, the design of rooms in almost every house often presented obstacles to the elderly or people with disabilities. Nowhere was this more true than in the bathroom. But a growing list of products engineered for easier use plus some basic design changes now can be combined to create an accessible bath in any home. Often these changes benefit everyone in a household, as well as relatives and guests.

Careful planning

Planning a bath for an individual with special needs requires individualized planning. Base your design on what the family member can do, not on what can't be done. If you don't know specific likes and dislikes, ask questions. The first and most obvious requirement for an accessible bathroom is that it be located on the first floor of the house.

Floors

Floors can be potentially hazardous even for persons without special needs. If you're not replacing a tile floor, coat it with a slip-resistant glaze. If you're putting down a new floor, mosaic tiles and matte-finished vinyl are good choices because they provide some traction. They also reduce glare, which can make navigation easier for persons with impaired vision.

Make sure all bathroom floors are level and remove area rugs for wheelchair safety. Rubber-backed rugs are mandatory—even if no one in the house uses a wheelchair. Nothing slides across a floor more quickly than an unbacked rug.

Toilets

The least costly and quickest modification you can provide to an existing toilet is a height adapter, a snap-on accessory that raises the seat to a comfortable height. If you're replacing the toilet, you can attach a wall-mounted unit at any height. Other replacement options include a higher or lower profile fixture or an elongated or oval seat. The important thing is that you tailor the fixture to individual needs.

Vanities and sinks

Improve access to vanity and cabinet doors with contoured handles or magnetic catches. Install cabinets with pull-down shelving for persons in a wheelchair.

The height of countertops is also a matter for individual design. The height that's perfect for a wheelchair will be too low for another family member. The easiest solution is sectional countertops, each installed at a different height. A height of 34 to 36 inches is standard. Install a section 30 to 32 inches above the floor for seated users.

Adding a new sink to your bathroom allows you to customize it for accessibility. Faucets at the rear of the sink can be hard to reach. As a rule, mount the sink with its rear edge 21 inches from the front of the vanity. If such a location would still not be accessible, mount a single-handled faucet or wide-set faucets with lever handles at the side of the sink. The open space under the sink and counter should be 29 inches high and 32 to 36 inches wide. In some bathrooms the easiest solution may be to

This hidden niche underneath the sink is easily pulled out and houses a shelving unit for storing bathroom items at a level that is easy to reach for everyone—regardless of age or limitation.

The height adapter attached to this toilet allows the user to rise to a comfortable height, and the grab bars are strategically placed next to the toilet and tub. The matte-finished vinyl will help guard against slipping.

fasten a wall-mounted sink at a height of 30 to 32 inches.

Tubs and showers

Traditional tubs and showers come with impediments that are natural to the design of the fixture. They're slippery, have high sides, and controls that might be out of reach. There are a number of accessories, however, that will improve the safety of these fixtures.

First, tape slip-resistant adhesive strips to tub and shower floors. Install grab bars *(pages 218–219)*, removing a section of the wall to install blocking, if necessary. Add shower seating—transfer seats, backed seats, and stools are available at hospital supply stores. If you're tiling your tub or shower surround, add a permanent seat 18 inches high and 15 inches deep.

If your plans call for a new tub or shower, your options for making the bath accessible increase dramatically. Side-mounted fixtures allow the water to be turned on and adjusted before getting into the tub. Side-

access tubs feature doors that eliminate stepping over the side. A curbless shower makes wheelchair entry safe and easy.

Doorways and open areas

The first priority for persons using a wheelchair is easy access. Make the doorway in your new bathroom 34 inches wide, and hinge the door so it swings out, not in. Doors wider than this can be difficult to open, and narrower doorways make access difficult or impossible.

Remove any high thresholds and replace them with low-profile transitions. Round doorknobs might prove difficult to turn. Install lever handles.

Inside the bathroom, a wheelchair needs an open area of at least 5 feet in diameter to turn easily. The amount of open space in front of and between fixtures is important too. You'll need at least 4 feet of clear space in front of the sink and the toilet, if both are on the same wall.

The elongated oval toilet and the grab bar provide comfortable transitioning and the counter height is set at the correct height and depth for someone in a wheelchair to easily access the sink area.

This sink has large, easy-to-use handles and roll-under space beneath. The tub and shower unit, right, has solid, well-placed grab bars, a stable and slip-resistant seat, and a handheld shower unit.

UNIVERSAL DESIGN (continued)

Customize your plan

Don't just follow the rules; make sure your layout and fixtures will be useful for everyone in your family now and in the future. Whenever possible test a product or layout ahead of time to make sure it can be used easily by a person in a wheelchair or walker.

Purchase ADA-approved grab bars and position them with these two purposes in mind: A grab bar should enable a person to easily enter and exit an area; there should be a grab bar at a convenient location so a person can reach it in case of a slip or fall. Be sure to anchor grab bars with screws driven deeply into studs.

This shower features an adjustable showerhead, strategically placed grab bars, a bench for sitting, and a mosaic tile floor to provide traction.

The roll-in shower allows for easy access for a wheelchair into the shower area.

This bathroom features a curbless shower with grab bar and an adjustable showerhead. The sink is placed at the front of the vanity to allow easier reach to the sink and faucet valves.

This bathroom mirror can be adjusted at an angle so that it can be used by someone sitting in a wheelchair.

Tilting mirrors over both sinks offer flexibility and improved visibility to their users. This vanity also features easy-to-grip faucet handles recommended for universally accessible bathrooms.

Planning an accessible bathroom

The Americans with Disabilities Act (ADA) of 1991 establishes accessibility standards for commercial and public facilities. Some of these regulations pertain directly to plumbing fixtures and the design of bathrooms and kitchens.

The ADA standards are not required for private residences, but they are a valuable source of information. Visit the ADA web site at www.usdoj.gov/crt/ada/.

Your local building department should be able to help you design kitchens and baths that are universally accessible. Some plumbing companies carry a line of accessible products. Other companies specialize in ADA-approved sinks and other fixtures, which include those with pedal-operated controls.

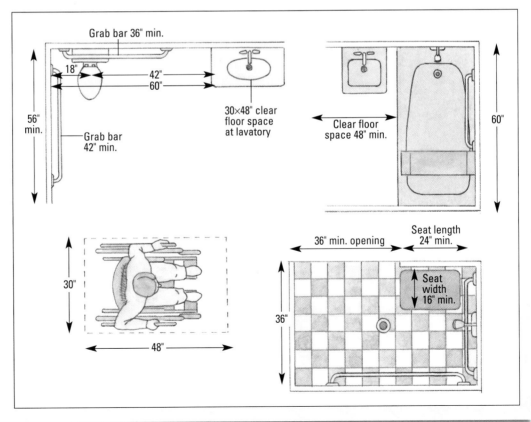

BUILDING CODES

Renovating a bathroom cuts across several areas of construction—plumbing, wiring, and structural work, and in almost every locality, the work you do on your bathroom will be subject to building codes. Codes are established to ensure the safety and quality of materials and their installation. Any major, and sometimes even minor, work will require you to take out a permit, submit plans, and arrange for inspections. Do-it-yourself renovation done without the benefit of inspections often turns out to be not only faulty, but also dangerous and unhealthy.

Local codes are based on national codes which apply generally to the entire country. Local codes—which may be more stringent—are the ones that most concern you. At the beginning of the planning process, visit or call your building department and obtain any printed information about local plumbing codes. Have the plans approved before starting work and perform all work to the satisfaction of the inspector. Draw a detailed plan that includes a list of all materials.

Valves, fixture controls, cleanouts, and compression pipe fittings must not be covered by a wall or floor surface. Since you may need to work on the plumbing in the future, install an access panel. The most common location is behind a tub or shower *(page 69)*.

Codes require that all receptacles be GFCI-protected. Any light fixture should have a sealed globe or lens to shut out moisture. A fan/light/heater may pull enough amps to require its own circuit.

Common electrical codes

Here are some of the most common general requirements for home electrical systems.
- **Boxes:** Plastic electrical boxes are common throughout much of the United States and Canada; some localities require metal boxes.
- **Receptacles, fixtures, and appliances:** All new receptacles and appliances must be grounded. Fixtures and appliances should be approved by Underwriters Laboratories (UL).
- **Cable:** Nonmetallic (NM) cable is the easiest to run and is accepted by most building departments. Wherever cable will be exposed rather than hidden behind drywall or plaster, armored cable or conduit may be required.
- **Circuits:** Most 120-volt household circuits are 15 amps, and all lights must be on 15-amp circuits. In kitchens and utility areas, 20-amp circuits may be required.
- **Wire size:** Attach #14 wire to 15-amp circuits and #12 wire to 20-amp circuits.

Common plumbing codes

The following represents code considerations found in most remodeling projects.
- Fixtures must not be placed too close together (see *page 41* for specifications).
- Drains, vents, and supply lines must be sized appropriate to their application.
- In most cases drain pipes must slope at least ¼ inch per running foot. Codes may require that vent pipes slope at ⅛ inch per foot.
- The installation of plumbing must not weaken the structure of a house. The inspector may require that you reinforce joists that have been cut to accommodate various pipes.

Other requirements include the use of fire caulking around pipes and placement of protective plates over pipes.

If you're simply replacing an existing fixture there's usually no need to contact the building department. But when you run new lines, be sure to work with a building inspector and comply with all local codes.

STANLEY PRO TIP

Work with the building department

Working with your building department ensures safe and reliable plumbing. Here are some tips for getting off to a good start:
- Find out if your building department requires a licensed plumber or electrician to do your work.
- An inspector may be willing to offer advice but don't ask for it. Instead, propose a plan and present it for feedback.
- Draw up professional-quality plans, with a complete list of materials. Make an appointment with the inspector to go over your plans. Take notes, and don't be afraid to ask questions.
- Schedule inspections and be prepared for them. Don't make an appointment until the work is done.

Above all, do not cover up any rough plumbing or electrical work until the inspector has signed off on it. Doing so runs the risk of having to tear out brand-new walls to revise the plumbing.

Standard specifications

Specifications for the placement of plumbing fixtures and the dimensions of pipes are intended to make the bathroom a comfortable room with plenty of capacity for incoming water and outgoing drains and vents. The specifications shown here will meet the requirements of most building departments, but check local codes to be sure. You will notice that in some cases these specifications are different from those required for accessibility. ADA standards represent minimums for accessibility.

Bathroom layout

Where you place the toilet, sink, and tub may depend partly on the existing plumbing. Most homes have a "wet wall," an interior wall that is thicker than most walls because it contains the main stack. Minimize long horizontal runs of drain and vent pipes by installing fixtures close to the wet wall.

Also plan for a layout that is comfortable and convenient. The illustration below shows a basic 5×8-foot bathroom— just enough room for the three major fixtures with adequate space between them.

Most codes require that no fixture be closer than 15 inches from a toilet's centerline. There must be at least 24 inches of space in front of the toilet (it's OK for a door to swing into this space).

Sinks and vanity sink tops range from 20 to 30 inches in width. A standard bathtub is 60 inches by 32 inches. If your plans call for a larger tub, alter the layout to fit it.

Framing for a tub—not the finished wall— must be 60 inches wide to accommodate a standard tub length. If the opening is any smaller, the tub will not fit; if the opening is more than ¼ inch too long, making a tight seal along the wall will be difficult. Framing must be almost perfectly square.

Choosing materials

Most codes call for 3-inch PVC pipe for the main drain and the short length leading from the toilet to the drain, and 2-inch PVC for the other drain lines and the vents. Some local codes may require a 4-inch main drain; some plumbers prefer to run larger vent pipes.

Cast-iron drainpipe is making a comeback in some areas because it's quieter than plastic pipe. However, cast-iron should be installed by a pro. (You can reduce the noise of water draining through PVC by wrapping the pipe with insulation.)

Rigid copper pipe is the most common material for supply lines. However, PEX or other plastic materials may be permitted in your area. Bathrooms are usually supplied with ½-inch pipe. For maximum water pressure, however, run ¾-inch pipe to the bathroom and use ½-inch for short runs only.

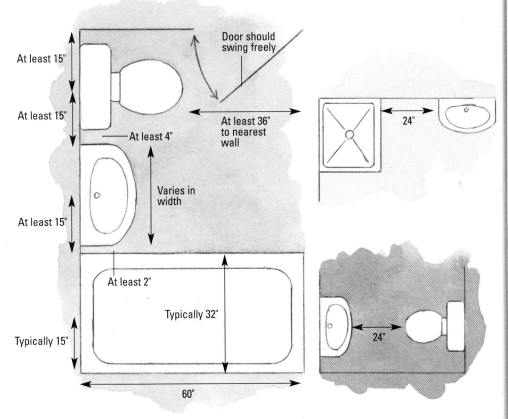

MINIMUM CLEARANCES

At least 15"

At least 15"

At least 4"

Door should swing freely

At least 36" to nearest wall

Varies in width

At least 15"

At least 2"

Typically 32"

Typically 15"

60"

24"

24"

A bathroom with a 5×8-foot interior space allows the minimum clearances that most municipal codes require for fixtures. While exploring layout options, maintain these clearances in your plan to ensure ease of use and installation.

Standard dimensions

Make sure your plans follow these standard specs:

Drain and vent pipes

- Toilet: 3–4 inches; 2-inch vent
- Sink: 2-inch drain, connecting to 3-inch horizontal run; 2-inch vent
- Tub/shower: 2-inch drain, connecting to 3-inch horizontal run; 2-inch vent
- Main stack: 3–4 inches
- Sink drain: 19 inches above floor
- Toilet drain: 12 inches from wall

Supply pipes

- Tub/shower: ¾-inch pipe
- Sink, toilet: ½-inch pipe
- Sink stubout: 19 inches above floor, 8–10 inches apart
- Toilet stubout: 8 inches above floor

Tub/shower fittings

- Tub control(s): 28 inches from floor
- Spout: 6 inches above top edge
- Showerhead arm: About 76 inches above floor
- Shower control: 48 inches above floor

DRAWING PLANS

Carefully drawn plans help show the building inspector that you've thought through your project. What's more, spending an extra hour or two with pencil and paper will help you spot potential problems before you begin tearing into walls, saving you time and expense in the long run.

The necessary tools are simple: A ruled straightedge will help you draw parallel lines. You'll also need a compass, colored pencils, an eraser, and a 30-60-90-degree triangle.

Use grid paper so it's easy to establish a scale, like ½ inch to 6 or 12 inches. Such a scale makes it easy to note any problems with the layout and is a useful guide for estimating materials.

Make a scale drawing of the room, including features such as counters and cabinets. If you have architectural drawings, make several photocopies of them. If you have no architectural drawings, make several copies of your scale drawing.

Drawing a plumbing plan

You may think that a rough sketch of a plumbing project is all you need. After all, you can figure out the details as you work, right? Even professional plumbers have to make on-the-fly changes after they start doing the work. The framing they find may differ from what they expected, or they may discover that their plan was faulty. Pros usually map a job in painstaking detail to avoid as many surprises as possible.

It's fairly easy to produce plan views and riser drawings that use official plumbing symbols. The effort expended making detailed drawings will save time and expense later. The drawing process helps you think through the project in detail. That may enable you to spot a mistake you might otherwise overlook. It will almost certainly minimize extra trips to the plumbing supply store. Also a clear, professional-quality plan will make your initial meeting with the building department more pleasant.

A plan for new plumbing service starts with a map of the existing plumbing. Use color codes when drawing a plan to indicate the function of each pipe.

Drawing plumbing plans

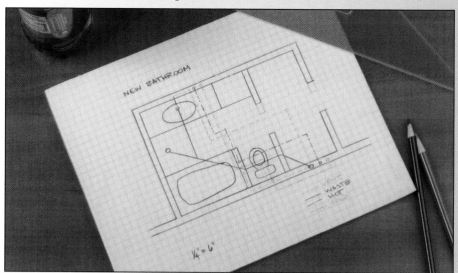

1 Start by drawing a floor plan of the existing space on graph paper. A scale of ¼ inch to 1 foot usually allows plenty of detail. Show all the walls, doorways, and windows. Once you have completed your floor plan, make tracing paper overlays to test out possible designs. Avoid erasing—if you make a mistake or if you don't like the way something looks, make another overlay. Better to make your mistakes on paper than on the jobsite. Solid lines indicate drainpipes, and broken lines indicate hot and cold water lines. Because this is an overhead view, notes must indicate any vertical runs. Different colored lines make clear the function of each pipe.

Drawing a framing plan

1 If you're adding a new wall to your bathroom, make a scale elevation of the framing. A scale of ¼ inch to 1 foot works well here too. Create an overlay for the elevation drawing. Show the critical dimensions and note potential problems or special circumstances.

2 Consult your framing diagram to make a materials list. Keep in mind the bottom plate of a wall runs the length of the wall—even if you plan to include doors. You'll cut the part that runs across the doorway after the wall is in place.

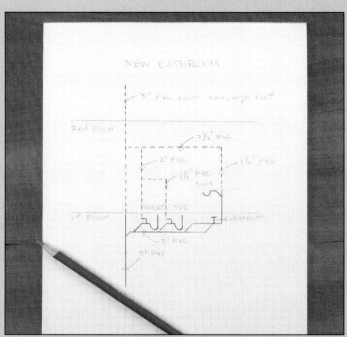

2 Draw a drain-waste-vent (DWV) elevation to illustrate the upward path of the stack, vents, and revents, the length of drainpipe runs, and traps. The primary purpose of a DWV elevation is to show how the fixtures will be vented. It doesn't have to be drawn over an architectural drawing.

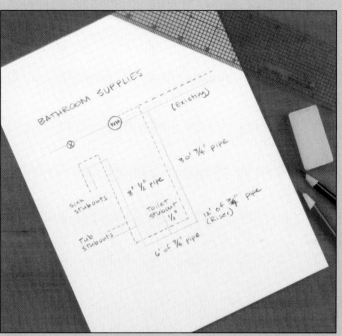

3 Draw a supply drawing to show the approximate length of supply pipes. The main purpose is to determine the minimum size of the pipes. Order supply pipe in excess of your estimates. You can only determine the exact length as you install them.

BATHROOM SUPPLY, DRAIN-WASTE-VENT OVERVIEW

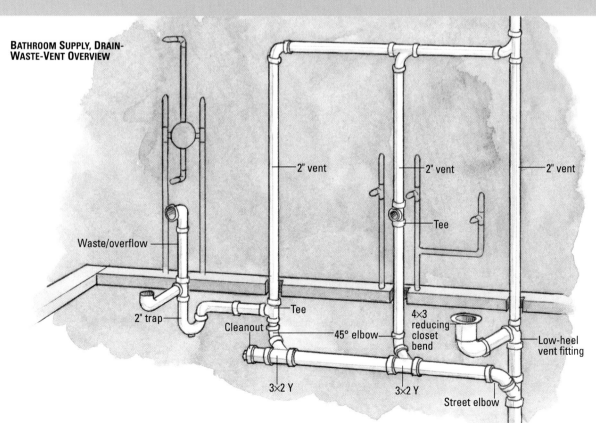

The pipes supplying hot and cold water can run in any convenient configuration. However, by running separate 3/4-inch lines from near the water heater to the shower, water pressure (and temperature) will not be affected when someone uses another fixture in the house.

Drawing Plans *(continued)*

Drawing a wiring plan

First make a rough drawing. Use the symbols shown below or get a list of symbols from your local building department. Make a quick freehand drawing, using colored pencils to indicate each circuit. Are the switches in convenient locations? Are all the circuits correctly loaded? Do you have enough receptacles, and will they be easy to reach? Once you've made your final decisions, draw a neat, final version of the plan.

Final drawings

To make a plan drawing, first draw all fixtures to precise size and make sure they are not too close together (see *page 41*). Then put in the drain lines with fixtures; then the supplies. Make riser drawings as well.

Use the drawing to make a list of materials. Indicate the exact type of every fitting so the inspector can approve them. Indicate pipe sizes, including valves, to match the pipe dimension.

Create a clear materials list

Use your drawings to list the materials you need. Divide your project into three sections—framing, plumbing, and wiring. In each section you'll make a list of the specific items you need, again according to category—lumber, trim, sheet stock under framing, supply pipe, fittings, drainpipe and fittings under plumbing, and so on.

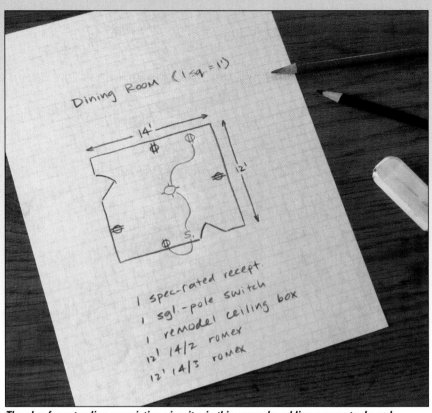

The plan for extending an existing circuit—in this example, adding a receptacle and a switched light fixture—is easy to draw. Don't take the task lightly: Use the correct symbols and make the drawing clear and neat.

Electrical symbols

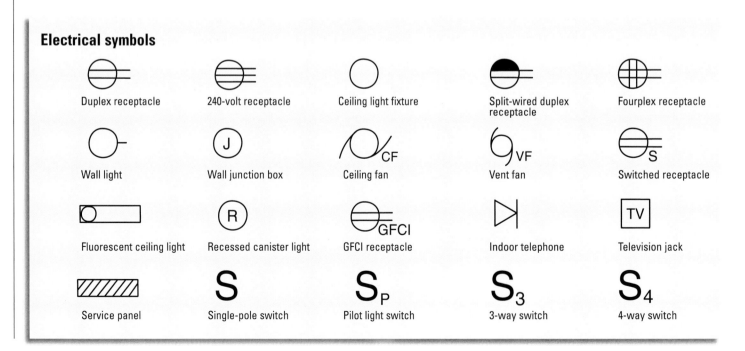

Duplex receptacle	240-volt receptacle	Ceiling light fixture	Split-wired duplex receptacle	Fourplex receptacle
Wall light	Wall junction box	Ceiling fan	Vent fan	Switched receptacle
Fluorescent ceiling light	Recessed canister light	GFCI receptacle	Indoor telephone	Television jack
Service panel	Single-pole switch	Pilot light switch	3-way switch	4-way switch

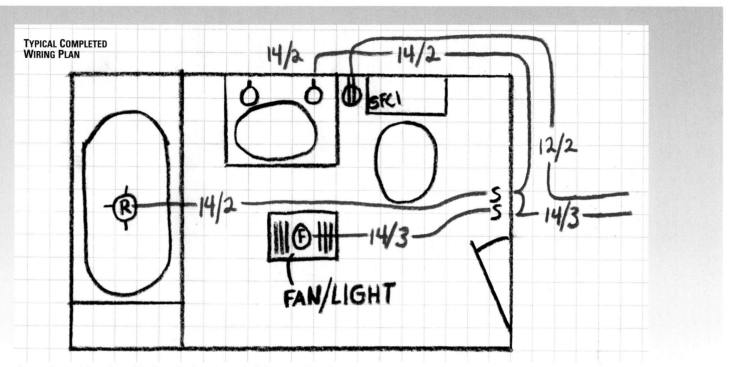

TYPICAL COMPLETED
WIRING PLAN

A complete wiring plan will show the locations of all fixtures, the wires that feed them, the load they will carry, and the name and type of each item. Color coding illustrates feed, return, and ground wires.

Plumbing symbols

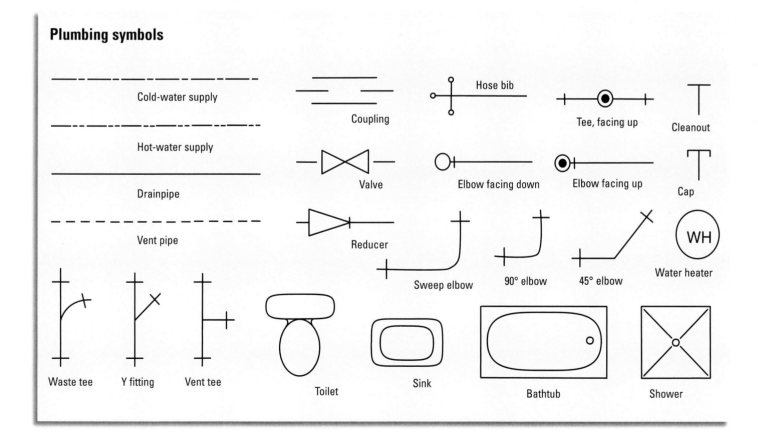

Cold-water supply

Hot-water supply

Drainpipe

Vent pipe

Waste tee

Y fitting

Vent tee

Toilet

Coupling

Valve

Reducer

Sink

Hose bib

Elbow facing down

Sweep elbow

90° elbow

45° elbow

Bathtub

Tee, facing up

Elbow facing up

Cleanout

Cap

WH
Water heater

Shower

CHOOSING TOOLS

A bathroom remodeling project pulls together several kinds of construction skills—carpentry, plumbing, wiring, and perhaps some drywall and tilework. Each of these skills requires its own set of tools, many of which you may already have. However, you'll probably need to make a trip to your home center to fill in a few vacancies.

If you're on your first tool-buying trip, the tool choices you'll find in a well-stocked home center might seem overwhelming. A few pointers will help you sort things out.

First, buy the best tools you can afford. It won't take but one trip to the hardware store for a new hammer to replace a cheap shattered one to convince you that spending a little more for quality beats the outlay for another tool—plus the trip and your time.

Second, treat the cost of new tools as an investment, not an expense. Even with new tools, your DIY budget will be less than if you contracted the work. Besides, you're certain to use these tools in future projects, and if you amortize their cost over their total usage, that expense becomes minimal.

Third, trust your instincts and do a little research. Quality comes with its own "feel," and it quickly distinguishes itself from inferior items. Examine top-of-the-line tools and you'll quickly see the difference between them and the cheap ones. The metal on all hand tools should be flawlessly machined; handles should be tight-fitting and hefty. A good hammer will have a drop-forged and heat-tempered steel head; the handle will be ash, hickory, or fiberglass; or it will be one-piece, all-steel construction.

A well-made power tool will feature a precisely assembled housing, smoothly finished steel or aluminum parts, user-friendly triggers and controls, and sturdy electrical cords.

To shore up your instincts, especially before buying a power tool, read tool reviews in home remodeling and woodworking publications.

When shopping for power tools, don't buy more features than you need. And if you don't expect to use a tool often in the future, rent it until your project is done.

Buy as complete a set of the best-quality tools you can afford—they pay off in the long run.

CHAPTER PREVIEW

Carpentry tools
page 48

Tiling tools
page 51

Drywall finishing tools
page 51

Plumbing tools
page 52

Wiring tools
page 55

STANLEY PRO TIP: **Buy a circular saw**

If you don't have a circular saw, now's the time to buy one. You can't do much remodeling without one. Here are a few tips on what to look for.

First, look for a name-brand saw and find the model that's most comfortable for you. Make sure you like the grip and the position of the switch and safety.

Second, don't concern yourself with horsepower rating—it's usually measured when the saw is not under load. How many amps a saw draws is a better indication of its power. Buy a saw rated at 12 or 13 amps or more.

The saw should have a solid extruded or cast base, not a light stamped-steel base. Make sure the tilt and height adjustments work smoothly, tighten easily, and stay tight. Large knobs or wing nuts tighten easily; levers work even better.

A remodeling project involves a variety of tools and supplies. To protect your investment, store tools in toolboxes when not in use. Keep like tools together in individual carriers so they are easier to find when you need them.

CARPENTRY TOOLS

You probably already have some basic carpentry tools around the house. To handle the demands of your bathroom project, make sure the tools you have are good quality and in good condition.

Use a **carpenter's level** to level and plumb long sections of framing and pipe. Use a **torpedo level** for short sections. A **16-ounce framing hammer** is essential—heavy enough to drive framing nails, yet light enough for trim work. Add a 22-ounce framing hammer for heavy work.

A **tape measure** provides a compact ruler for all measuring tasks. A 25-foot model is standard.

Use a ⅜-inch **variable speed electric drill** to bore holes. For installing screws buy a **magnetic sleeve** and several **screwdriver bits**. A **cordless 18-volt drill** is portable and keeps the workplace free of extension cords. Buy several **spade bits** for drilling holes for water supply lines. When you need the extra reach, attach spade bits to a **bit extender**. A **quick-change sleeve** speeds

switching **twist bits** for small holes. Make finder holes with a **long bit**. For cutting holes larger than 1 inch, buy a **hole saw**. Renting or buying a **hammer drill** will speed tough-to-bore holes in concrete.

A **stand-up flashlight** will light up cramped, dark quarters. You'll find a **nail set** handy for finishing nails below the surface of moldings and extending your reach into hard-to-hammer places.

A **plumb bob** provides a vertical reference. A **chalk line** marks long, straight lines.

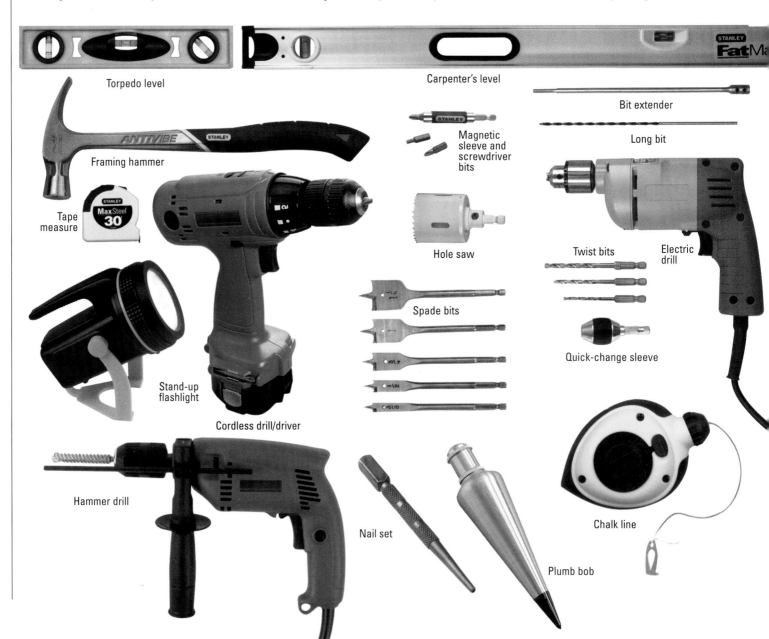

Torpedo level

Carpenter's level

Bit extender

Long bit

Framing hammer

Magnetic sleeve and screwdriver bits

Tape measure

Hole saw

Spade bits

Twist bits

Electric drill

Quick-change sleeve

Stand-up flashlight

Cordless drill/driver

Hammer drill

Nail set

Plumb bob

Chalk line

A **stud finder** will find studs in the walls. Get one that locates the stud by sensing its density, not the presence of nails.

For cutting miters in trim, you'll need either a **miter box** or a power mitersaw. Equipped with a fine-cutting blade, it will cut PVC pipe precisely. A **coping saw** is indispensable for cutting moldings at inside corners. A pair of heavy-duty **metal snips** comes in handy for a variety of cutting tasks, including the installation of metal studs.

Demolition tools

To cut away a small section of concrete, a **small sledge** and **cold chisel** may be all you need. To chisel out a large area, rent an **electric jackhammer** and **jackhammer chisel.** For cutting through subflooring or framing, a **reciprocating saw** is indispensable. Its long blades reach in to cut awkward spots and can even slice through nails and screws. Several types of blades are available, including metal-cutting blades. Buy several; they often break.

For pulling nails nothing beats a **cat's paw.** A **12-pound sledgehammer** is also useful for demolition and for nudging wayward walls into position. A **flat pry bar** will enable you to disassemble most nailed-together framing members. Occasionally you may need a longer **ripping bar** for heavy-duty work.

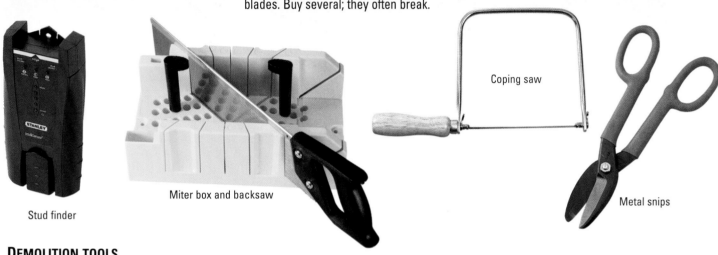

Coping saw

Miter box and backsaw

Metal snips

Stud finder

DEMOLITION TOOLS

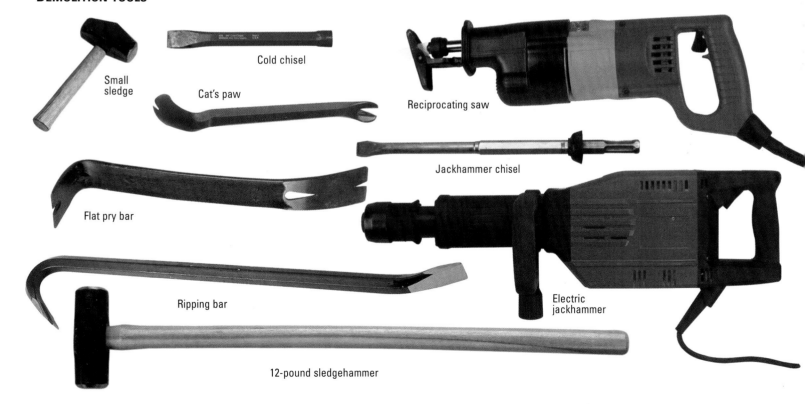

Cold chisel

Small sledge

Cat's paw

Reciprocating saw

Flat pry bar

Jackhammer chisel

Ripping bar

Electric jackhammer

12-pound sledgehammer

CARPENTRY TOOLS *(continued)*

A **combination square** allows you to mark boards for crosscutting. A **layout square** does many of the same tasks and can serve as a guide when crosscutting with a circular saw or jigsaw. Use a **framing square** for larger layouts. A **T-bevel** transfers angles from one place to another.

To get to pipes inside a wall, you'll need to cut through drywall or plaster. For small jobs a **drywall saw** is adequate. A full-size **hacksaw** is useful for cutting steel and copper pipes and for removing rusted fittings and old sections of pipe. Have a **close-work hacksaw** for working in tight areas. Most use full-size hacksaw blades as well as shorter metal-cutting blades. A **utility knife** does everything from sharpening pencils to cutting drywall.

Keep plenty of blades on hand and change them often so you always have a sharp edge.

Use a **circular saw** for cutting framing lumber and, with a metal-cutting blade, for cutting cast-iron pipe. For quick work a **toolbox handsaw** packs a lot of cutting capability into a compact size. For cutting access panels, flooring, and holes for sinks, use a **jigsaw**.

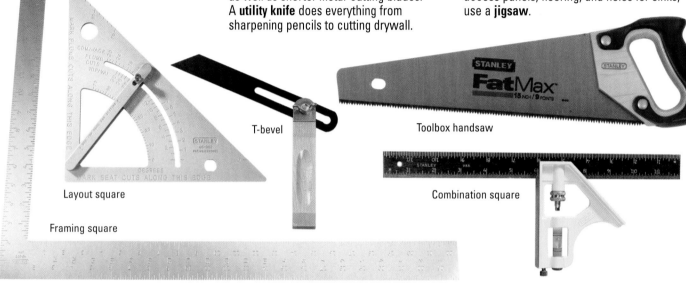

T-bevel

Toolbox handsaw

Layout square

Combination square

Framing square

Close-work hacksaw

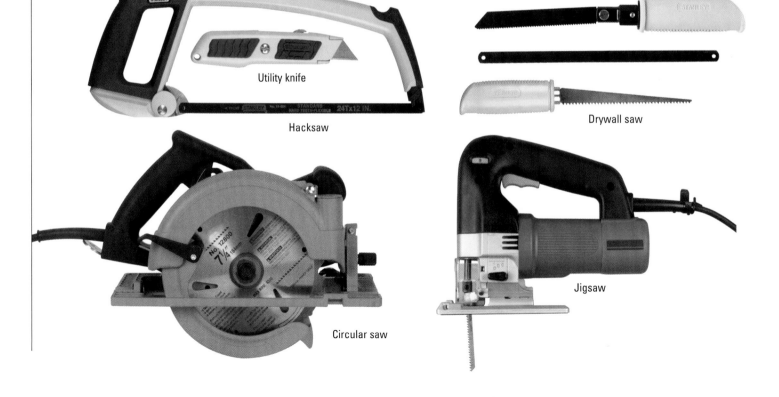

Utility knife

Hacksaw

Drywall saw

Circular saw

Jigsaw

TILING TOOLS

Installing ceramic tile requires tools made for the job. To mix thinset mortar, use a **heavy-duty drill** and a **mixing paddle**. Different jobs require different **trowels**, and filling the joints properly calls for a **grout float**. You'll need a **sponge** to clean the grout off the surface of the tiles. Cutting tiles is easy with a **snap cutter**. A **wet saw** makes quick work when you have lots of cuts to make. Use **tile nippers** to chip away small pieces of tile when cutting circular or unusual patterns. A **masonry stone** removes rough or sharp edges.

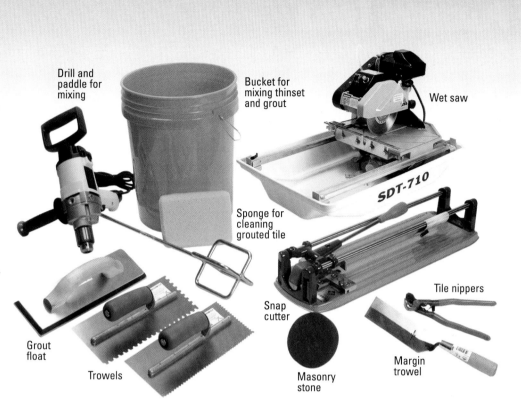

Drill and paddle for mixing

Bucket for mixing thinset and grout

Wet saw

SDT-710

Sponge for cleaning grouted tile

Grout float

Trowels

Snap cutter

Masonry stone

Tile nippers

Margin trowel

DRYWALL FINISHING TOOLS

Finishing drywall also requires specialized tools. For laying out and guiding cuts on a drywall sheet, nothing beats a **drywall square**. For light trimming such as planing an edge flush at a corner, use a **Surform plane**. Tools used for spreading joint compound over drywall joints are called **taping** or **drywall knives**. These come in a variety of widths. For most purposes a 6-inch, a 10-inch, and a 12-inch will handle

the task. Along with the knives, get a **mud pan** to hold a supply of joint compound (often called mud).

To smooth dried joint compound, use **sanding screens** mounted in a **holder**. For an almost dust-free environment, smooth the walls with a wet **drywall sponge**—it has a tough abrasive plastic layer laminated to one side.

Drywall square

Mud pan

6-inch drywall knife

10-inch drywall knife

12-inch drywall knife

Sanding screen holder

Sanding screens

Surform plane

Drywall sponge

PLUMBING TOOLS

For a modest amount of money—probably less than a single visit from a plumber—you can assemble a tool kit that will tackle most jobs in your house. Invest in quality tools. They will stand up to tough tasks and be more comfortable to use.

General plumbing tools

These tools are useful no matter what material your pipes are made of. An **adjustable wrench** adjusts to grab nuts and bolts. Its one-size-fits-all jaws save you from rooting around in your toolbox for the right size open or box-end wrench. A **locking adjustable wrench** is a handy variation on the same theme that quickly tightens on stubborn nuts and bolts. Press the lever for a quick release. A pair of **groove-joint pliers** is useful for tightening and loosening all sorts of joints. A 14-inch **pipe wrench** is the ideal size for most projects. (To add to its persuasive force,

slip a 1¼-inch steel pipe over the handle to increase the leverage.) If you will be working on steel pipe, buy a pair of pipe wrenches (add an 18-inch size).

A **putty knife** scrapes away old putty and other types of hardened debris. You'll need both **phillips** and **slot screwdrivers** to disassemble fixtures and fittings—a **4-in-1** combines both types. Use a **wire brush** to clean parts and encrusted pipe threads.

A **strainer wrench** will help you twist out

Adjustable wrench

Putty knife

Locking adjustable wrench

Pipe wrench

Groove-joint pliers

SAFETY FIRST
Tools that protect

Whenever doing work that creates sparks or flying debris, wear **safety goggles.** And preserve your hearing when using power tools—or even a simple hammer—with **ear protectors.**

Protect your hands with **leather gloves** when working with rough framing or cut pipes. When removing traps and toilets, wear long-sleeved clothing and **heavy-duty rubber gloves.**

Plug power tools into a **GFCI-protected extension cord,** which will shut off the moment it senses danger from exposure to water. (Cordless tools are safest.) When sweating joints, have a **fire extinguisher** nearby.

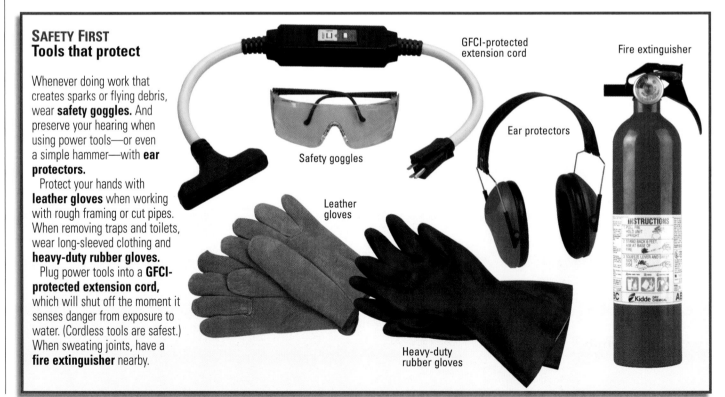

GFCI-protected extension cord

Fire extinguisher

Safety goggles

Ear protectors

Leather gloves

Heavy-duty rubber gloves

the upper part of the drain assembly in a sink or tub. To remove a large nut like that beneath a kitchen sink basket strainer, a **locknut wrench** is easier to use than groove-joint pliers. When repairing a faucet, you may need to get at the seat, a small part located inside the faucet body. Use a **seat wrench**. A **basin wrench** reaches into small spaces to loosen or tighten hold-down nuts. Without this tool, removing a kitchen or bathroom faucet is nearly impossible.

Tools for plastic pipe
You can use just about any kind of saw to cut plastic pipe—a hacksaw, a standard backsaw, an ordinary handsaw, a circular saw, or even a power mitersaw. However, an inexpensive **plastic pipe saw** (also known as a PVC saw) cuts easily and leaves few burrs. Use it along with a **miter box** to ensure straight cuts in smaller pipe. For larger pipe mark the cut line and keep the saw perpendicular in all directions.

After cutting, burrs must be removed completely in order for the joints to fit tightly and to stay that way. A **deburring tool** does the job better and more quickly than a utility knife.

To cut supply pipe (1 inch and smaller), you can also use a scissors-action **plastic pipe cutter.** Be sure to get a heavy-duty model made for PVC pipe. For PEX and other flexible tubing, a **plastic tubing cutter** makes a quick, clean cut.

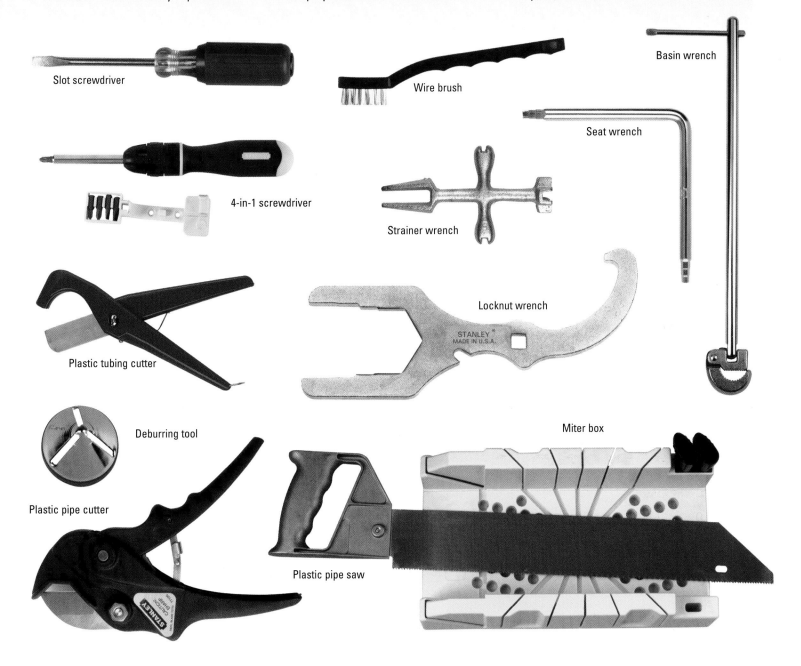

Slot screwdriver

Wire brush

Basin wrench

Seat wrench

4-in-1 screwdriver

Strainer wrench

Plastic tubing cutter

Locknut wrench

STANLEY
MADE IN U.S.A.

Deburring tool

Miter box

Plastic pipe cutter

Plastic pipe saw

PLUMBING TOOLS (continued)

Tools for copper pipe

A **tubing cutter** cuts copper pipe cleanly, quickly, and without bending the pipe out of round. For working in tight spots, you might need a **small tubing cutter** as well. (A hacksaw can cut copper pipe, but a dull blade may cause you to dent the pipe, making it very difficult to add fittings.)

To bend flexible pipe without crimping, use a **tubing bender.** Choose the size that tightly slips onto the pipe. A **flaring tool** may be needed for certain types of compression fittings, particularly in outdoor installations. A **handle puller** smoothly detaches faucet handles without strain or damage.

To sweat copper pipe and fittings, buy a **propane torch.** A model with an **electric igniter** is easiest—and safest—to use. To protect flammable surfaces from the propane torch flame, use a **fiber shield** or prop an old cookie sheet behind the joint being heated.

The ends of copper pipe and the insides of fittings must be burnished before soldering. A **multiuse wire brush** does both jobs. Or buy a **reamer brush** for the fittings and a roll of **plumber's emery cloth** for the pipe ends. Before joining pipes, paint **flux** on the pipes using a **flux brush.**

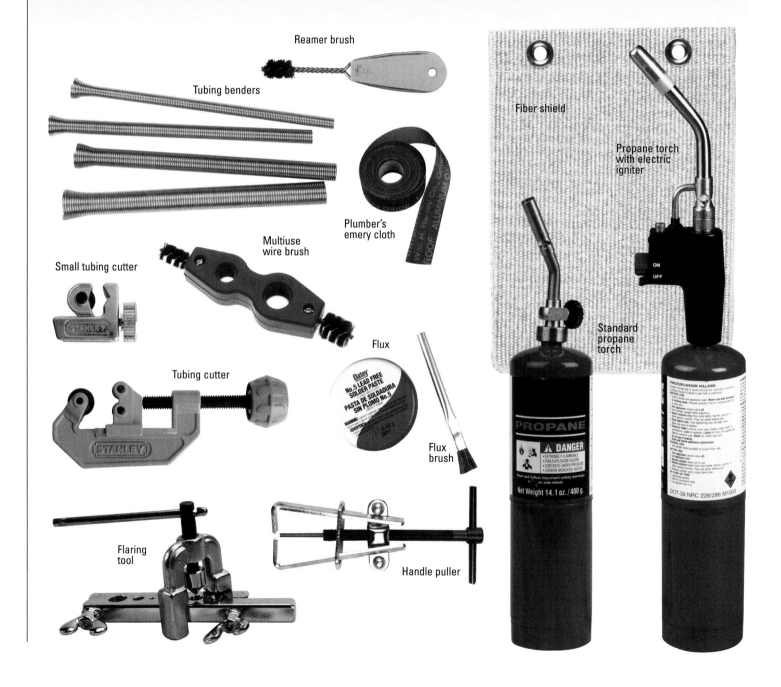

Reamer brush

Tubing benders

Plumber's emery cloth

Multiuse wire brush

Small tubing cutter

Flux

Tubing cutter

Flux brush

Flaring tool

Handle puller

Fiber shield

Propane torch with electric igniter

Standard propane torch

WIRING TOOLS

Assembling a complete kit of quality electrician's tools will cost far less than hiring a professional to do the job.

Wiring tools

A pair of **diagonal cutters** makes working inside a crowded electrical box or snipping off sheathing from nonmetallic cable easier. **Cutting pliers** help with general chores such as snipping armored cable. Use **long-nose pliers** to bend wires into loops before attaching them to terminals. The **Combination stripper** shown below— with wire holes near the tip—is easier to use than those with holes near the handle. Use **lineman's pliers** to twist wires together; no other tool works as well. A **rotary screwdriver** drives screws quickly; use it to install several cover plates.

Fishing tools

These tools help minimize damage to walls and ceilings when running cable. In addition to a standard ¾-inch **spade bit,** buy a **fishing bit,** which can reach across two studs or joists and pull cable back through the holes it has made *(pages 168–171).*

You can use a straightened coat hanger wire to fish cable through short runs, but a **fish tape** is easier to use *(pages 168–171).* Occasionally you may need to run one tape from each direction, so buy two. Also use a fish tape when pulling wires through conduit *(page 165).*

Testers

For most work you will need a **voltage tester** to test for the presence of power. A **multitester** tests for voltage, checks devices for damage, and performs other functions. A **receptacle analyzer** shows if a receptacle is grounded and polarized.

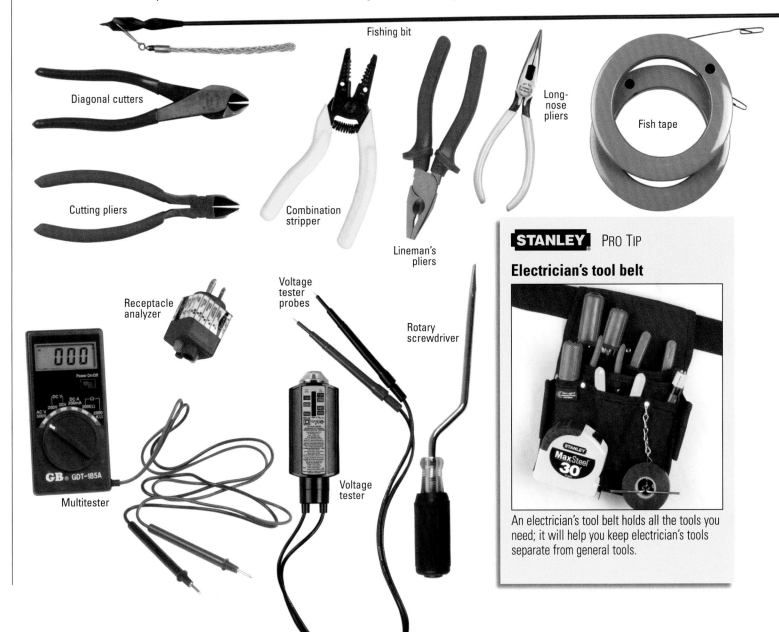

Fishing bit

Diagonal cutters

Long-nose pliers

Fish tape

Cutting pliers

Combination stripper

Lineman's pliers

Receptacle analyzer

Voltage tester probes

Rotary screwdriver

Voltage tester

Multitester

STANLEY PRO TIP

Electrician's tool belt

An electrician's tool belt holds all the tools you need; it will help you keep electrician's tools separate from general tools.

PREPARATION & DEMOLITION

The first stage of a remodeling job typically is demolition—tearing out the old to make way for the new. Demolition is messy work, but it can be rewarding. It moves along quickly, progress is visible, and knocking things apart can be fun—remember how flattening a sand castle was more fun than building it?

Demolition with forethought

Before you start swinging away, decide whether you want to salvage anything. Wood moldings, for example, can be difficult to match, and even if the profiles are readily available, you can save money by reusing them. You can also reuse framing lumber—but watch out for nails. After deciding what to salvage, your primary objective should be to contain dust and debris in your work area.

Dust doctoring

Some easy methods will help you isolate the work site from the rest of the house.
■ If you are tearing out a wall in a carpeted room or over finished flooring, protect it with a layer of ¼-inch plywood or reinforced plastic tarps. Tape the tarp to the floor to keep it stationary.
■ Lay tarps on hallways outside the work area to keep floors from being scratched by tracked-in dust.
■ Tape plastic sheets over open entries or tack up an old bedsheet to allow access to another room.
■ If the demolition room has a window, open it and prop up a box fan so it blows out airborne dust.
■ Prevent dust from spreading into other rooms by taping cardboard over heat and return-air ducts or wrap them with plastic and replace them.

■ Set a small rug (a carpet sample works well) just outside the door of the work area to remove debris from your shoes. Slip into a pair of slippers and leave your work boots behind at the end of the day.

Cleanup

For small jobs bag the debris and put it out with the trash. Be warned: Construction debris is heavy. Don't overfill containers. Use heavyweight or doubled bags. For larger jobs rent a waste container.

A shop vacuum makes quick work of construction dust, but most stock filters can't deal with the fine dust generated by remodeling projects. Some vacuum makers sell bags that fit over the regular filters for dealing with fine dust. Or you can retrofit your vacuum with an after-market filter.

CHAPTER PREVIEW

Is this wall structural?
page 58

What's in the wall?
page 59

Removing drywall
page 60

Removing plaster
page 61

Removing framing members
page 62

Removing toilets and sinks
page 64

SAFETY FIRST
Pull nails as you go

As you remove each piece of
wood, pull protruding nails—
they're hazardous. Keep a cat's
paw handy for prying up
nailheads and a pair of end
nips to lever out the nails.

**Removing shower
and tub fixtures**
page 66

Removing a tub
page 68

**Removing an old
vanity**
page 71

**Removing
resilients, ceramic
tile, and carpet**
page 73

**Installing new
underlayment**
page 75

**Installing cement
backerboard**
page 76

IS THIS WALL STRUCTURAL?

Planning a remodeling job will cause you to see your house in a whole new light. Many things you considered permanent before—walls, for example—may not seem that way anymore. You'll soon realize that almost any alteration is possible if you are willing to do the work and bear the expense. Before you get carried away and start knocking down walls, however, you need to understand that house walls come in two varieties—bearing (or structural) and nonbearing (or partition) walls.

Bearing walls help carry the weight of materials and contents of the upper stories to the ground. **Partition walls** only divide interior space. It is far easier to remove or relocate a partition wall than it is to alter a bearing wall. Removing a bearing wall is costly and time-consuming. If not done correctly, it can weaken the structure of the house and make it unsafe. In many cases you may want to rethink your project before deciding to remove or modify a bearing wall.

How to spot the difference

One of the first steps in planning a remodeling project is to determine whether an interior wall is a bearing wall.

If the wall runs parallel to the ceiling and floor joists, it is probably not a bearing wall. Short closet walls, for example, usually are not bearing. If the wall runs perpendicular to the ceiling and floor joists, there is a good chance it is a bearing wall.

How can you tell which way the joists run? Most of the time joists run perpendicular to the roof's ridgeline. If the wall is under an attic, go up and see if the joists cross over the wall. If joists end on top of a wall, it definitely is a bearing wall. If the attic has floorboards, you'll see the nail lines where they are fastened to the joists. If your roof is supported by trusses, the answer is simpler. Trusses have diagonal members that run from the attic floor to the rafters. They transfer the weight of the roof to the outside walls, so all the interior walls in the story directly below are probably partition walls.

If you can't check above, check below. Is there a wall directly under the one you want to remove or modify? If there is, both are probably bearing walls. If there is a basement or crawlspace below the wall you want to change, check under the house and see if a beam supported by posts or piers is directly under the wall. If so, you can assume the wall above is bearing.

If you still have doubts, hire a carpenter or a structural engineer to help you. A small fee will buy you a lot of comfort.

IDENTIFYING A BEARING WALL

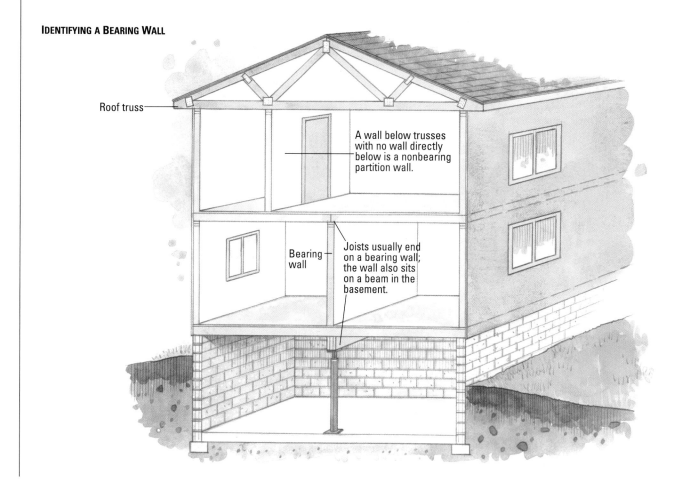

Roof truss

A wall below trusses with no wall directly below is a nonbearing partition wall.

Bearing wall

Joists usually end on a bearing wall; the wall also sits on a beam in the basement.

WHAT'S IN THE WALL?

When you start thinking about modifying existing walls, you need to consider what runs through them, hidden behind the drywall or plaster. The walls in most houses are strung with a network of wires, pipes, and ductwork. Moving or getting rid of a wall may require rerouting one or more of these hidden systems. The only way to be absolutely sure of what's inside is to strip the surface. But before you remove the drywall, do a little sleuthing so you know what you might run into.

At the very least, most walls will contain electrical wiring—a certainty if there are receptacles or switches on the surface. Even if there aren't any, the wall can still harbor wiring, so use caution when poking or cutting the surface.

The best way to determine if the wall contains plumbing and ductwork is to go to the basement or crawlspace and see what goes up into the wall. Check along the entire surface of the wall, even where it spans rooms next to your project area. If you don't see ducts or pipes running up into the wall, there's a good chance there's no plumbing or ductwork in it.

Mark the new routes for wires, ducts, and pipes on your plan, and if you decide not to do the work yourself, call in a trade professional. Most will want to see the original layout after you've stripped the covering from the surface.

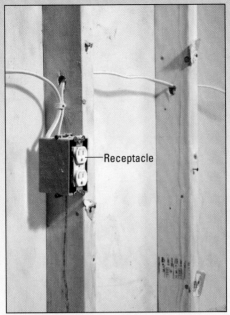

—Receptacle

Electrical wiring is found in most walls. Most receptacles are wired to circuits in other walls, so you may have to reroute the wiring in more than one room. Check both sides of a wall as well as those in neighboring rooms.

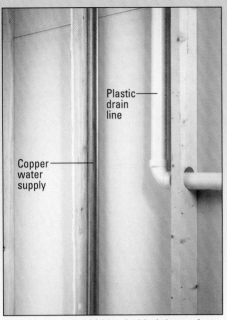

Plastic drain line

Copper water supply

Plumbing can be hidden behind the surface too. If a bathroom or kitchen is located directly above (and sometimes below) the wall you intend to work on, you will probably find pipes in that wall.

Air duct

Heating and air-conditioning ductwork is difficult to trace. Often second-floor vent lines and return air lines pass through stud bays but are difficult to spot from underneath because other ducts block them from view.

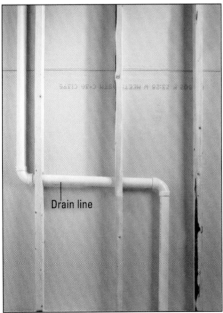

Drain line

Drain-waste-vent lines can be trickier to locate than plumbing supply lines; they take less direct routes. Besides being much larger than supply lines, drains and vents often run from the basement through the roof, requiring extensive rerouting.

REMOVING DRYWALL

Before you remove drywall, take off the trim and baseboards. Slide a wide putty knife under the trim and pry it until you can get a flat pry bar behind the wood. Move along the trim with the pry bar, keeping the putty knife behind it for added leverage.

By now you should know if the walls contain any pipes, ducts, or wiring *(page 59)*. If you're in doubt, tap the wall with a screwdriver handle until you find a spot that sounds hollow. That's where you want to make your first hole with the hammer.

This is a messy job, so work carefully to avoid creating excessive debris and dust. Drywall is inexpensive, so don't try to save it. Use a heavy-duty paint scraper or chisel to remove construction-adhesive residue. Construction-adhesive remover will soften troublesome residue spots. Provide plenty of ventilation and give the remover time to do its job.

Be sure to wear a dust mask rated for fine dust, not just nuisance dust. A fine-dust mask has two straps and is thicker than a nuisance-dust mask.

PRESTART CHECKLIST

☐ **TIME**
About 1 to 2 hours per sheet (32 square feet) of drywall from start to final cleanup

☐ **TOOLS**
Hammer, flat bar, end nips, utility knife, power drill/driver (for removing drywall screws), reciprocating saw (for removing parts of walls), handsaw

☐ **SKILLS**
Prying, pulling nails, removing screws, cutting with a reciprocating saw

☐ **PREP**
Isolate the work site to contain the mess; determine what utilities may be contained within the wall

1 **Shut off power at the service panel** and remove cover plates from the wall boxes. If the drywall section you're removing ends at a corner, slice through the joint compound and tape with a utility knife. If the section ends in the middle of a wall, cut along a stud with a utility knife.

2 Punch a line of hammer holes high along the stud bays to create handholds for pulling off the drywall. Work carefully to ensure you don't damage concealed plumbing lines, heat ducts, or wiring.

3 Grip the drywall and pull it away from the wall, prying it free of its fasteners as you go. Remove the material in large pieces. Drop the pieces directly into a disposal container instead of on the floor. That way you will greatly reduce cleanup chores.

4 Clean up the studs by yanking nails or backing out screws. To make sure you find every fastener, slide a putty knife or the edge of your hammerhead along the stud. Even if you're completely removing the wall, fastener removal makes the studs safer to handle.

REMOVING PLASTER

The walls of many older houses are finished with plaster, and removing it proceeds easily with some understanding of how it was applied.

Old-style plaster was troweled as a wet paste over thin horizontal wood strips (lath) nailed to the studs. Plaster squeezed between the lath formed "keys" that held the dried plaster to the wall.

Newer techniques rely on a base of expanded metal mesh (metal lath) rather than wood strips. Use tin snips to cut through metal lath.

In both cases the trickiest part of removing plaster is avoiding damage to adjacent walls. Tack battens to the perimeter as shown in Step 1.

Before removing plaster **turn off the power at the service panel.** Remove all receptacle and switch cover plates. Wear a dust mask rated for fine dust.

PRESTART CHECKLIST

☐ **TIME**
About 1 to 2 hours per 8-foot section of wall

☐ **TOOLS**
Hammer, pry bar, power drill/driver (for attaching reinforcing 1×2s), handsaw, reciprocating saw (for removing parts of walls)

☐ **SKILLS**
Prying, pulling nails, cutting with a reciprocating saw and handsaw

☐ **PREP**
Isolate the work site to contain the mess; determine what utilities may be contained within the wall

☐ **MATERIALS**
1×2s to reinforce surrounding plaster, if necessary

1 Plaster is a tough wall surface, but too much pounding and vibration can jar it loose in places you don't want to remove. To reduce such peripheral damage, attach 1×2s in the corners of walls and in the ceiling adjacent to the wall you are removing.

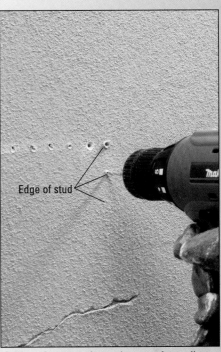

Edge of stud ◄

2 If you're removing only part of a wall, stop at a stud on both sides of the opening. That way the remaining lath and plaster will be supported. To find the edge of a stud, drill ⅛-inch holes across the waste section until the drill hits a stud. Attach a 1×2 along the stud as a nailing surface.

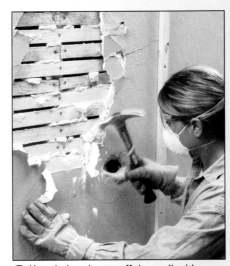

3 Knock the plaster off the wall with a hammer. Then shovel up the loose plaster before removing the lath. If the lath continues past the end stud, cut the lath flush to the edge of the stud with a handsaw or reciprocating saw.

4 Remove the lath with a pry bar and pull the nails from the studs as you go. Try not to break the lath—small pieces mean more cleanup time. Pile the lath neatly, then bundle it with twine for disposal.

REMOVING FRAMING MEMBERS

With the drywall or plaster and lath removed, the framing is the last thing to go. It's not difficult to beat the studs from their positions with a sledgehammer, but a neater and safer method is to cut the nails at the bottom, then pry and twist the pieces free. This way you'll be able to reuse the pieces if you need them; just remember they still have nails in one end. After removing the studs, you can remove the top and bottom plates.

Keep in mind **the directions here apply to nonbearing walls only.** Removing load-bearing walls requires the skills of a master carpenter and sometimes a structural engineer. See *page 58* to learn how to determine if a wall is bearing.

PRESTART CHECKLIST

☐ **TIME**
About 5 to 15 minutes per framing member

☐ **TOOLS**
Reciprocating saw with metal-cutting blade, hammer, pry bar

☐ **SKILLS**
Sawing with a reciprocating saw, pulling nails

☐ **PREP**
Remove trim and drywall or plaster and lath

If you don't own a reciprocating saw, consider renting one the day you remove framing.

Plate

1 Cut through the nails between the bottom of the stud and the plate with a reciprocating saw. Be sure to use a metal-cutting blade.

Top plate

2 Knock the bottom of the stud sideways with a hammer to free the bottom. With the bottom loose, twist and lever the stud free of the nails that hold it to the top plate.

WHAT IF...
You have to remove a doorway?

Top plate

Header

Use a reciprocating saw to cut the nails at the bottom of one of the two sets of doubled studs the same way you did for single studs. Then lever that leg of the doorway free of the bottom plate. Knock the doubled studs sideways with your hammer to free them from the header and the top plate. Pry the header free of the cripple studs above and the doubled studs on the other side. Then cut the nails holding these doubled studs to the bottom plate and twist this leg free as well.

Removing the top plate

1 The top framing of most walls will consist of two 2×4s—a top plate covered by a cap plate. Drive a flat pry bar between the two and pry off the top plate (the bottom 2×4). If the wall you're removing is tied to a perpendicular wall, the cap plate will overlap the adjacent framing at the corner. Use a handsaw to cut off the cap plate from the adjacent corner.

2 If joists run perpendicular above the wall you are removing, drive a flat bar between each joist and the cap plate and pry the plate free. Place a scrap piece of plywood under the bar to protect the ceiling.

WHAT IF...
You find wiring in the wall?

Once you've opened up a wall that contains wiring, you'll usually want to remove the wall before rerouting the circuits. But what do you do with the existing circuits if you need to keep them powered for lights or equipment? Here's an easy way to get wiring out of the way so you can continue working.

Start by turning off the electricity by removing the fuse or throwing the circuit breaker that protects the circuit. Check to make sure the power is off by plugging a light into all of the receptacles and operating all of the switches. Nothing should happen if the power is off.

Next unscrew the receptacles and switches and pull them out of their boxes. Sketch how the wires are connected, noting which color wire attaches to which terminal.

Reassembled boxes

Detach the receptacles and switches from the wires. Pull the wires out of the boxes and back through any holes in the framing. Remove the boxes from the studs. Run the wires back into the now loose boxes and reattach the wires. Screw the receptacles back into the boxes and replace the cover plates. With the wiring removed from the framing, you can proceed with demolition.

WHAT IF...
You're removing part of a wall?

Plate to be removed

If you're removing only a section of a wall, cut the bottom and top plates of the section with a handsaw. Then pry them from the floor and ceiling with a flat pry bar. Be careful to avoid marring the ceiling and finished floor.

REMOVING TOILETS AND SINKS

Most bathroom remodeling projects will require removal of the toilet and sink. Even if you think you can work around them, the job will go more smoothly with the fixtures out of the way. You'll have more working room, and if you're tiling the floor, you'll have substantially fewer tiles to cut and install, and fewer exposed joints to maintain. Besides, removing the fixtures keeps them from getting damaged.

Over time toilet and sink anchor bolts often rust, bend, and otherwise undergo alterations that make their removal a stubborn chore. Don't give up; a close-working hacksaw can come to the rescue.

PRESTART CHECKLIST

☐ **TIME**
About 30 to 45 minutes each for toilet, wall-mounted sink, and pedestal sink (more if anchor bolts prove stubborn)

☐ **TOOLS**
Plumber's plunger, groove-joint pliers, locking pliers (optional), adjustable wrench, straight and phillips screwdrivers, allen wrenches, narrow putty knife, hacksaw, mini hacksaw (optional), pipe wrench, tape measure, bucket

☐ **SKILLS**
Removing screws with screwdrivers, removing fasteners with wrenches

☐ **PREP**
Turn off water supply valve(s) for each fixture removed

☐ **MATERIALS**
Bleach, rags, plastic bag, penetrating oil, wood shims, duct tape

Removing a toilet

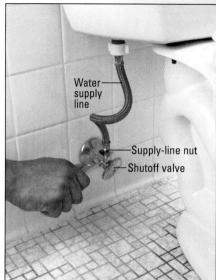

Water supply line — Supply-line nut — Shutoff valve

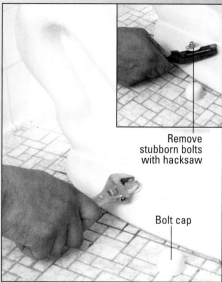

Remove stubborn bolts with hacksaw

Bolt cap

1 Pour a quart of bleach into the tank, flush, and let it refill. Close the shutoff valve and reflush, holding the handle down until the tank empties. Push the water out of the trap with a plunger and stuff the bowl with rags. Disconnect the supply line with a wrench or groove-joint pliers.

2 Pry off the anchor-bolt caps. Remove the anchor bolts with an adjustable wrench or groove-joint pliers. If the bolts spin, snap, or won't come off, cut them with a hacksaw. You can replace the bolts when you reinstall the toilet.

Removing a pedestal sink

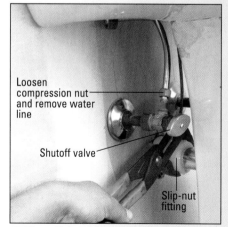

Loosen compression nut and remove water line

Shutoff valve

Slip-nut fitting

1 Shut off the water valves, loosen the compression nuts on both supply lines, and pull the supply line out of the valve. Place rags under the trap to catch any water. Loosen the slip-nut fittings with groove-joint pliers and pull the trap off. Pour the trap water into a bucket.

2 Remove any bolts attaching the top to the pedestal. Lift the top off. If the sink is hung on wall brackets, grasp it near the wall and pull up. Unbolt the pedestal from the floor and lift it off. If the sink is a one-piece unit, unbolt it from the wall and floor. Remove the wall brackets.

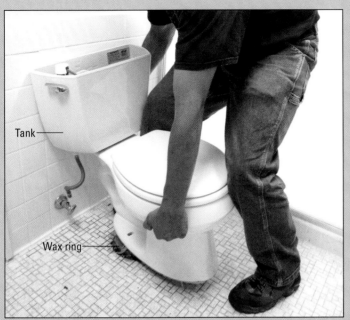

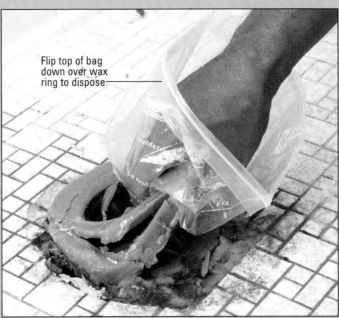

Flip top of bag down over wax ring to dispose

Tank

Wax ring

3 The bottom of the toilet trap fits snugly over a wax ring that seals it against the closet flange in the floor. To break the seal of the wax ring, rock the toilet gently back and forth as you lift it off the floor. Newer, low-capacity toilets may be light enough for you to lift by yourself, but older toilets can weigh up to 60 pounds. Remove the tank bolts and tank first or get help to avoid injury. Lift the toilet off the floor and carry it to another room.

4 With one hand in a plastic bag, grab the inside bottom edge of the ring. Pull it out, pulling the bag over the ring with your other hand. Dispose of the ring. With a putty knife scrape residue from the flange. Stuff a large rag into the drain to keep out debris and duct-tape it in place to keep it from being dislodged as you work.

Removing a wall-mounted sink

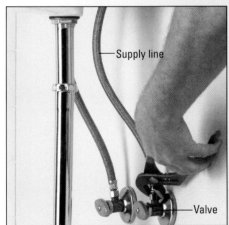

Supply line

Valve

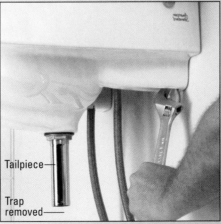

Tailpiece

Trap removed

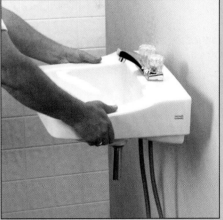

1 Shut off the hot and cold water valves and loosen the compression nuts on both supply lines with groove-joint pliers or a wrench. Pull the supply line out of the valve. If you have fixed-length supply lines, remove the compression nut and move the lines out of the way.

2 Set a bucket under the trap to catch any water released as you remove the pipe. Loosen the slip-nut fittings on both ends of the trap with groove-joint pliers or a pipe wrench and pull the trap off the tailpiece. Dump the trap water in the bucket and remove the sink mounting bolts.

3 Remove any legs that support the front of the sink. Grasp the sink with both hands near the wall and pull it up and off the brackets. If the sink won't come loose, try loosening the wall-bracket bolts a couple of turns, then pull the sink off the brackets. Remove the brackets.

REMOVING SHOWER AND TUB FIXTURES

If you're not replacing or refinishing the walls surrounding a tub or shower, or not removing the bathtub, you can, of course, leave the fixtures in place. But if you want your bathroom to exhibit a unified style, the old fixtures will have to come off. And if you're tiling or otherwise replacing the surrounding walls, you must remove the fixtures.

Tub and shower fixtures can be as temperamental and stubborn as toilet bolts, but with a few deftly placed tools, you'll have them off in short order.

PRESTART CHECKLIST

☐ **TIME**
About 15 minutes for tub and shower fixture set

☐ **TOOLS**
Groove-joint pliers, locking pliers (optional), adjustable wrench, straight and phillips screwdrivers, allen wrenches, narrow putty knife, pipe wrench

☐ **SKILLS**
Removing screws with screwdrivers, removing fasteners with wrenches

☐ **PREP**
Turn off water supply valve(s) for each fixture removed

☐ **MATERIALS**
Rags, penetrating oil, duct tape, pipe nipples, and caps

Removing a showerhead

Duct tape protects gooseneck from damage

1 If you are replacing the plumbing or valves to a shower, you must first turn off the water supply. Remove the showerhead with an adjustable or open-end wrench. If the showerhead is not machined for a wrench, use groove-joint pliers, protecting the collar with duct tape or rags.

2 Wrap the gooseneck with several layers of duct tape about 1 inch from the wall to protect it. Adjust a pipe wrench so it just fits over the gooseneck and position the jaws so the wrench will pull counterclockwise. Pull the wrench firmly, keeping it perpendicular to the pipe.

Removing a tub spout

Grasp the spout firmly with both hands and unscrew it from the fitting. If the spout is fastened to the pipe with a clamp, loosen the clamp screw—usually accessible from the plumbing access door on the other side of the wall behind the shower. Pull off the spout.

Cap the pipe

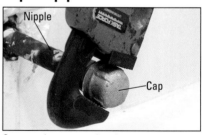

Nipple

Cap

Once you've removed a shower gooseneck or tub spout, screw a pipe nipple into the fitting. A nipple is a 5- to 6-inch length of water pipe threaded on both ends. It temporarily replaces the fixture and allows you to cut the backerboard in the exact location for the pipe. It also protects the fitting threads from becoming clogged with adhesive. Take the gooseneck or tub spout to the hardware store so you find the right nipple size. Cap the nipple with a cap of the correct size.

Removing shower faucet handles

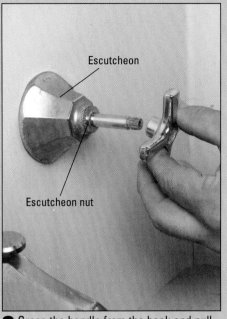

Escutcheon

Escutcheon nut

1 Most faucets fit on a valve stem and are held in place with setscrews. If the screw is not visible, you'll find it under a cover plate. Insert a thin screwdriver blade or putty knife under the cover plate and pop it off. Cover the drain to make sure you don't lose the cover plate or screw.

2 Select the proper size screwdriver (usually a phillips head) and remove the screws from each faucet.

3 Grasp the handle from the back and pull it toward you. Wiggling sometimes helps. So does penetrating oil. If the handle is especially stubborn, rent a handle puller. Remove the escutcheon nut and escutcheon. Tape the parts together and store them out of the way.

Measure the thread length

If you are tiling over existing wall tile or installing new tile with backerboard, the combined thickness of the new materials may exceed the length of the threads on the faucet valves. The threads of the valves need to extend beyond the new wall.

Measure the depth of the threads. If they are less than the thickness of the new materials, you'll have to install new faucets—a job best left to a plumber.

WHAT IF ...
A faucet has only one handle?

Plastic screw cap

Escutcheon plate

1 Remove the setscrew (on the underside of the handle or under a plastic cap) with a screwdriver or allen wrench. If you can't find a setscrew, try unscrewing the handle itself.

2 Pull the handle off the stem and remove the escutcheon-plate screws. Pull off the escutcheon plate and any other plates under it, tape the parts together, and store them.

REMOVING A TUB

Bathtubs sustain heavy use and are frequently scoured, so it's not surprising they eventually need to be replaced. If your tub is chipped, difficult to keep clean, or just plain ugly, you can refinish it, but you'll get more years from a new tub. Besides, by installing a new tub, you get to choose one whose style is in harmony with the rest of your new bathroom design.

Plan and prepare
You can cut a fiberglass, polymer, or pressed-steel tub with a reciprocating saw and remove the pieces. Cast iron can be broken with a sledgehammer or, like a steel tub, will have to be carried out in one piece. If you decide to remove and preserve your old tub, measure it and make sure you will be able to get it past other fixtures and out the door. Remove the sink or the toilet if they will be in the way. Cut and tape pieces of plywood to the floor and cover with a drop cloth.

If the tub surround is tiled, you might be able to reuse the tiles. If some break, either find tiles to match or plan to retile the walls. Or you can install a prefab tub surround (*pages 190–191*).

PRESTART CHECKLIST

☐ **TIME**
A full day to remove a bathtub

☐ **TOOLS**
Groove-joint pliers, flat pry bar, crowbar, hammer, drill, screwdriver, utility knife

☐ **SKILLS**
Basic carpentry skills, dismantling a trap

☐ **PREP**
Locate access to the tub plumbing in the basement below or in an adjacent room; if necessary, install an access panel (*page 69*)

☐ **MATERIALS**
Plywood and drop cloth to protect the floor

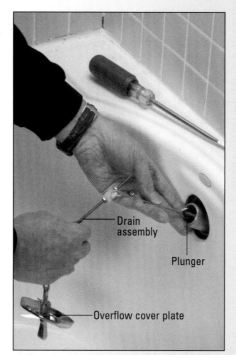

Drain assembly
Plunger
Overflow cover plate

1 From inside the tub, unscrew and remove the overflow cover plate. If a drain assembly is attached to it, pull it out. (A drain assembly with a plunger is shown.) If there is one, unscrew and remove the mounting bracket.

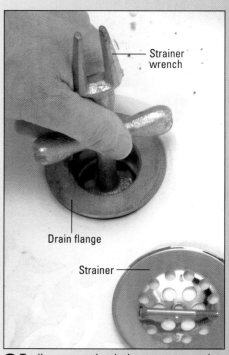

Strainer wrench
Drain flange
Strainer

2 To disconnect the drain, you may need to remove a screw or two and remove the strainer. Or you may need to lift out a stopper and a rocker assembly (*page 187*). Use a strainer wrench to remove the drain flange from the tub.

WASTE-AND-OVERFLOW INSTALLATIONS

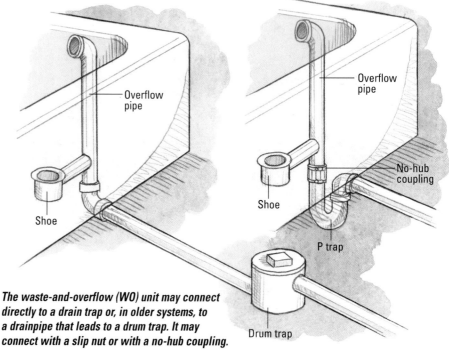

Overflow pipe
Shoe
Overflow pipe
No-hub coupling
Shoe
P trap
Drum trap

The waste-and-overflow (WO) unit may connect directly to a drain trap or, in older systems, to a drainpipe that leads to a drum trap. It may connect with a slip nut or with a no-hub coupling.

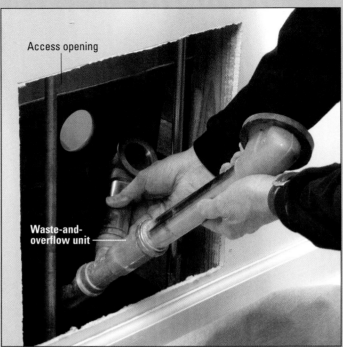

3 From an access panel behind the tub or from below, disconnect the waste-and-overflow (WO) unit from the drain line. Depending on the installation, you may need to unscrew a slip nut or loosen the screws on a no-hub coupling (see *pages 186–188* for alternatives). If the parts are cemented plastic, you'll have to cut through a pipe. Remove the WO unit from the tub. (You may not need to remove the old WO unit if it will fit exactly on the new tub. Measure carefully.)

4 Remove the tub spout and remove the wall surface all around the tub to a height of about 8 inches. (If there are tub faucet handles, leave them in place if they are at least 8 inches above the tub.) Use a flat pry bar or putty knife to pry off tiles. Cut through drywall with a drywall saw. If the wall is plaster, use a reciprocating saw, taking care not to cut into the studs. Pry off or unscrew nails and screws.

WHAT IF...
You need to install an access panel?

Add a ready-made panel

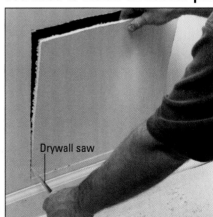

1 If there is no easy access to the plumbing behind the tub, install an access panel in the adjacent room. Use a drywall saw to cut a hole in the wall surface, spanning from stud to stud.

2 Screw 2×2 cleats to either side of the opening. Cut a piece of plywood 2 or 3 inches larger than the opening. Paint it to match the wall and attach it with screws.

Purchase a ready-made plumbing-access panel for a quicker installation and a neater appearance. Follow the manufacturer's instructions for cutting the hole and installing it.

Removing a tub *(continued)*

Crowbar

Tub flange

5 Pry out or unscrew any nails or screws anchoring the tub flange to studs. Where the tub rests on the floor, use a utility knife to cut through a bead of caulk, if there is one. Use a crowbar to pry the tub an inch or so away from the back wall.

6 Unless the tub is an old-fashioned claw foot or other type of stand-alone, it will fit fairly tightly between studs on either side. That means you probably can't slide it outward unless you cut away the wall surface on both sides. The best way is usually to lift the tub up on one end. Pry up one end of the tub first with a crowbar, then with 2×4s. Working with a helper, stand the tub upright.

STANLEY PRO TIP

Remove a cast-iron tub

A cast-iron tub weighs 300 to 400 pounds—a bear to remove. If you plan to discard it anyway, break it into manageable pieces. Wear eye protection and gloves. Cover it with an old drop cloth (to prevent pieces from flying) and hit it repeatedly with a sledgehammer.

Choosing a new tub

Acrylic or fiberglass tubs are inexpensive, light, and easy to install. Some have finishes that are fairly durable, but they may become dull in time. An enameled steel tub has a sturdier finish but lacks insulating properties; bathwater will cool quickly. Enameled cast iron is the most expensive and heaviest material but may be worth the cost because it retains a gleaming finish for decades, fills quietly, and keeps water warm the longest.

Enameled steel

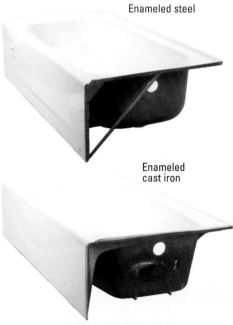

Acrylic

Enameled cast iron

REMOVING AN OLD VANITY

Although you may find many reasons for tiling over or otherwise renovating an existing vanity, removing the old one and installing a new model is generally the wiser option. A new vanity provides you with the opportunity to integrate all aspects of your bathroom design.

As a compromise, and if you plan a tiled vanity, you may want to remove the existing countertop and build a new base for the tile *(pages 222–223).* One of the main advantages of making a new base as opposed to tiling over it is that you will not raise the height of the countertop. That may not sound important, but the addition of even the thickness of a new tile surface can disrupt the comfortable use of your bathroom.

Whether you leave the sink in or out of the counter when removing it is a matter of personal choice. Removing the sink reduces the weight.

PRESTART CHECKLIST

☐ **TIME**
From 45 minutes to one hour; total time will vary with the length and configuration of the countertop

☐ **TOOLS**
Removing countertop: wrenches, groove-joint pliers, cordless drill and bits, utility knife, pry bar, hammer, putty knife

☐ **SKILLS**
Removing nuts with wrench, scoring with utility knife, prying, driving screws

☐ **PREP**
Shut off water to house if no supply valves are present

Removing a vanity countertop

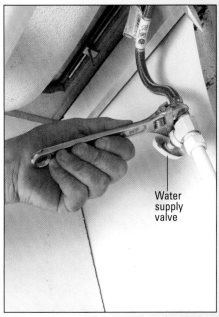

Water supply valve

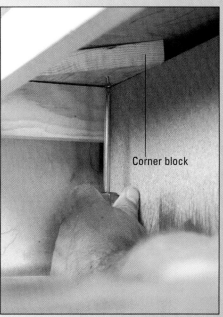

Corner block

1 Turn off the supply valves to the sink and disconnect the lines. To disconnect the lift rod that controls the sink stopper, pull off the clip and loosen the setscrew that holds the strap to the rod. Loosen the compression nuts on both supply lines and pull the supply lines out of the valves.

2 Locate corner blocks or cleats that fasten the countertop to the cabinet. Using a screwdriver or cordless drill, unscrew the fasteners. Do not unscrew the fasteners that attach corner blocks to the cabinet frame.

Removing the vanity base

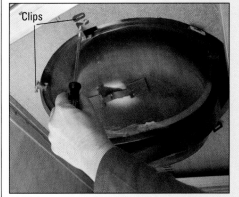

Clips

Enlarge openings

1 If the weight of a sink makes removing the countertop difficult, remove the sink first. **Shut off the water;** disconnect the supply lines and drain pipe. Loosen any retaining screws and remove the clips.

2 Enlarge the back-panel openings around the shutoff valves and drain extension with a utility saw. Unscrew the fasteners that hold the vanity to the wall. Cut any caulking or adhesive along the wall and floor. Then pull the cabinet away from the wall and floor.

Removing a vanity countertop *(continued)*

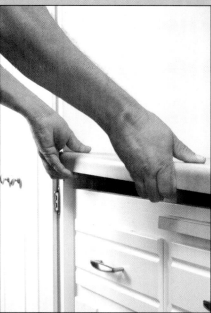

3 Score the joint between the backsplash and the wall with a sharp utility knife. Then score the joint between the countertop and cabinet to break the bond of any glue or caulk. Keep the blade of the knife as perpendicular to the cabinet frame as possible to avoid cutting the wood.

4 Pry off any trim at the countertop edge. Force a pry bar between the countertop and cabinet and pry up the countertop. If the countertop is too heavy to lift, cut it into sections with a reciprocating saw. Saw carefully to avoid cutting the cabinet frame.

Removing a solid surface countertop

Synthetic resin countertops are fastened to the cabinet frame with glue. Use a sharp utility knife to cut the glue line where the countertop meets the cabinet. Tap a pry bar into the joint and pop the countertop free.

WHAT IF...
The existing countertop is tiled?

With a cold chisel and hammer, break the center of one tile. Chip out the pieces until you get to a joint. Tap the blade of a wide cold chisel under the tiles and pop them loose. If the tile is set on backerboard, remove the tile and backerboard on the entire countertop. Hire a pro to saw out a mortar-bed installation.

Removing a drop-in sink

1 If the weight of a sink makes removing the countertop difficult, remove the sink first. Shut off the water; disconnect the supply lines and drainpipe. Loosen any retaining screws and remove the clips.

2 Cut any caulk along the edge of the sink with a utility knife. Either push up on the sink from below so you can lift it out or insert a wide putty knife under the edge of the sink and pry it up until you can grasp it with your hands. Lift the sink up and out of the countertop.

REMOVING RESILIENTS, CERAMIC TILE, AND CARPET

Removing existing floor surfaces allows you to properly prepare for tile or other finished flooring, and gives you a chance to inspect the condition of the underlayment. Don't expect to rush this stage of your demolition. Properly applied flooring is meant to stay down, not come up. Removing it can be slow, patient work.

Before you tackle the flooring, remove the baseboards and shoe molding. Starting at a corner, slide a small pry bar behind the shoe. Loosen the shoe until you can insert the pry bar next to a nail. Pry each nail out a little at a time.

To take off the baseboard, work a wide putty knife behind the board and use it as a prying surface at each nail, prying the baseboard away with a pry bar. Remove vinyl cove molding with a putty knife, softening the adhesive with a hair dryer.

PRESTART CHECKLIST

☐ **TIME**
From 30 to 45 minutes per square yard, depending on the type of flooring

☐ **TOOLS**
Resilient floors: heat gun, wide putty knife, floor scraper, utility knife
Carpet: utility knife, pry bar, hammer, screwdriver, floor scraper
Ceramic tile: grout knife, cold chisels, hammer, margin trowel, sanding block

☐ **SKILLS**
Cutting with circular saw, using pry bar, using hammer and cold chisel

☐ **MATERIALS**
Resilient floors: adhesive remover

Removing resilient tile

Warm the adhesive with a heat gun. If you don't have a heat gun, use a hair dryer set on high heat. Warm a corner first, insert a floor scraper or wide putty knife, and with the heat on, lift up the tile. Scrape the adhesive from the floor with a floor scraper.

Removing sheet flooring

Start at a corner. Insert a floor scraper or wide putty knife under the sheet and pry it up. Work down each strip of the material, rolling the strip as you go, using a hair dryer to soften the adhesive. Then spray them with adhesive remover. Let the remover work, then scrape the residue from the floor.

Removing conventional carpet

1 If the carpet is not tacked or glued to the floor, work a straight screwdriver under a corner or grab the corner with groove-joint pliers and pull the carpet off the tack strips. Once you get started, the carpet should tear up easily.

2 Cut the pad into strips with a utility knife. Then grab each section of pad and pull it from the floor. Roll the pad as you go and dispose of the rolls. Then work a pry bar under the tacking strips and pry them up.

Using existing floor tile as substrate for ceramic tile

1 With a high-quality hammer or small sledge and cold chisel, break out any damaged tile, working from the center of the tile to the edges. Pull out the broken chips and scrape off any remaining adhesive. Vacuum the area.

2 Using a margin trowel or wide putty knife, apply adhesive in the recess and back-butter a replacement tile. Push the tile into the recess until the adhesive oozes up from the grout joints. Make sure the tile is level with the rest of the floor, wipe off the excess thinset, and let it cure.

3 Use a sanding block and a coarse grit of abrasive paper to roughen the entire surface of the tile. This will give the tile a "tooth" for the adhesive and strengthen its bond with the floor.

Removing floor tile set in thinset

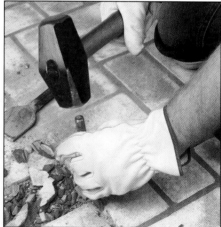

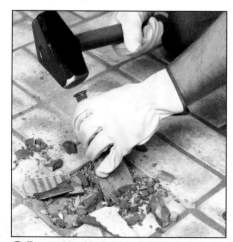

1 Create a starting point in a central area of the floor by cracking one tile with a small sledge and cold chisel. Grip the chisel firmly and strike it with a sharp blow of the small sledgehammer. **Wear eye protection.**

2 Break out the remaining area of the tile with the sledge and brush the loose pieces out of the recess. Chip out the grout along the edge of an adjacent tile.

3 Tap a wide chisel at an angle under the edge of the adjoining tile and pop off the tile. Repeat the process for each tile until you have removed the entire floor. Dispose of the tile and scrape off any remaining adhesive.

INSTALLING NEW UNDERLAYMENT

No matter how you finish your bathroom floor, it will only be as good as its underlayment—the supporting layer fastened to the joists. Underlayment provides a smooth, stable surface for the finished floor.

You can lay ceramic tile over hardwood and ceramic floors—if the surface and subfloor are stable and in good condition. The same is true for uncushioned resilient tile or sheet materials on a wood frame floor. But new ceramic tile over an existing floor will raise the surface by at least ¾ inch. Removing the existing floor will minimize any change in floor levels and reveal any hidden faults that need repair.

If your underlayment shows signs of rot or is not thick enough to support the finished floor, or if you're working in new construction, you'll have to install new underlayment, typically ¾-inch exterior plywood. Bring the plywood into the room a few days before installation to acclimate it, which will reduce shrinkage or expansion.

PRESTART CHECKLIST

☐ **TIME**
From 30 to 45 minutes per square yard

☐ **TOOLS**
Circular saw, cordless drill, screwdriver bit, tape measure, chalk line

☐ **SKILLS**
Driving fasteners with cordless drill, cutting with circular saw, measuring and marking

☐ **PREP**
Remove existing flooring as necessary

☐ **MATERIALS**
¾-inch exterior grade plywood, galvanized screws, construction adhesive (optional)

1 Set up 2×4s as a work surface—in an area where they won't be in the way. Start with a full sheet in a corner, squaring it with the room and centering its edges on the joists. When cutting pieces, measure from the edge of the board to the center of the joist, and snap a chalk line for the cut.

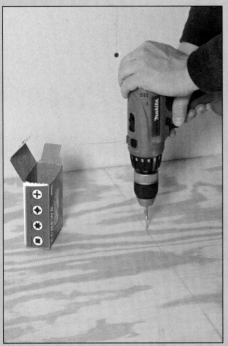

2 With old underlayment, locate the joists and mark their positions on the wall. Lay the new sheet down and snap perpendicular joist lines to guide the placement of fasteners. Apply a bead of construction adhesive (optional) and drive screws long enough to penetrate the joists.

3 Set half sheets next to full sheets so the joints are offset. Leave at least a ⅛-inch gap between the sheets (an 8d nail makes a good spacer) and ¼ inch at the walls.

Removing a hardwood floor

To remove hardwood or parquet flooring, start by making several plunge cuts in one or two strips or planks. Chisel out the cut area. Tap a pry bar under the flooring and pry the material up. Insert the bar fully under the strip or plank, not the tongue.

INSTALLING CEMENT BACKERBOARD

Cement backerboard is made expressly as a substrate for ceramic tile. Installed over plywood or other underlayment on floors, countertops, or walls, it provides a solid, stable surface that is unaffected by moisture or temperature changes.

Center the backerboard edges on joists and studs. Mark the joist and stud locations before you start. Because you won't be able to see marks after you have troweled on the thinset, mark joist locations on the wall and stud locations on the ceiling.

Offset the joints by half a sheet where possible. Leave at least a ⅛-inch gap between sheets and a ¼-inch gap at the walls (about the diameter of a pencil).

Scoop thinset out of the bucket with a margin trowel, then spread it with the notched trowel recommended by the adhesive manufacturer.

PRESTART CHECKLIST

☐ **TIME**
About 30 to 45 minutes per square foot of surface

☐ **TOOLS**
Drywall square, carbide scriber, utility knife, rasp, tape measure, cordless drill, carbide hole saw, compass, hammer for large holes, trowel, margin trowel, corner drywall knife

☐ **SKILLS**
Precise measuring and cutting, driving fasteners with cordless drill, troweling

☐ **PREP**
Prepare, vacuum, and damp-clean surfaces; install waterproofing membrane in wet locations

☐ **MATERIALS**
Thinset, backerboard, 1¼- and 2-inch backerboard screws, 2-inch gummed fiber mesh tape, 2×4 lumber for blocking (walls only), 8d nails

Cutting backerboard sections

1 Protect finished floors with a tarp. Backerboard particles will easily scratch a floor. Mark the line to be cut and position a drywall square or metal T square on the line. Using a carbide backerboard scriber and firm pressure, scribe the cut line. Make several passes.

2 Stand the sheet on edge or turn it over. Working from the side opposite the scored line, brace the board with your knee on the line and snap the board.

Cutting small holes

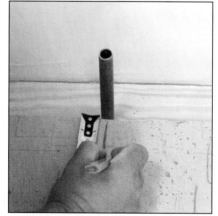 

1 Set the board against the pipe or other obstruction. Mark the diameter of the hole to be cut. Use a tape measure to locate the center of the hole. For faucets measure the location of each faucet hole from the wall and from the tub or floor.

2 Use a cordless drill and carbide-tipped hole saw or coring saw to cut small holes in backerboard. Place the drill point of the saw on the mark you made, and use light pressure and high speed to cut through the backerboard.

3 Keeping the pieces at an angle and using a utility knife, cut through the board to separate the two pieces. Depending on how deeply you made your first cut, you may have to make several passes with the knife to separate the pieces.

4 Backerboard cuts are rough, whether made with a carbide scriber or a utility knife. Pieces being joined should have as smooth an edge as possible. Use a contour plane with a serrated blade, a rasp, or a masonry stone to smooth out the edge. Keep the tool perpendicular to the edge of the board and pass over the board several times until its surface is flat.

Cutting large holes

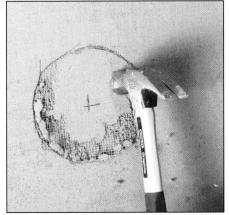

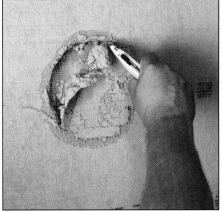

1 When the diameter of a hole to be cut exceeds the size of available hole saws, measure the obstruction and use a compass to mark its location on the backerboard. Then score completely through the backerboard mesh with a utility knife or carbide scriber.

2 Support the cutout with the palm of one hand, if necessary, and tap the scored edge with a hammer. Continue tapping until the surface around the circumference crumbles. Alternatively, drill a series of small holes around the circumference.

3 Using a utility knife, cut through the mesh on the opposite side of the board. Push the cutout through and smooth the edges with a rasp, serrated contour plane, or masonry stone.

Installing backerboard on floors

1 Mix and pour thinset *(page 121).* Hold the smooth side of a notched trowel at a 30-degree angle and spread the mortar in a thick, even coat, forcing it into the subfloor. Then, keeping the notched side of the trowel in contact with the floor and at a 45- to 75-degree angle, work the mortar into ridges.

2 While the mortar is still wet, tip the board on a long edge and hinge it toward the floor. Line the first board on a joist and keep a gap of ⅛ inch between boards, ¼ inch at walls. Manufacturers' directions may vary, but typically you should stagger the joints. Walk on the board to set it in the mortar.

3 Using a cordless drill and phillips bit, drive backerboard screws through the board and into the subfloor at about 8-inch intervals. Use 2-inch backerboard screws at the joists and 1¼-inch screws in the field. Set the screws so they are flush with the surface of the board.

Installing backerboard on walls

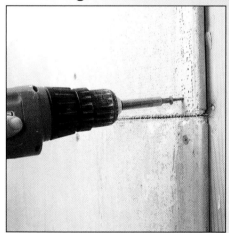

1 Nail blocking between studs to support joints, if necessary. Apply construction adhesive to the studs. Screw the board to the studs and blocking. Rest the next pieces on ⅛-inch spacers (8d nails) before fastening.

2 Use 2- or 4-inch gummed tape over each backerboard joint. Press the tape into the joint and unroll it as you go. Use a utility knife to cut the tape at the end of the joint.

3 Apply a thin coat of thinset mortar to the taped joint with a margin trowel. Trowel on enough mortar to fill the joint and level it with the backerboard. Feather the edges until they are smooth.

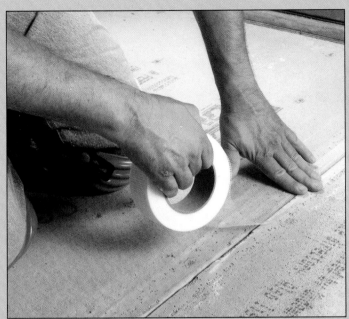

4 Apply 2-inch pregummed fiberglass mesh tape over each joint, pressing the tape firmly on the backerboard. The tape cuts easily with a utility knife. Use 4-inch tape (if available) for increased strength. Alternatively you can embed ungummed tape in a thin coat of mortar applied to the joints. Use this method where stronger joints are required—in stone-tile installations, for example.

5 Whether you have used ungummed or pregummed tape, finish the joint by applying a thin coat of thinset mortar over the tape. Use a margin trowel to scoop mortar from the bucket. Apply the mortar so it levels the recess in the joint from side to side. Feather the edges to avoid creating high spots under the tiled surface.

Taping corners

Tape corners with either 2-inch or 4-inch gummed fiberglass mesh tape. In either case do not precut the tape to length. Unroll it as you press it into the joint and cut it when you reach the end. Precut lengths of gummed tape may roll up and stick to themselves before you get them on the board.

If using 2-inch tape, place one length along one edge and another length along the other edge. Bridge the central edges of the corner with a third length of tape. Four-inch tape hastens the job. Fold the tape in half as you press it into the corner.

If using ungummed tape, first spread a thin coat of mortar into the corner joint and smooth it with a drywall corner knife. Then embed the tape in the mortar. With any kind of tape, finish the joint with a thin coat of mortar, feathering the edges smoothly.

STANLEY PRO TIP

Fix backerboard screw snaps

Backerboard fasteners, unlike drywall screws, are made to withstand the rigors of tile installations. Occasionally, however, one will snap off. Check the torque setting of your cordless drill to make sure the clutch slips when the screw just dimples the board. If a backerboard screw snaps, remove the loose piece and drive another about 1 inch away from the first one.

FRAMING & FINISHING WALLS

Framing a wall is satisfying work. The pieces go together quickly and progress seems significant. Assembling the wall is actually the easiest part of the job. What takes time is the accurate layout of its parts.

An accurate layout assures you of a wall that is plumb and straight, with studs on 16-inch centers. A properly laid out wall, in turn, makes drywall installation and finishing easier.

Choosing lumber

A well-made wall actually starts in your lumberyard or home center. Get the straightest and most defect-free stock you can find. Examine each 2×4 carefully. A few loose knots might be OK, but splits and severe bows are not. Even though you might be picking through the "stud-grade" bin, you'll find a lot of latitude within that grade. With a little patience, you'll go home with lumber that won't cause you construction problems and send you looking for the sledgehammer.

Partition walls (the most common in a remodeling project) are typically framed with 2×4 studs fastened between 2×4 top and bottom plates. If your bathroom remodeling plan calls for the new wall to house large drainpipes, use 2×6 stock throughout.

Wood or metal framing?

Wood is the traditional material for interior walls, and wood walls are generally easier to preassemble than to build in place. If you're short on assembly space, as many remodeling projects are, consider metal framing. Made of lightweight, galvanized steel, metal framing is easy to handle, won't burn, and is rust-resistant. It's ideal for building in place; it's not designed for preassembly. The studs are still called "studs," but the plates are called "tracks."

After you've added utilities to the wall, add insulation for soundproofing.

CHAPTER PREVIEW

Anatomy of walls and ceilings
page 82

Laying out a new wall
page 84

Framing a wall
page 86

Building a wall with metal framing
page 90

Hanging drywall
page 92

Finishing drywall
page 96

**Framing a
built-in cabinet**
page 100

**Installing
wainscoting and
tileboard**
page 102

Tiling walls
page 104

**Tiling a
window recess**
page 108

**Installing
crown molding**
page 110

ANATOMY OF WALLS AND CEILINGS

If the bathroom remodeling project you're planning involves the construction or modification of interior walls, it will help to become familiar with how walls are framed and some of the terminology associated with their construction.

Most houses in this country are stick-framed; that is, their skeletons are built from a framework of relatively small pieces of wood. Typically interior walls are framed with 2×4s. This makes walls about 4½ inches thick (3½-inch framing covered on both sides by ½-inch-thick drywall). The illustration on *page 83* shows how the assembled pieces form a wall and names each framing member.

Terminology

All 2×4s look basically the same, but in home construction they have different names depending on how they are used within the wall. **Studs** are the vertical members that make up most of the framing and provide support for the floors above the wall. The cavities in between the studs are called **bays** (or stud bays). The horizontal 2×4 fastened to the floor and tying the studs together at the bottom of the wall is called the **bottom plate.** The corresponding 2×4 at the top of the wall is the **top plate.** It is often capped by a 2×4 **cap plate** whose function is to provide additional strength and to tie the wall to perpendicular walls.

In new construction, walls are usually assembled on the floor of the structure with a single top plate. The cap plate is added after the walls are raised into position and need to be tied at the corners. Sometimes **blocking** is added to provide a solid surface between the studs for attaching cabinets or handrails. In some localities codes require blocking as a fire-stop in any stud bay that extends between floors. This keeps the bay from acting as a chimney that could allow a fire to spread quickly from floor to floor. Blocking and extra studs are also added at corners and where stud spacing is irregular so drywall has a fastening surface.

Openings for doors or windows

Openings for doors or windows have their own set of terms. The opening itself is called the **rough opening.** The size of the rough opening required for a particular door or window is specified by its manufacturer. Typically it's 1 inch larger than the outside dimensions of the door or window itself. Doubled studs stand on both sides of the opening. One stud of each pair, called the **king stud,** runs from plate to plate. The **jack stud,** or **trimmer,** supports the **header,** a doubled 2×4, 2×6, or 2×8 that defines the height of the rough opening and carries the load of the upper floors across it.

In most walls, headers are topped by short studs known as **cripple studs,** which transfer weight to the header and help support drywall and trim.

Types of walls

A wall that supports the weight of the stories above it is a bearing wall and is said to be structural *(page 58).* If a wall merely divides the interior space, it is not structural but simply a partition wall.

The framing members in the floor and in the ceiling are called joists. Underfoot, a subfloor is nailed to the **joists.** The walls are usually fastened to the subfloor. Overhead, drywall can be attached to the underside of the ceiling joists, or if you prefer, the grid for a dropped ceiling can be attached to them.

Furred "walls"

Certain "walls" are not walls at all, as the term is used to describe a vertical structure framed with 2×4s or 2×6s. Furred walls are constructed with 2×2s or 1× stock to provide a nailing surface for covering concrete block or masonry. Such "furred out" walls are often used in basements where a more attractive surface than concrete is desired. They are not structural, and though they are often called "walls," they are more properly considered a nailing base for paneling and other wallcoverings.

Why 16 inches?

In much residential construction, wall studs and floor and ceiling joists are spaced 16 inches on center. (On center, or OC, indicates the distance from the center of one member to the center of the next.) Why 16 inches? Plywood or oriented strand board used to sheathe the outside of the walls and the drywall used to finish the inside all come in sheets 48 inches (4 feet) wide. The 4-foot width spans four studs spaced 16 inches apart, with the edges of the sheet at the middle of the outer studs. This allows the edges of the sheet goods to be firmly supported by a stud and still leave room for the adjoining sheet. Spacing studs on 16-inch centers allows efficient use of 4×8 sheet stock.

FRAMING TERMINOLOGY

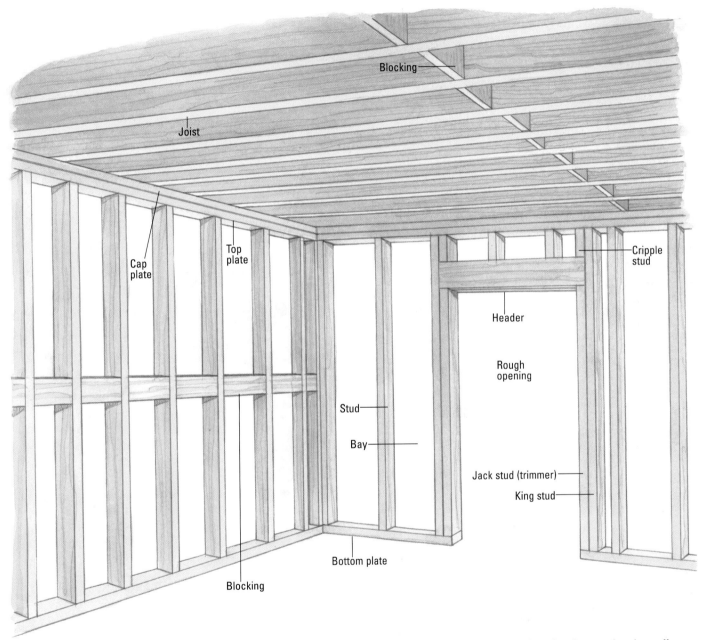

Blocking

Joist

Cap plate

Top plate

Cripple stud

Header

Rough opening

Stud

Bay

Jack stud (trimmer)

King stud

Bottom plate

Blocking

Before planning your interior wall project, learn the names and functions of all wall-framing members.

LAYING OUT A NEW WALL

Erecting a new wall starts with the installation of the cap plate on the ceiling. Once you've marked the position of the cap plate and fastened it, you can turn your attention to assembling the wall and attaching it to the cap plate and the floor.

The job of putting up a new wall ranges from simple to complex, depending on whether the wall runs parallel to the ceiling joists or perpendicular to them. A wall running perpendicular to the joists is easier to build because you can fasten the cap plate to the joists without adding any structural support in the ceiling.

Building a wall that runs parallel to the joists is somewhat more involved. Unless you are lucky and your wall falls directly under a joist, you'll have to open up the ceiling to install blocking to provide a surface to which you can fasten the cap plate. You'll need to install blocking between the floor joists too. If moving your proposed wall an inch or two would place it under a joist, consider doing so.

If you are attaching a cap plate on a plaster ceiling, predrill the plate and fasten it with 3-inch wood screws to minimize damage to the surrounding plaster.

PRESTART CHECKLIST

☐ **TIME**
About 1 hour for a simple wall that's perpendicular to the joists

☐ **TOOLS**
Tape measure, chalk line, hammer, circular saw, power drill/driver, utility knife, layout square

☐ **SKILLS**
Measuring, snapping a chalk line, hammering, crosscutting

☐ **PREP**
Complete remodeling plans

☐ **MATERIALS**
2×4 for top plate, 16d nails

Installing the cap plate

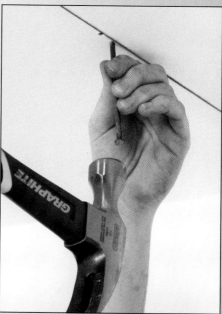

1 Start by marking the ends of the new wall on the ceiling using the dimensions you worked out on your bathroom plan view *(pages 42–45)*. With a helper snap a chalk line between the two points. Make sure the chalk line represents the edge of the cap plate, not the center.

2 Locate the joists with a stud finder. Drive an 8d nail through the ceiling to double-check. If it punches through easily, you've missed the joist; move over an inch and try again. Mark the center of each joist on the ceiling.

WHAT IF...
You don't have room to preassemble the wall?

If you don't have room to preassemble the wall and set it up, you'll have to build it in place. Mark the top and bottom plates for the stud positions, including any doorway framing. Then locate and fasten the top and bottom plates using the techniques shown above. Measure the stud length at each position and cut it. Toe-nail the studs while a helper plumbs them. At doorways fasten the king studs, jack studs, headers, and cripples.

3 With the joist locations marked, cut a 2×4 cap plate to the length of the new wall. Measure the distance of the first joist from the corner and transfer this measurement to the plate. Measure and mark each joist position on the plate.

Joist location

4 Starting a nail at each joist location is easy while the plate is still on the floor. Use predrilled 3-inch bugle-head screws if you're fastening the plate to a plastered ceiling or if you prefer screws over nails.

5 With a helper hold the cap plate in place along the chalk line and nail it through the ceiling into the joists. Start fastening at one end and work down the plate, forcing it if necessary to lay straight on your chalk line.

Running a wall parallel to the joists

1 Use a drywall saw or reciprocating saw to cut away the drywall flush with the inside faces of the joists where the wall will attach. (For cutting plaster see *page 61*.) Snap a chalk line along each joist ¾ inch from the edge. Then use a utility knife to cut away a ¾-inch strip of drywall. This will expose surfaces on the joists for attaching the new drywall.

2 Cut blocking to fit snugly between the joists. Use four toenails to attach each block with its wide face down. Use a ⅛-inch-diameter bit to predrill the ends of the blocks for the toenails.

3 Nail or screw the blocking in place between the joists. Space them 16 inches on center to provide support for the new drywall as well as convenient nailing for crown molding. Cut and fasten drywall to the blocking and joists. Install blocking between the floor joists also, then fasten the cap plate to the blocking at the location shown on your dimensioned plan.

FRAMING A WALL

The basic strategy for building a wall is comprised of four steps:

- Cut the framing members to length.
- Assemble the frame on the floor.
- Raise the wall into place.
- Fasten it to the top and bottom plates.

This method allows you to attach the studs by nailing through the bottom and top plates. That's much easier than toe-nailing, especially toe-nailing overhead. If you don't have enough room, you'll have to attach the top and bottom plates to the ceiling and floor and toe-nail each stud in place.

Measure the distance between the cap plate and the floor and subtract 3¼ inches. This is your stud length, and it accounts for the combined thickness of the top and bottom plates (3 inches) plus ¼ inch. Without that extra margin the wall will hang up on the cap plate when you raise it.

If your wall includes a doorway, select the straightest studs you can find for the opening. And make sure the rough opening coincides with the door manufacturer's specifications—buy the door before you build the wall or get the measurements from the distributor.

PRESTART CHECKLIST

☐ **TIME**
About 1 hour for an 8×8-foot wall, slightly more with a door opening

☐ **TOOLS**
Tape measure, layout square, circular saw, hammer, chalk line, plumb bob, level

☐ **SKILLS**
Measuring and marking, crosscutting, driving fasteners

☐ **PREP**
Install cap plate; get dimensions for rough opening

☐ **MATERIALS**
2×4s, 16d, 10d, 8d nails

Assembling the wall

1 Start by measuring from the underside of the cap plate to the floor to determine the wall height. Measure in several places along the cap plate and use the smallest dimension.

2 Cut the studs to the length of your measurement less 3¼ inches. This accounts for the thickness of the two 2×4 plates (1½ inches each) plus a small amount of clearance so the wall doesn't hang up on the cap plate when you raise it.

Framing a doorway

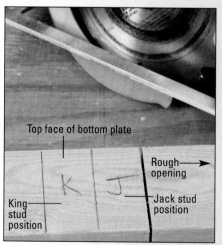

Top face of bottom plate

King stud position

Rough opening

Jack stud position

1 Mark the positions of the jack and king studs on both the top and bottom plates. Set a circular saw to a depth of 1⅛ inches and cut across the bottom plate. Cut on the waste side of the jack stud.

Jack stud

King stud

2 Fasten the king studs and cut the jack studs to the rough opening height less 1½ inches (thickness of the bottom plate). Nail the jack studs plate with 16d nails and to the king studs with 10d nails.

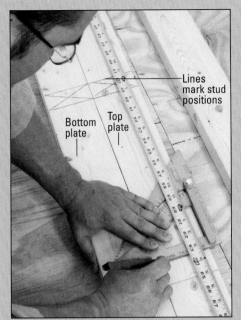

3 Cut the plates and clamp them side by side. Then mark the stud positions on 16-inch centers. This will keep the studs plumb when the wall is up. Measure ¾ inch on both sides of your center marks and mark the edges of the stud locations.

4 Lay out the framing loosely on the floor with the studs in place between the plates. Hold each stud on your marks and nail them through the plates. Make sure the edges of the studs are flush with the edges of the plates.

5 If necessary for your installation, cut and fasten blocking to provide a solid nailing surface for moldings or cabinets. Set the blocking with its wide face out. Toe-nail one side of each block. Here the pieces are positioned to support a chair-rail molding.

3 To assemble a header in a nonbearing wall, fasten a doubled 2×4 between the king studs with 16d nails. Make a bearing-wall header from doubled 2× stock as specified by local codes.

4 Nail one cripple to each king stud with 10d nails to hold the header firmly down on the jack studs. Attach cripples on 16-inch centers to the top plate with 16d nails and to the header with 8d toenails. Raise the wall into place as described on *pages 88–89.*

Raising the wall in place

Plumb bob line

1 Drop a plumb bob from the corner of the cap plate to transfer the wall position to the floor. If you are working alone, hang the plumb bob from a nail in the plate. Let the plumb bob come to rest and mark the position on the floor. Repeat at the other end.

2 Snap a chalk line between the two marks you made using the plumb bob. This line represents the edge of the bottom plate. Use a framing square to make sure the line is perpendicular to the adjoining wall and resnap the line if necessary.

WHAT IF…
You are anchoring to concrete?

To anchor the plate to a concrete slab use masonry nails. Be sure to **wear safety goggles** when driving nails into concrete—to avoid damage to your eyes from flying concrete chips. Lay down a generous amount of construction adhesive on the slab for additional holding power.

Framing a corner

If your new wall turns a corner, frame it with four studs or with three studs and blocking as shown. This creates a sturdy structure that provides a 1-inch nailing surface for inside-corner drywall as well as solid nailing for drywall on the outside corner.

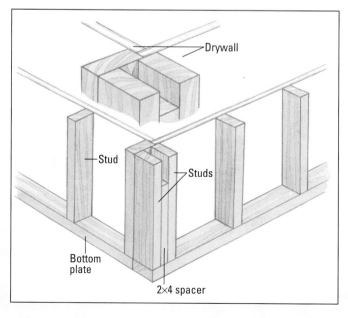

Drywall

Stud

Studs

Bottom plate

2×4 spacer

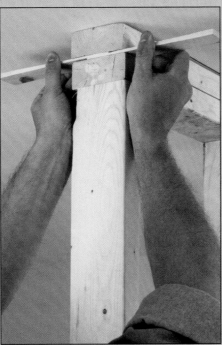

3 Position the wall so the bottom plate is about a foot away from the chalk line. Lift the wall by the top plate and tip it up until it is vertical. Slide it into position under the cap plate.

4 Slip in a pair of shims where there are spaces between the cap plate and the top plate. Drive them in until they are secure. When you fasten the wall to the cap plate, drive the fasteners through the shims to keep them from slipping out.

5 Anchor the wall by nailing through the top plate into the cap plate. Make sure the edges of the two plates are flush. Starting at the adjoining wall, plumb each stud with a carpenter's level, nailing the bottom plate to the floor as you work toward the other end of the wall.

Spacing studs accurately

Make stud layout easier and accurate—mark them with a between-stud-spacing of 14½ inches. That will put them 16 inches on center.

To mark the location of the first stud, measure 15¼ inches from the end of the plates. Mark the stud position on the plates and measure 14½ inches between the edges of each succeeding stud. This will center the fourth stud at 48 inches—just right for a 4×8 sheet of drywall.

The spacing for the last stud can be anything from a couple of inches to 14½ inches.

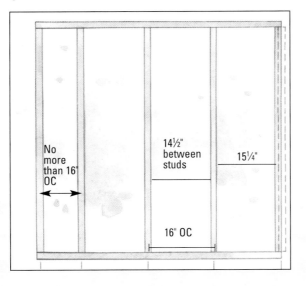

No more than 16" OC

14½" between studs

15¼"

16" OC

Removing the bottom plate

After the wall is anchored, use a handsaw to remove the section of bottom plate in the doorway. Be careful not to cut into the floor on either side of the doorway.

BUILDING A WALL WITH METAL FRAMING

Although steel framing was initially manufactured for commercial construction—largely because it's fire-resistant—it's gradually catching on with home remodelers.

Steel framing has some real advantages over wood. In addition to its fire-resistant properties, it's lightweight, inexpensive, and strong. In addition it won't rot, shrink, or warp. Steel framing is ideal for framing walls in a basement, where moisture can be a problem. It's also a practical alternative to wood when you don't have room to preassemble the wall.

Walls framed with steel are built in place, one piece at a time. The primary fasteners are sheet-metal screws; the primary tools are a power drill/driver and metal snips.

PRESTART CHECKLIST

☐ **TIME**
About 1 to 2 hours for a 12-foot wall

☐ **TOOLS**
Tape measure, chalk line, plumb bob, power drill/driver, metal snips

☐ **SKILLS**
Measuring and laying out, power-driving screws, cutting sheet metal

☐ **PREP**
Planning where walls are to go

☐ **MATERIALS**
Metal track and studs, concrete screws (for installation on a slab), pan-head sheet-metal screws for wood

1 Mark the ends of the wall on the floor and snap chalk lines between them. Predrill ⅛-inch holes in concrete with a masonry bit and attach the track with concrete screws. Use sheet-metal screws for a wood floor ("Fastening metal framing," *page 91*).

2 Transfer the layout from the floor to the ceiling with a plumb bob. If your wall runs parallel to the joists, install blocking to provide a fastening surface ("Pro Tip," *page 91*). Screw the track to the joists or blocking with pan-head sheet-metal screws.

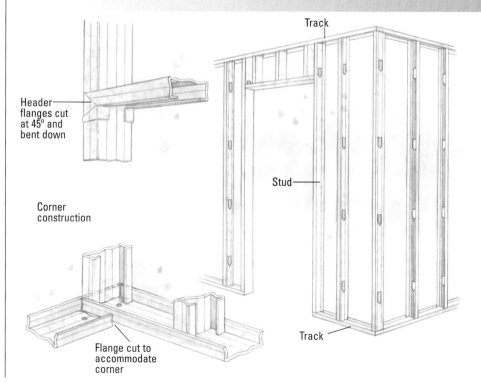

Header flanges cut at 45° and bent down

Corner construction

Flange cut to accommodate corner

Track

Stud

Track

3 Where track splices are necessary, cut a 2-inch slit in the center of the web of one track. Compress the flanges and slide the tracks together. For corners cut the flange from one of the tracks and overlap the webs as shown in the illustration *(page 90).*

4 Lay out the stud locations on the top and bottom tracks. Cut the studs to length and stand them in the tracks. Friction will hold them in place while you plumb them. Fasten them with short pan-head sheet-metal screws.

5 Make doorway headers from lengths of track. Measure the width of the opening and cut the web on both ends to form 1½- to 2-inch flaps. Bend the flaps at 90 degrees and cut the flanges at 45 degrees. Attach the header with a single screw driven through each of the four resulting tabs.

Fastening metal framing

Metal framing relies on various kinds of screws. You'll want to stock some of each. One type of screw is a **pan-head sheet-metal screw.** For attaching metal pieces together, use screws that are ½ inch long. Use longer sheet-metal screws to attach the track to a wooden floor and to the ceiling joists. If the ceiling is already covered with drywall, you'll have to use 1¼-inch screws to reach through the drywall into the joists. For attaching drywall to metal studs, 1¼-inch **drywall screws** are in order; for attaching trim use 1½-inch (or longer) **trim-head screws.** Trim-head screws have small-diameter heads that countersink neatly. The resulting holes are easy to fill. Finally if you have to fasten metal track to a concrete floor, use **gunpowder-actuated fasteners** or **concrete screws.** The powder-actuated fasteners are fired from a nail gun you can rent. Get a #3 load with a ½- or ⅝-inch pin.

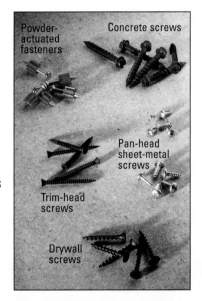

Add plywood blocking

If you will be hanging cabinets or trim on a wall that's framed with metal studs, install ¾-inch plywood blocking between the studs to provide a fastening surface. Likewise you can insert 2×4s into headers and studs at door openings for attachment of doorjambs.

HANGING DRYWALL

You can attach drywall to wood framing with nails or screws. Many carpenters argue that nailing is faster; others prefer driving screws with a cordless drill. Nails, however, sometimes pop loose under the paint, creating bumps on the wall surface. Screws cost a bit more but they rarely pop loose. If you're working with steel framing, screws are the only thing that will do. When working with phillips-head sheet-metal screws, set the clutch on your cordless drill to release just when the screw is tight.

Construction adhesive will also hold drywall to wood studs, reducing the time needed to fill fastener dimples. It also makes a stiffer wall and reduces nail pops.

You must also decide whether to attach the drywall sheets horizontally or vertically. Most drywall installers prefer to run the sheets horizontally, which makes a stronger wall, especially over steel studs, and covers the area with fewer seams. It also places single long joints 4 feet off the floor, a convenient height for finishing. Stagger the vertical seams if you can—doing so makes the wall stronger.

PRESTART CHECKLIST

☐ **TIME**
About 15 to 30 minutes per sheet of drywall, depending on the complexity of the shape

☐ **TOOLS**
Tape measure, chalk line, power drill/driver or hammer, drywall T square, utility knife, jab saw, Surform plane

☐ **SKILLS**
Measuring and laying out, driving screws or nails, cutting with a utility knife

☐ **PREP**
Framing completed; utilities in place

☐ **MATERIALS**
Drywall sheets, 1⅝-inch drywall nails or screws

Hanging horizontal pieces

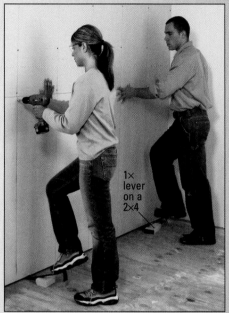

1 Screw a 2×2 ledger about 52 inches below the ceiling. Set the drywall on the ledger. Make sure the sheet ends on the middle of a stud; if it doesn't, cut it. Mark the stud locations and snap chalk lines. Then push up the sheet tight against the ceiling and fasten it.

2 Cut the lower sheet about 1 inch shorter than the open space below the top sheet. With the factory edge up, set the sheet on 1× levers. Step down on the levers, lifting the sheet tight to the sheet in place, and fasten it. Baseboard will hide the cut edge and gap at the floor.

DRYWALL APPLICATION

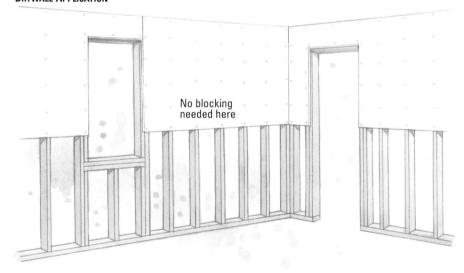

No blocking needed here

In general make as few seams as possible. For example, if you are working on 9-foot walls, use horizontal 54-inch sheets. Joints between ½-inch drywall sheets do not require blocking if the studs are spaced on 16-inch centers.

Cutting drywall

Front of sheet

Back of sheet

1 Mark the sheet about ¼ inch smaller than the space it needs to fit. Use a utility knife to cut the front face of the drywall about half the thickness of the sheet. Make a couple of passes to deepen the cut; you do not need to cut through the sheet.

2 To complete the cut, bump the back of the sheet at the cut line with your knee. This will snap the gypsum along the cut. Fold back the sheet and slice the back paper along the fold line with a utility knife.

Fastening drywall

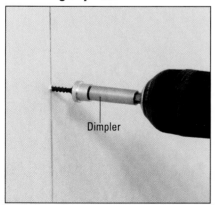

Dimpler

Screws: Use a screw gun with an adjustable clutch or a regular drill with a dimpler attachment. Both the clutch and the dimpler are designed to drive screws so they sink just below the surface without breaking the paper. Space the screws 12 inches apart.

Nails: Double-nail to prevent nail pops. Space ringshank drywall nails 12 inches apart, with a second set about 2 inches from the first. Along the edges use single nails 8 inches apart. When a nail is flush to the surface, hit it one more time to create a slight depression, but don't break the paper.

Cutouts for receptacles

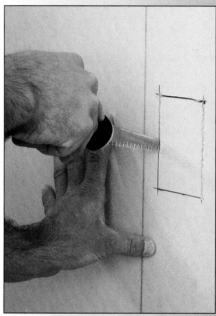

You'll need cutouts to fit drywall around electrical boxes and other obstacles in the wall. Start by measuring and carefully laying out the positions of the cutouts on the face of the sheet. Use a drywall saw or rotary cutout tool to make the cutout.

STANLEY PRO TIP

Cutting around an opening

When covering an opening, fasten the drywall over the opening and cut it out. If the sheet extends beyond the opening (as shown above), cut the drywall with a handsaw, guiding the saw against the framing. It doesn't matter if the cuts are ragged or a little uneven because they will be covered by trim or corner bead.

Applying corner bead

After all the drywall is up, the next step is to apply corner bead. The bead serves two purposes—it protects the corner from impacts and it provides a guide for your knife as you apply joint compound to the corner. You won't need to bead corners where you plan to install molding—the molding provides protection, and joint compound won't be used on those corners.

There are two styles of bead: standard, which makes a crisp, square corner; and rounded, which makes a soft, smooth corner. Both are available in white vinyl and galvanized steel. Both materials work well, so choose based on price and availability.

For an arched passageway or other curve, apply flexible bead. It is similar to standard corner bead but the flanges are cut to allow it to bend around a curve.

Whichever type of bead you use, it is better to fasten the flanges with drywall nails than with screws. Screws tend to make the bead pucker. Use nails that penetrate studs or other framing at least ¾ inch.

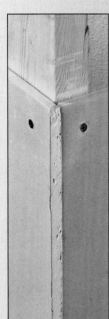

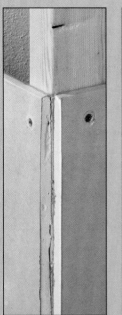
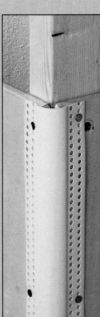

Standard corner bead: Lap one sheet of drywall over the edge of the other (left). Nail the bead in place through the holes in the flanges every 6 to 8 inches. Be careful to keep the flanges flat as you attach them.

Rounded corner bead: This style of corner bead is available in different radii, including some that call for overlapping drywall edges. In most cases, though, you'll need to attach the drywall flush with the edges of the stud (left). Then nail the bead every 6 to 8 inches.

Cut corner bead short

Cut corner bead about ¼ inch short of the floor-to-ceiling height. This makes it easier to put the bead in place. Hold the bead tight to the ceiling as you nail it in place. The baseboard will cover the gap.

WHAT IF…
You have to run drywall up against a post or other surface?

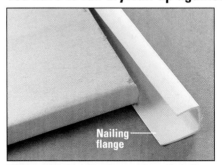
Nailing flange

When a raw drywall edge meets a dissimilar surface, such as wood, it is nearly impossible to get a clean fit. Two products create a crisp edge in this situation: J-bead and L-bead. J-bead is nailed into the wood before the drywall is installed. Prepaint it because it remains visible when the job is finished. (Spray paint works well.) J-bead is particularly useful where condensation might wick into the drywall. It encases the drywall, isolating it from the abutting material. L-bead is nailed to the face of the drywall. It is covered with joint compound (as corner bead is) after installation and painted with the rest of the wall. This bead does not extend over the back of the sheet.

Hanging drywall on a ceiling

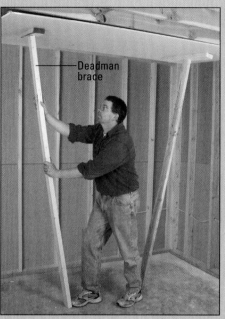

1 Since all edges of a drywall sheet must have a nailing surface behind them, you'll have to add blocking between the joists where a seam edge will fall. Toe-nail flat 2×4s between the joists.

2 Snap chalk lines or mark the location of the joists on the sheets before you hoist them into position. Use ⅝-inch drywall if the joists are more than 16 inches OC. Many drywall T squares have holes in their blades to ease marking. If yours doesn't, drill some on 16-inch (or as needed) centers.

3 Make a pair of deadman braces from 2×4s to help hold the sheets against the ceiling as you work. The length of the legs should be 1 inch more than the floor-to-ceiling height. This allows the braces to be wedged into position. As an alternative rent a drywall lift (see below).

Using long sheets

Drywall comes in 4×9-, 4×10-, and 4×12-foot sheets, and in 54-inch widths, as well as the standard 4×8 sheet. The larger sizes can make your project easier. For example if you have a room that is 12 feet wide, use 12-foot sheets for two walls and the ceiling to avoid butt (end-to-end) joints, which are more difficult to tape and mud.

Before you decide to use long sheets, make sure you will be able to maneuver them through your home and into the work area.

It's a good idea to have helpers on hand when you install long sheets. The sheets are awkward and heavy, and they may break under their own weight if not properly supported, especially when being raised to a ceiling.

Fixing a cracked plaster ceiling with drywall

Adding a layer of ⅜-inch drywall is an excellent way to restore a cracked or discolored plaster ceiling. Poke nails through the old ceiling until you locate all the joists (work carefully; there may be pipes or wires present), then snap chalk lines along their length. Apply construction adhesive to the back of the sheet. Use about half a tube of adhesive per sheet, applying it in S-shape beads about 1 foot apart. Fasten with 2½-inch drywall screws into the joists.

Rent a drywall lift—you'll be amazed at how easy it makes the job of drywalling a ceiling, even with 12-foot sheets.

FINISHING DRYWALL

Finishing drywall involves spreading joint compound over the joints and screw or nailheads to create a smooth surface. Joints are taped to prevent cracks, and the procedure varies with the tape you use.

Paper tape requires a precoat of joint compound, into which it is embedded. Pregummed fiber or jute tape goes directly on the drywall and is covered with compound.

Drywall finishing tools and techniques are easy, but creating a smooth surface requires lots of practice. A pro can finish a wall with three coats, but beginners sometimes need more. You'll need three drywall knives: a 6-inch knife for the first coat, a 10-inch for the second coat, and a 12-inch for the final coat. The three knives allow you to feather out the joint—making it gradually thinner toward the edges so it blends level with the wall surface.

Joint compound is commonly called mud and comes dry or ready-mixed in 5-gallon buckets. Use the ready-mixed variety and keep the bucket covered at all times so the mud won't dry out. Stir in any water that pools on the surface.

PRESTART CHECKLIST

☐ **TIME**
For an 8×8-foot wall, about 1½ hours for the first coat, 45 minutes for each subsequent coat

☐ **TOOLS**
Mud pan; 6-inch, 10-inch, and 12-inch drywall knives; sanding block or sponge

☐ **SKILLS**
Spreading and smoothing joint compound

☐ **PREP**
Check over wall to make sure all fasteners are sunk below surface

☐ **MATERIALS**
Joint compound, fiberglass mesh tape, paper tape (for corners), abrasives

1 Load some joint compound into a mud pan using a 6-inch drywall knife. Start filling the screw or nail dimples with a sweeping motion. Scrape the mud off so the dimple around the screw is filled flush to the surface. Closely spaced dimples can be filled or scraped in one motion.

2 Use fiberglass mesh tape on joints where two tapered edges come together. This self-adhesive mesh costs a little more than paper tape, but it is easier to use and prevents air bubbles. Start at one end and stick the tape evenly along the length of the joint.

Sponging to smooth a surface

After you apply the final coat of mud and it dries, the final step is to smooth the surface. You have two choices: sponging or sanding. Each method has its advantages. Sponging does not create dust but can be difficult to control, removing more mud than you want. Sanding does a better job of making the joint flat but creates a fine dust that can migrate throughout the house.

To sponge you'll need a bucket of water and a drywall sponge—it has a coarse mesh on one side that removes excess mud and a plain sponge on the opposite side for refining the surface. Wet the sponge and work it across the mudded surfaces. Rinse the sponge frequently to get rid of the mud that builds up in it.

Scrape off the ridges and lumps, then sponge the wall smooth. Be careful not to scrub too hard on the paper areas—you can actually wear away the paper and create a rough spot.

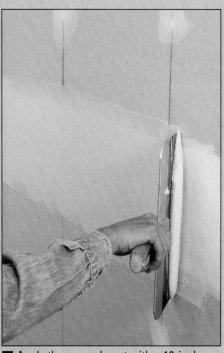

3 Cover the tape with a coat of joint compound applied with a 6-inch drywall knife. Level this first coat with the surface of the drywall. Resist the temptation to apply a thick coat—thick applications are hard to keep flat and they crack as they dry.

4 There is no need to sand between the first and second coats. Just scrape away the ridges and blobs with your knife after each coat has dried for 24 hours.

5 Apply the second coat with a 10-inch knife. After the coat dries, scrape the high spots and apply the third coat with a 12-inch knife. Feather out the edges of the mud as thinly and smoothly as possible.

Sanding a wall smooth

For an especially smooth, flat joint, you can't beat hand sanding. This method creates lots of dust, but the results are worth it. Be sure to seal off your work area with plastic sheeting and wear a dust mask to avoid breathing the dust. You might be tempted to use a power sander, but don't. Power sanders fray drywall paper and blast large amounts of dust into the air.

For small jobs a sanding block with regular sandpaper works well. For larger jobs invest in a sanding screen (a screen mesh impregnated with abrasive) and a holder. Some holders attach to a shop-vacuum hose, which helps contain dust during sanding.

Scrape the high spots, then scrub down the wall with a sanding screen. Safety gear is in order, including goggles, dust mask, and ear protectors (because of vacuum noise).

STANLEY PRO TIP

Use a pole sander

The universal pole sander extends your reach and allows you to work efficiently by making long strokes. Its name comes from the universal joint that attaches the pole to a sanding pad. This joint ensures that the pad is always flat on the wall. The pad is sized for a half sheet of sandpaper or a standard sanding screen and has clamps to hold the paper or screen in place.

Finishing butt joints

The long edges of drywall sheets are recessed on the finished side. The two tapered edges along a joint form a depression, which makes it possible to create a flat mud joint. The short sides of drywall sheets are not tapered; they meet at a butt joint.

Butt joints are more challenging to finish because all the drywall compound sits on the surface. That tends to create a slight, but noticeable, high spot over the joint. To make the high spot subtle enough to go unnoticed, you must feather the joint compound over a wide area.

Use the same fiberglass mesh tape and similar techniques for applying mud over butt joints.

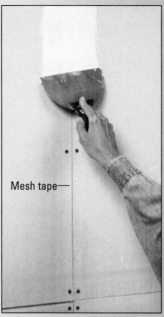

Mesh tape—

1 Cover the butt joint with fiberglass mesh tape. Use your 6-inch knife to spread a thin coat of mud over the tape.

2 When the first coat of mud is dry, apply the second coat along both sides of the joint using a 6-inch drywall knife.

3 Apply the third coat with a 12-inch drywall knife, feathering the edges out 8 to 10 inches on each side of the joint. You may leave a ridge down the center, but it can be scraped away later.

STANLEY PRO TIP: **Check the show coat**

A work light held at a raking angle helps reveal ridges, bumps, and depressions as you scrape and sand between coats. But your best—and last—chance to fix finish flaws is after you have applied a primer coat—the show coat—to the walls. At this point the walls are a uniform color and you'll see irregularities you might not have noticed before priming. The most common beginner's mistake is joints that are too thick. If you find joints like this, add another coat of mud and feather it out farther. Sand these joints again, apply primer to any bare mud, and you are ready to apply paint once the primer dries.

As an alternative you can spray or roll on a textured surface. The rough surface of the texture will hide minor flaws in your taping and adds interest to the appearance of the wall.

SECOND COAT
Try a drywall trowel

If your project includes several butt joints, consider investing in a drywall trowel. It looks like an ordinary mason's trowel, but the blade has a subtle bow that will form a slight mound over a butt joint. Use the trowel for the second coat only, running it once over the center of the joint.

Finishing corners

Covering corner bead at <u>outside corners</u> is easy because the bead itself guides the drywall knife. Run one side of your knife along the bead to produce a smooth, flat joint as the mud covers the nailing flange. As with other joints, apply at least three coats, sanding in between to feather the joint where it meets the drywall. The bead itself isn't hidden in mud. Scrape excess mud off the bead, then paint it along with the drywall.

Inside corners are more difficult. They require taping and mudding. The hard part is smoothing the mud on one side of the corner without messing up the mud on the other side.

Resist the temptation to try to get these inside joints perfect on the first, or even second, coat. Accept that there will be ridges you'll need to sand or knock off in the first two coats. To avoid ridges on the third coat, think of it as a filler coat; press hard on the knife so you fill imperfections instead of leaving behind a thick layer of joint compound. Remember there's no law against going over the joints a fourth time if necessary for a smooth finish.

Finishing inside corners

1 Apply mud to both sides of the corner. Fold a length of paper tape in half (it is precreased) and press it into the mud with a 6-inch knife.

2 Bed the tape in the mud by drawing down the knife along both sides of the corner. Repeat this process to apply additional coats of mud. Sand to smooth the final surface.

OUTSIDE CORNERS
Let the bead be your guide

For outside corners, mud the flanges of the corner bead. Apply several coats, sanding the final coat for a smooth surface.

WHAT IF...
There are bubbles under the paper tape?

If there are bubbles under the tape, the tape doesn't stick to the mud, or it wrinkles, peel it off and apply more mud underneath. This is one time when applying a little too much mud is not a problem.

STANLEY PRO TIP

Consider using a corner knife

One way to achieve straight, smooth inside corners is to use a corner knife. First embed and cover the tape in mud using a 6-inch knife, but don't attempt to smooth the joint. Next hold the corner knife at the top of the joint, angling it slightly away from the wall, and pull it down to near the floor. Do this in one even stroke. The corner knife leaves ridges on both sides of the joint. When dry, scrape off the ridges before you apply a second coat.

FRAMING A BUILT-IN CABINET

The space inside the walls of a typical home is underutilized. If you're looking for a place to put a bathroom display cabinet, a medicine cabinet, or even an ironing board, consider tapping into this unused real estate. Don't put cabinets in exterior walls, though. The gain in storage isn't worth the loss of insulation.

Start by locating the studs with a stud finder. Be as certain as you can about the existence and location of any wiring or other utility lines *(page 59)*. Then determine if your built-in will fit between the studs (in a wall framed 16 inches OC, the space between the studs is 14¼ inches), or whether you will have to rework the framing and possibly reroute some utilities.

PRESTART CHECKLIST

☐ **TIME**
About 1 to 2 hours for a basic cutout; up to 8 hours or more for a cutout that involves cutting studs and reframing

☐ **TOOLS**
Tape measure, framing square, level, jab saw, circular saw, drill/driver, hammer

☐ **SKILLS**
Measuring and laying out, cutting drywall, cutting studs in place, toe-nailing

☐ **PREP**
Locate studs and utilities; determine opening size

☐ **MATERIALS**
2×4s, 10d nails, drywall screws, woodscrews

Framing a cabinet between studs

1 A standard medicine cabinet fits between existing studs. Lay out the opening on the wall. Drill holes at the corners to help start the cuts. Saw along the lines with a drywall saw.

6-inch-long blocks

Space for header

Space for sill

2 Using 2-inch drywall screws, fasten 6-inch 2×4 blocks to the studs to provide support for a header and sill. Use four screws per block and position the blocks 1½ inches from the top and bottom of the opening.

Header

Sill

3 Attach the header and sill at each end with one toe-nailed fastener into the stud and one driven into the support block. Install the cabinet with 1¾-inch woodscrews.

WHAT IF...
The cabinet is too deep for the wall?

A regular 2×4 stud wall with drywall on either side can accommodate a cabinet about 4 inches deep. A wall with plaster and lath can be as much as 1 inch deeper. If you have an even deeper cabinet, allow it to protrude from the wall and use extension pieces to bridge the gap between the wall and the cabinet front. Predrill and screw the pieces to the cabinet or wall.

Extension pieces

Framing a wide cabinet

Limiting yourself to narrow cabinetry that fits between studs can unnecessarily reduce your bathroom storage space. Wider cabinets require that you cut away a stud or two to accommodate them. If the wall you are cutting into is load-bearing, you'll have to brace the ceiling before you cut and add a stout header to distribute the load.

For spans up to 3 feet wide, a doubled 2×4 header is adequate; for spans from 4 to 5 feet, you'll need a doubled 2×6. Insert ½-inch plywood spacers between the 2×6s so the header thickness is 3½ inches—the same as the thickness of the wall. For walls that don't bear a load, a single 2×4 header is fine.

The cabinet opening shown here is in a bearing wall and requires that two studs be cut. Install the new framing so the opening is ¼ inch larger than the cabinet.

Unlike a cabinet that fits between studs (page 100), wider cabinets require you to remove drywall beyond the final opening so you can attach the frame to the nearest studs. Patch the areas with new drywall and finish the joints before you install the cabinet. You may also want to paint the new drywall before installing the cabinet.

— Cutting line

Cabinet opening

1 Lay out the cabinet opening on the wall. Then lay out the cut lines around the cabinet outline. You'll need to allow 1½ inches for a sill underneath and, in this case, 5½ inches for a header above. The side cut lines appear along the inside edges of the nearest studs. Cut along the lines with a jab saw or other handsaw.

2 If you are cutting into a bearing wall, construct bracing on both sides of the wall. Cut through the necessary studs that are even with the opening. Start the cuts with a circular saw; finish with a handsaw. Be careful not to damage the drywall at the rear of the cavity.

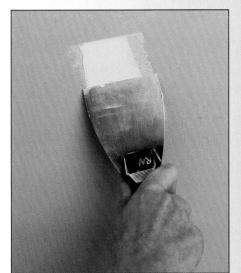

3 After the studs are cut, they will still be attached to the drywall on the opposite side of the wall. Pry them out; you will probably damage the drywall on the back of the opening as the fasteners pull through. Fill the holes using joint compound and a 2- or 3-inch putty knife.

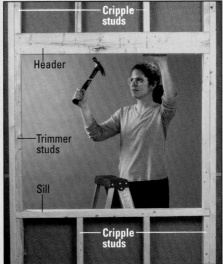

Cripple studs

Header

Trimmer studs

Sill

Cripple studs

4 Nail four new cripple studs to the inside faces of the full studs: two at the top and two at the bottom. Nail the sill in place. Add trimmer studs on both sides of the opening and a header across the top. Toe-nail up through the outside face of the header to catch the bottoms of the cripples.

Cripple jack studs

Spacer blocks

5 Cut spacer blocks to position the cripple jack studs that will make the sides of the opening. Nail the spacers in place to the sill and header, then nail the cripples to the spacers. Make the opening ¼ inch wider than the intended cabinet. Install drywall to close in the rest of the wall (pages 92–99).

INSTALLING WAINSCOTING AND TILEBOARD

A wall treatment that lends a quiet quality and warmth to a bathroom, wainscot paneling also resists dents and scuffs better than drywall.

The tongue-and-groove beaded board in this project is one of the most popular styles. Prefinish the backs and end-grain edges with a high-quality polyurethane varnish or paint. When installed, the outer surface should be sealed with three coats of the same finish.

Technically "wainscoting" includes any wooden paneling applied to the bottom portion of a wall. The term, however, is commonly used to describe any wallcovering on the lower portion of the wall—including ceramic tile and tileboard. Tileboard is hardboard surfaced with a melamine or PVC coating and finished tile patterns. It is tough, water-resistant, and easy to clean, and its low cost makes it an attractive substitute for ceramic tile.

PRESTART CHECKLIST

☐ **TIME**
About 6 hours for an 8-foot section of wainscoting, 3 hours for a similar tileboard installation

☐ **TOOLS**
Tape measure, chalk line, chop saw, hammer, nail set, circular saw, jigsaw, block plane, adhesive trowel

☐ **SKILLS**
Measuring and laying out, crosscutting, driving finish nails, applying mastic

☐ **PREP**
Empty room of all furnishings

☐ **MATERIALS**
Beaded tongue-and-groove boards, tileboard panels, 4-inch baseboard, cap molding, 8d and 4d finishing nails, construction adhesive, wood glue, tileboard adhesive

1 If your project includes a cap rail, snap a level chalk line ½ inch below the height of the cap rail (measure up from the highest point on the floor). Cut the tongue-and-groove beaded board ¼ inch shorter than that.

2 Apply construction adhesive to the back of the first board and set it on the wall level with the chalk line. If manufacturer's instructions specify toe-nailing the tongue, use a pneumatic nailer. Repeat the procedure for the remaining boards, snugging the boards with a piece of scrap.

3 Before fitting the boards around an electrical box, **turn off power to the box**. Disconnect the receptacle or switch. Use a jigsaw to cut boards to fit around the box. Insert a box extender to move the box out flush with the wall. Reconnect the switch or receptacle and replace the cover plate.

4 When you get to an inside corner, put the second-to-last piece in place without adhesive. Measure from the top and bottom edge of the board to the wall. Even if the measurements differ, use a saber saw to cut the last piece to fit the opening.

5 In many installations the last two pieces at a corner must be snapped in place as one unit. Put adhesive on the wall. Snug the last two pieces together. Bend them a bit at the joint and fit them to the last board on the wall. Press at the joint to snap the last two boards into place.

6 Before installing the first length of cap rail that turns an inside corner, shave the tongue off with a block plane. Install the piece so that the planed edge is toward the corner.

7 Attach a baseboard at the bottom of the wainscoting, driving two 8d finishing nails into each stud. Attach cap rail over the top edge. At the corner use carpenter's glue and 4d nails driven at a slight angle toward the wall to ensure they don't come through the face of the top molding.

Cap rail

Installing tileboard

1 Locate the position of the tileboard on the wall by marking its height from the highest point on the floor. Snap a level line across all surfaces to be covered. (See Step 1, *page 102.*) Cut the panels to fit each wall, and where fixtures will come through the board, cut cardboard templates. Use a jigsaw to cut the fixture holes.

2 Test-fit the panels and connector strips in each section and tape the panels in place. Following the manufacturer's instructions, outline the panels and remove them. Again following the instructions, apply adhesive to the wall inside the outline or to the back of the panel. Spread adhesive to any connector strips and apply them to the wall.

3 Refer to the manufacturer's instructions for the preferred method for applying the panel to the wall. Most panels slide into a connector strip. Make sure the entire surface of the panel is adhered to the wall—press it firmly to ensure a tight bond. Wipe off any excess adhesive and caulk the joint where the panel meets the floor.

TILING WALLS

To make your installation of wall tile easier, you'll need to make sure it's smooth and level and free of any substance that would interfere with the action of the adhesive. Once you've prepared the surface, establish layout lines in both a vertical and horizontal plane.

Wall tiles are affected by gravity and tend to slide down the wall during installation. Organic mastic is one solution—tile sticks to it almost immediately. Mastic is not as strong as thinset mortar, however, and not as water-resistant. You can keep tile that's embedded in thinset in place with spacers, nails, or tape.

If you are tiling a wall and a floor, tile the floor first so you can continue the grout joints up the wall in the same pattern as the floor. Install a cove base, then start wall tile at the cove base. If you are tiling adjacent walls, set the back wall first. Tapered edges on a side wall are less visible.

PRESTART CHECKLIST

☐ **TIME**
About 30 to 45 minutes per square yard to prepare and set tile

☐ **TOOLS**
Wide putty knife, 4-foot level, sanding block, small sledge and cold chisel, stud finder, tape measure, chalk line, utility knife, carbide scriber, margin trowel, notched trowel, straightedge, cordless drill/driver, grout knife, snap cutter or wet saw, tile nippers, masonry stone, caulk gun, hammer, grout float

☐ **SKILLS**
Reading level, troweling, laying tile, grouting

☐ **PREP**
Repair structural defects

☐ **MATERIALS**
Deglossing agent, release agent, bucket, thinset, dimensional lumber for battens, backerboard, screws, tape, tile, spacers, caulk, grout, rags, sponge, water, tile base or bullnose, nylon wedges, nails

A. Preparing the wall

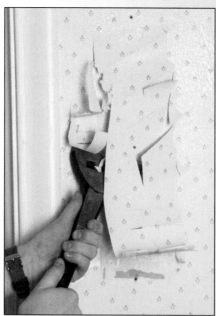

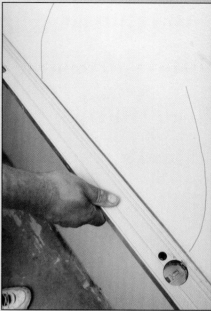

1 Remove any wallcovering and degloss paint. If removing wallpaper, sand or use a wet sponge to clean off the residue of glue and paper. Make sure the surface dries completely before applying adhesive to it.

2 Using a 4-foot level, examine the wall in sections, marking high spots, depressions, and other defects that would interfere with the tile. Pay close attention to corners to check for plumb *(page 107)*. Use care in your survey of the wall at this stage—it will save time later.

WHAT IF...
There's a window on the wall?

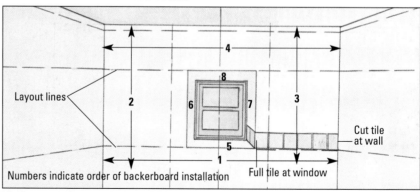

Layout lines

Cut tile at wall

Full tile at window

Numbers indicate order of backerboard installation

Windows complicate wall layouts. If possible arrange the pattern with a full tile around the perimeter of the window and cut tiles at the edges of the wall. You can achieve this balance fairly easily if the window is centered and if tile covers the surface evenly or leaves at least a half-tile at the corners.

If a perfectly balanced layout won't work, try adjusting the grout lines or inserting decorative tile. Trim tiles at the window's edge might even out the layout. Install the window tiles first to establish the grout lines for field tile, then tile the remainder of the back wall, working upwards.

3 Skim-coat a layer of thinset on any walls that are out of plumb and fill depressions. If installing backerboard on studs, mark stud centers on the ceiling. Cut and fasten backerboard, centering its edges on the studs. Position the backerboard sheets in a pattern that will minimize cutting and waste.

B. Marking layout lines

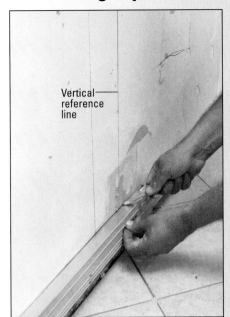

Vertical reference line

1 Set a 4-foot level vertically on the wall about 2 feet from a corner, over a grout joint. If the wall meets at an outside corner, set the level where the inside edge of a bullnose will fall. Pencil a line down the level; extend it to the floor and ceiling. Repeat the process on the horizontal plane.

2 Measure up from the horizontal line a distance equal to the size of your tile and mark the wall at this point. Continue marking the wall in the same increments. Using a 4-foot level, mark the wall across from these points and snap layout grids so you can keep each horizontal course straight.

REFRESHER COURSE
Installing backerboard on walls

1 Nail blocking between studs to support joints, if necessary. Apply construction adhesive to the studs. Screw the board to the studs and blocking. Rest the next sheets on ⅛-inch spacers (8d nails) before fastening.

2 Use 2- or 4-inch gummed tape over each backerboard joint. Press the tape into the joint and unroll it as you go. Use a utility knife to cut the tape at the end of the joint.

3 Apply a thin coat of thinset mortar to the taped joint with a margin trowel. Trowel on enough mortar to fill the joint and level it with the backerboard. Feather the edges smooth with a square trowel or drywall knife.

C. Laying the tile

Spacers

1 Mix enough adhesive to cover the size of a section you can lay within its working time (the amount of time it takes for the mortar to set and become unworkable). Work from the bottom up, spreading the adhesive evenly and combing it with the notched edge of the trowel. Start at the bottom, pressing the tile into the mortar with a slight twist.

2 Continue laying the pattern of your choice, using spacers if your tile is not lugged. Note the placement and position of the spacers (above). Setting the spacers flush with the surface of the tile will make them difficult to remove. Inserting them with one tab in the joint makes them easy to remove. When the field tile is set, cut and install the edge tiles.

Keeping the tiles on the wall

Batten holds
first row level

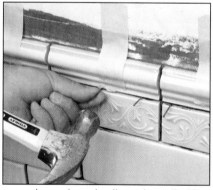

If you're not using a coved base and your layout results in cut tiles at the floor, tack a level 1× or 2× batten along the plane on which your first full tiles will be laid. The batten will keep the first row level and prevent the tiles from sliding down the wall. Even with a coved base or a batten and spacers, you may have to take extra precautions to keep the tile on the wall while the adhesive cures. Drive nails partway into the wall at least every third of each tile's length and tape the tiles with masking tape. If your layout calls for a coved-tile base, install it first, leveling it with nylon wedges. Then tile up the wall.

WHAT IF...
Tiles are lugged (prespaced)?

Lugs

Lugged tiles make it easy to space wall installations. They come with small bisque lugs raised on the edges and don't require additional spacers to keep them aligned.

Because the lugs are fired into the tile at the time of manufacture, they don't allow you to make the grout joints narrower. Determine the actual dimensions of the tile when you purchase it so you know how much space each tile actually covers.

D. Grouting the tile

1 When the adhesive has cured to the manufacturer's specifications, inspect the joints for excess adhesive. Use a utility knife or grout knife to remove any adhesive left in the joints and clean any excess off the tile surface. Mix enough grout to cover a section and force it into the joints with a grout float, keeping the float at a 45-degree angle. Work the float in both directions to fill the joints; work diagonally to remove excess grout.

2 When the grout has cured enough that a damp sponge won't pull it out of the joints, scrape off the excess with the float held almost perpendicular to the surface. Clean the surface and smooth the joints with a damp sponge, then repeat the cleaning with clean water and a clean sponge. When a haze forms, wipe it with a clean rag. You may have to wipe with some pressure to remove the haze.

WHAT IF...
The wall has electrical outlets on it?

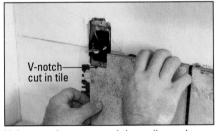

V-notch cut in tile

Unless you have removed the wall covering, the finished tile surface will extend beyond the edges of electrical outlet boxes. As a result the receptacle screws may be too short to anchor the receptacle. A box extension will remedy the problem, but if local codes don't require an extension, you can fix the problem by using longer screws.

First **turn off the power to the circuit** and remove the cover plate and receptacle screws. Remove one receptacle screw completely so you can take it to the store to buy a screw ½ inch longer. Push the receptacle into the box and out of your way.

Cut the tiles to fit around the box. Then cut V-shape notches (use tile nippers) that line up with the tabs and screw holes on the top and bottom of the box. Spread adhesive to within ¼ inch of the box and embed the tile. When the mortar cures, pull out the receptacle from the box and fasten it with the longer screws inserted through the notches.

Turning an outside corner

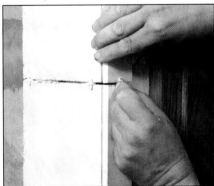

Outside corners can present problems, especially if they are not plumb. You can hide slightly out-of-plumb situations by skim-coating the wall with thinset. Then overlap bullnose tiles or edge tiles on the full tiles on the other wall. As long as the tiles meet crisply, the out-of-plumb wall should not be as noticeable.

TILING A WINDOW RECESS

Tiling a window recess adds a whole new feeling to the design scheme of a room. With the right color, texture, and shape, window tiles can make the room look like you've made it over without the actual expense of redecorating. And a tiled window adds a practical dimension as well: Tiles won't rot or stain, and they won't get scratched by cats seeking a sunny refuge.

Choose the color first, then the texture (most often they go hand in hand). A neutral color will cause the window to recede or blend in with the wall. Terra-cotta tiles are a good choice. If you want to call attention to the architecture of the window, use decorative tiles, but design the pattern judiciously. Too many bright colors and designs can overwhelm a room and defeat the purpose.

If the window is situated on a wall that you're going to tile, your color choice is already made. Use bullnose tiles to round off the edges of the window frame and tile the wall first. That way you can make sure the grout lines of the recess are on the same plane as the wall.

1 Remove the window casing with a pry bar and hammer, inserting a piece of scrap wood under the pry bar to keep from damaging the surfaces. Remove the stop molding if the tile will extend all the way to the sash. Remove the sill, cutting it with a handsaw if necessary.

2 Stuff insulation into the gap between the jamb and the wall but don't hinder the movement of the sash weights in an old double-hung unit. If you're tiling the wall, apply fiberglass drywall tape and compound. Feather the compound level with the wall. Let it dry and sand smooth.

PRESTART CHECKLIST

☐ **TIME**
About 4 to 5 hours for a standard 36×40-inch, double-hung window

☐ **TOOLS**
Pry bar, hammer, handsaw, margin trowel, notched trowel, grout float, wide putty knife, caulking gun, bucket, sponge

☐ **SKILLS**
Prying, troweling, sanding, setting tile, grouting

☐ **PREP**
Repair structural defects

☐ **MATERIALS**
Joint tape, joint compound, mortar, tile, caulk, sandpaper, spacers, grout, rags, water, nails, fiberglass insulation

WHAT IF...
You're painting the wall?

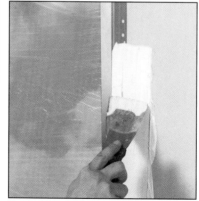

If you plan to paint the wall around the window, fasten metal corner bead to the jamb and trowel on two coats of joint compound. Feather the compound level with the wall. Let each coat dry and sand it smooth.

Create a tiled molding

You can achieve an eye-catching effect with a tiled molding. Pry off the trim and build a molding from milled stock. Make the space between the molding and the trim ¼ inch larger than the tile. Set the tile in thinset (with a margin trowel) or silicone adhesive.

3 Spread and comb thinset on the sill plate and set sill tiles before the sides. Then mortar the jambs and set the side tiles, holding them in place with 8d finishing nails *(page 106)*. Pounding nails into hardwood will shift the tiles, so insert finishing nails in a drill and spin them in. Grout tiles with a float.

4 To create a straight grout line at the edge, install wall tiles flush with the jamb. Then set the ceiling tile in mortar and support it with three boards (battens). To avoid pushing the end tiles too deeply into the mortar, don't force the supports. Let the mortar dry.

5 Caulk the joint between the tiles and the window to prevent water damage. Choose a caulk that's the same color as the grout and smooth it with a caulking tool or a wet finger.

Edging options

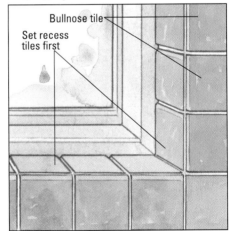

Bullnose tile

Set recess tiles first

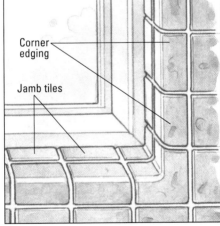

Corner edging

Jamb tiles

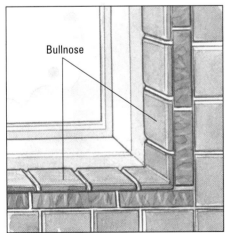

Bullnose

To finish the edge of a tiled window, you have several options other than the one shown at the top of the page. Instead of setting bullnose inside the recess, set it on the wall surface. Set the recess tiles first, then the bullnose.

Use corner edging tiles, similar to countertop V-caps (but without the raised lip that forms the front edge of the counter). Mark the wall where the edges of the corners will fall. Set the wall tiles, then the corners, then the jamb tiles.

Apply a decorative border strip around the recess with bullnose or rounded field tiles on the jambs. Use bullnose if the border tile does not have a finished edge. Set the wall tiles and border first, then set the jamb tiles.

INSTALLING CROWN MOLDING

Crown molding is installed at the juncture of the wall and the ceiling. Although it looks like a hefty piece of wood, most crown molding is relatively thin material. The secret of its appearance is the way it is installed. Rather than being a solid block nailed into the corner, crown moldings are installed on the diagonal between the wall and ceiling—there is nothing in the corner. Moldings installed this way are said to be sprung into place.

The tricky part about installing crown molding is cutting the joints. Because the molding is installed at an angle, it cannot be cut lying flat in an ordinary miter box. As you make the cuts, you must hold the molding at an angle. To cut crown molding flat, you need a compound mitersaw.

PRESTART CHECKLIST

☐ **TIME**
About 4 hours for a regular room with four straight walls

☐ **TOOLS**
Tape measure, framing square, miter box or mitersaw, hammer, nail set, coping saw, utility knife

☐ **SKILLS**
Measuring and laying out, driving nails, crosscutting moldings, mitering moldings, making coped joints

☐ **PREP**
Walls and ceiling should be finished and painted; molding can be prefinished

☐ **MATERIALS**
Crown molding, 8d finishing nails, wood for blocking

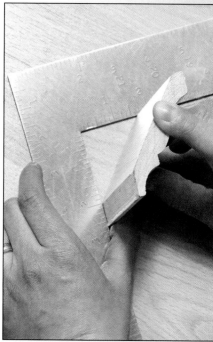

1 Start by determining how far out from the wall the edges of the molding will fall. Place a piece of the molding inside a framing square to find this measurement. Mark this distance on the ceiling near the corners and at several points along the length of the wall.

Square-cut both ends of the first piece

2 Start with the wall opposite the door. Cut the molding to length with square cuts on both ends. Hold it in place and nail it first to the wall studs with 8d nails and then to the ceiling joists.

WHAT IF...
You need to end crown molding without running into a wall?

90° cut

Inside miter cut

You may need to end a run of crown molding that doesn't turn a corner or run into a wall. If so, stop the molding with a triangular return piece. To cut this piece, place a scrap of crown upside down in the chop saw or miter box and make an outside miter cut. Then set the saw to 90 degrees and cut off

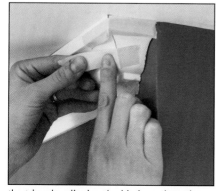

the triangle, aligning the blade to the point where the miter ends at the back of the molding. Attach the return piece with yellow carpenter's glue. Use masking tape to hold the piece in place until the glue sets.

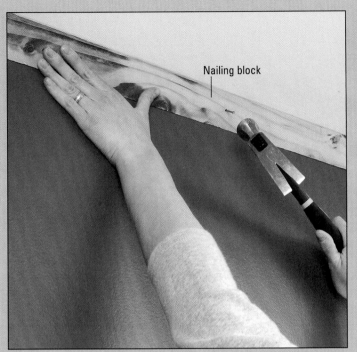

3 If the wall runs parallel to the ceiling joists, there may be no framing members in position to nail the molding to the ceiling. In this situation cut some triangular nailing blocks to attach to the wall studs. Size the blocks to allow a ¼-inch gap between the front of the block and the back of the crown.

4 The second piece of crown is cut square on one end and coped on the other. To cut the cope, start with an inside miter cut. Hold the crown in your miter box upside down (as if the base of the box were the ceiling and the fence were the wall) and backwards (if the cope is on the right end of the piece, the cut will be on the left as the piece rests in the miter box).

5 Cope the edge by undercutting the joint with a coping saw. Test-fit it against a piece of scrap and fine-tune the edge with a utility knife. Nail the piece in place. Proceed around the room, making square cuts on one end and coped cuts on the other end. Cope both ends of the last piece.

6 For outside miters, the pieces also are held in the saw upside down and backwards, but the cut is angled in the opposite direction. To get a tighter fit in both outside and inside corners, flex and twist the pieces slightly before driving in the nails closest to the joint.

STANLEY PRO TIP

Burnish corners to cure gaps

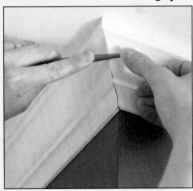

In spite of careful work, not every joint will fit perfectly. If you find a slight gap in an outside miter, force a little glue into it, then burnish the edges using the side of a nail set. Burnishing the corners folds over the thin wood fibers, bridging the gap.

FINISHING FLOORS

With the possible exception of the kitchen floor, no floor in your house takes more abuse than the bathroom floor. It is subject to a constant parade of wet feet and has to suffer heavy foot traffic, dirty shoes, the occasionally overflowing sinks and tubs, and periodic misdirected shower sprays. Fortunately there are plenty of hardy floor surfaces that can stand up to the abuse and do so with style.

Shore up the floor

Whether it be ceramic tile, natural stone, resilients, or laminates, your bathroom floor will only be as durable as the subfloor beneath it. Before installing any finished flooring material, you'll need to inspect the condition of the subfloor and the supporting joists.

Decayed subflooring, especially around the toilet and tub, is so common in older homes that you can almost assume you have a little repair work ahead of you. After you remove the toilet and sinks *(pages 64–65)*, and perhaps the bathtub *(pages 68–70)*, the areas under them require some careful inspection.

Rotted wood will automatically give itself away. It will be stained gray or black, and if you poke it with a screwdriver, it will feel mushy. Water-damaged plywood may have begun to separate at the layers. Inspect the joists, too, and if you can't get at them from below, pull up the existing subfloor.

You can cut out damaged areas with a circular saw and replace them piece by piece. Set the saw to the depth of the underlayment and cut sections that leave half of the joist exposed. You'll probably have to install blocking to support the edges of the patch, and if the damage is extensive, it's easier and safer to pull up the whole underlayment and replace it *(page 75)*. Weak joists can be fixed by fastening (sistering) new joists to them.

Even if the floor is in good shape, ceramic tile and stone call for an extra measure of caution. They are heavy, and if you're in doubt about the subfloor and joists, call in a tiling contractor before you proceed. You have to get the floor right before you do the rest of your remodeling.

Acclimate the materials

Before laying your floor, bring the materials into the room so they can adjust to the ambient temperatures. Unroll resilient sheet flooring, and pull tiles out of the box. That way they'll do whatever expanding or contracting they need to before they're on the floor.

Choose and install your flooring carefully. Floors are crucial to bathroom design and comfort.

CHAPTER PREVIEW

Preparing a floor for tile
page 114

Installing electric radiant heat
page 116

Installing ceramic floor tile
page 120

Grouting, caulking, and sealing
page 124

**Installing
mosaic tile**
page 126

Installing stone tile
page 128

**Installing dry-
backed
resilient tile**
page 130

**Installing sheet
vinyl flooring**
page 132

PREPARING A FLOOR FOR TILE

Ceramic and stone tile need a sound, level base to keep them from cracking. You may need to repair the surface of the underlayment or subfloor, and shore up the substructure as well. Inspect the subfloor and make repairs that will ensure it provides a stable bed.

Dimensional lumber—1×4 or 2×6 planking—is not suitable as a bed for any tile. Planks expand and contract with changes in temperature and humidity, as does tile, but at different rates. The result is cracked tile, broken grout joints, or split seams. Install plywood or backerboard on planks *(pages 75–79)*. If the resulting floor will be too high for smooth transitions to adjacent floors, tear up the planking and install ¾-inch exterior-grade plywood, followed by backerboard.

PRESTART CHECKLIST

☐ **TIME**
About 30 minutes to check defects in an average-size room; repair time will vary with size and condition of floor—could average 45 minutes per square yard

☐ **TOOLS**
Repair subfloor: 4-foot level, cordless drill/bits, hammer, circular saw
Repair surface: mason's trowel, belt sander, nail set
Install membrane: roller, trowel

☐ **SKILLS**
Driving nails with hammer, removing fasteners with cordless drill, sawing with circular saw, troweling, using a belt sander

☐ **PREP**
Remove or repair finished flooring

☐ **MATERIALS**
Subfloor: 2×4 lumber, 2½-inch coated screws, 8d nails, wood shims
Surface: thinset mortar, membrane, adhesive

1 Divide the floor into imaginary 6-foot sections and within each section rotate a 4-foot level. Use a carpenter's pencil or chalk marker to outline sags, <u>low spots, high spots</u>, and other defects. Then walk the floor to test it for squeaks and weak spots. Mark these areas.

2×4 bridging

2 If the entire subfloor is weak, cut 2×4 bridges to fit between the floor joists. Measure the joist spacing across the floor, and if the dimensions are equal, cut all the bridges at one time. If the spacing varies, cut the pieces to fit. Nail the bridges in place, offsetting each one by 24 inches.

LOW SPOTS, HIGH SPOTS
Level the subfloor

Vacuum the floor thoroughly. Trowel thinset into depressions and chips in a slab with a mason's trowel. Feather the edges of the repair so it is level with the floor. After it dries sand the edges of the repair if necessary.

Before you level any high spots on the floor, make sure the heads of all nails and fasteners are set below the surface. Level high spots on the floor with a belt sander. Keep the sander moving when it is in contact with the floor.

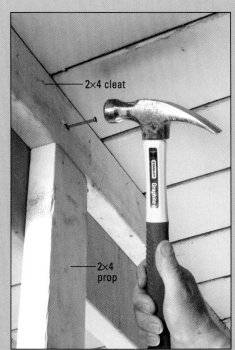

3 Shore up broken or sagging joists by nailing a 2×4 cleat up against the subfloor. Force the cleat snugly against the subfloor with a 2×4 prop, nail the cleat in place with 8d nails, and knock the prop out to remove it.

4 Fill minor sags and separations between the subfloor and joists by driving shims or shingles into the gap. Tap the shim gently until it's snug—forcing it may cause the flooring above to bow.

5 Fasten loose subflooring material securely by screwing it to the joists. Drive screws into any repairs you have made with shims. You can use ringshank or spiral-shank nails as an alternative, setting the nailhead below the surface with a hammer and nail set.

REFRESHER COURSE
Install backerboard

Anchor the backerboard to the floor by driving 2-inch backerboard screws into the subfloor at 8-inch intervals. Set the screws so they are flush with the backerboard. Cover the

joint with fiber tape and spread thinset over it with a margin trowel or mason's trowel. Apply the mortar until it levels the recess in the joint and feather the edges.

Install waterproof membrane

Although many tiles and setting materials are impervious to water, virtually no tile installation is completely waterproof without a waterproofing membrane.

Water that penetrates a tile bed weakens the adhesive, promotes rot, and nourishes organisms destructive to the wood subfloor. Bathrooms, kitchens, and surfaces that require frequent cleaning are especially vulnerable.

One of the easiest membranes to apply utilizes an adhesive that spreads with a roller. To install it, start at a wall opposite a doorway and apply the adhesive in sections with a roller (top). Let the adhesive cure, spread the fiber membrane over the adhesive (middle), and then trowel the membrane into the adhesive (bottom).

INSTALLING ELECTRIC RADIANT HEAT

If you are planning to install an interior floor of ceramic or porcelain tile, brick, or stone, consider adding the warming influence of electric radiant heat. Installed directly over the substrate (cement board, plywood, a mortar bed, or a concrete slab), this system uses a plastic mat with interwoven heater cable. The mat is embedded in thinset before the final flooring material is installed. Controlled by a wall-mounted thermostat or timer, the heater cable radiates warmth at a preset temperature.

The 120-volt circuit or power source for the radiant heat mats must be GFCI protected. Mats are available in a variety of lengths. Check the manufacturer's specifications for the wattage your situation will require. It will increase as the size of the room increases.

PRESTART CHECKLIST

☐ **TIME**
About 8 hours to install mat, wire, and tile for an average bathroom

☐ **TOOLS**
Digital ohmmeter, drill, ½-inch bit, drywall saw, fish tape, chisel, hot-glue gun, ⅜-inch trowel, screwdriver, stripper, long-nose pliers, lineman's pliers, tools for laying the flooring

☐ **SKILLS**
Stripping, splicing, and connecting wires to terminals; installing boxes; running cable into boxes; setting tile

☐ **PREP**
Rough in the plumbing; install the subfloor

☐ **MATERIALS**
12/2 cable, mat, box, armored power cable, thermostat and/or timer, thinset, flooring, mortar or grout

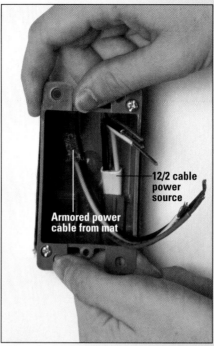

12/2 cable power source
Armored power cable from mat

1 Install a large-capacity box for the thermostat 60 inches above the floor. Using 12/2 cable, add a new circuit or extend an existing circuit, but **do not connect the power source.** Pull it to the box cable provided with the mat.

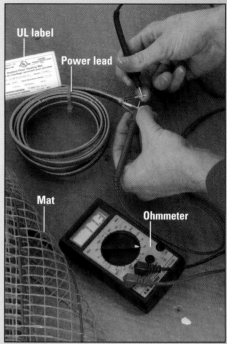

UL label
Power lead
Mat
Ohmmeter

2 Unpack the mat. Check the resistance using an ohmmeter. The reading should be within 10 percent of the rating shown on the UL label. This will be your benchmark for confirming that the heat cable has not been nicked during installation. Write the reading on a piece of paper.

INSTALLING UNDER-FLOOR ELECTRIC RADIANT HEATING

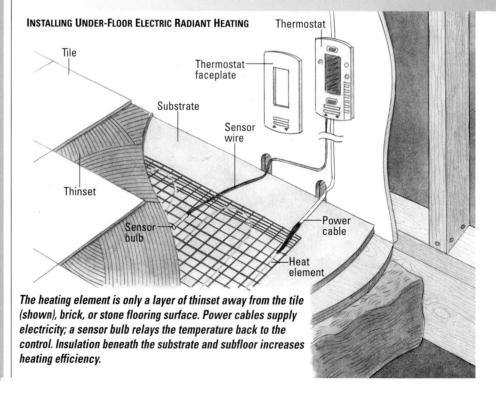

Tile
Thermostat
Thermostat faceplate
Substrate
Sensor wire
Thinset
Sensor bulb
Power cable
Heat element

The heating element is only a layer of thinset away from the tile (shown), brick, or stone flooring surface. Power cables supply electricity; a sensor bulb relays the temperature back to the control. Insulation beneath the substrate and subfloor increases heating efficiency.

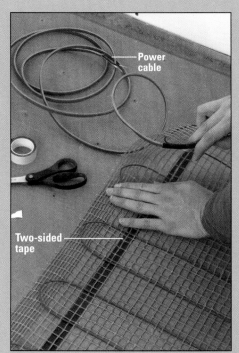

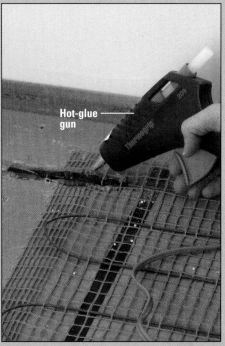

3 Clean the floor of debris and tighten any protruding screw or nailheads. Roll out the mat so it's no closer than 3 to 6 inches to walls and fixtures. Staple the mat to the floor with ½-inch staples or fasten it with double-sided tape every 12–24 inches.

4 If the power lead is thicker than the mat (some come with ribbon leads), you can sink it into the substrate if you've used backerboard. Use a cold chisel to cut a channel for it. If you don't recess the power lead, you must make sure it's adequately covered by mortar.

5 Hot-glue the power cable to the substrate. Mark along the power cable and slide it to one side. Working a few feet at a time, run a continuous bead of hot glue. Press the lead into the bead of hot glue. Make sure the lead wires don't cross each other or run perpendicular to a heater wire.

Strategies for running cable through walls

Go downstairs for power by drilling a finder hole directly in front of the wall through which you want to run the cable. Use a wire to mark the spot. Drill a ¾-inch hole and use a fish tape to pull the cable to where it is needed. See *pages 168–171*.

By cutting away drywall (save the piece for replacing and taping later), you can run cable horizontally. This allows you to tap into a receptacle (check that the circuit can bear the additional load) in the same room.

If you have attic space above, drop power down to the room where you need it. Drill a finder hole to locate the wall plate. Drill an access hole, run fish tape, then pull cable to extend a circuit or create a new circuit. See *page 170*.

See *pages 168–171*.
See *page 170*.

WHAT IF...
There's a toilet or vanity?

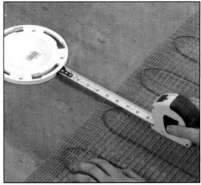

Mats can run under a toilet but must be 3 inches from the toilet ring. In addition, a mat can run beneath the kickplate of a vanity. Never overlap mats, never cut a mat to fit, and never attempt to repair a cut or nicked heating wire. If the wire is damaged the entire mat must be replaced.

INSTALLING ELECTRIC RADIANT HEAT (continued)

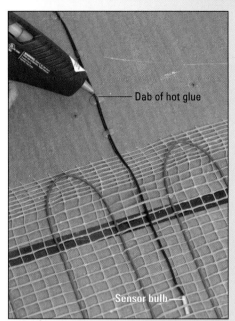

Dab of hot glue

Sensor bulb

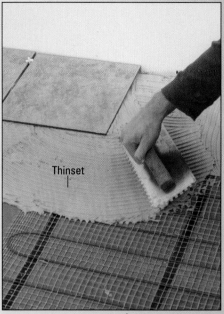

Thinset

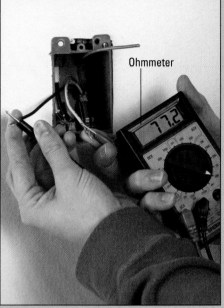

Ohmmeter

6 If your system uses a thermostatic sensor, weave the sensor bulb between two heating elements. Adhere the bulb wire with dots of hot glue. Now check the mat resistance with an ohmmeter. If the reading falls outside the manufacturer's tolerance, find the damaged mat and replace it.

7 With the flat side of a ⅜-inch notched trowel, apply thinset over an area of the mat. Then turn the trowel over and rake the thinset to ¼-inch uniform depth. Be careful not to snag the mat. Do not clean the trowel by banging it on the mat. Tile the area of the floor covered with thinset.

8 Check mat resistance once again using the ohmmeter. If the ohm reading drops to zero or infinity, the heating element has been damaged. The tile must be removed and the mat replaced.

Radiant heat for most floors

You can install almost any finished flooring over radiant heat, but the key to the system's performance is how well the flooring material conducts heat.

Ceramic tile and stone are the best conductors and will allow the system to run more efficiently than other materials. Parquet and laminate are also good conductors. Carpet tile is thinner than broadloom carpet, but still acts as insulation and won't distribute heat as well as solid materials. Vinyl tile has almost no R-value at all, so it's a good choice, but it should not be heated above 85°F.

No matter which system you install, put separate thermostats in each room. That way you can customize the heat for maximum comfort and efficiency.

Plan ahead for wiring

Carefully sketch the system wiring on a dimensional plan. Note the location of the thermostat and any other electrical switches or outlets in the room. Measure the location of the switch/thermostat from a reference point such as an adjoining wall and transfer this measurement to the subfloor in the room below.

If possible locate the thermostat on an interior wall; this will make drilling through the floor plate easier. Place the thermostat as close to the power source as possible. Long lead wires from the power source can reduce the efficiency of the system.

Bathroom heating plan

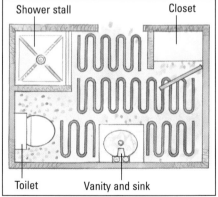

Shower stall | Closet | Toilet | Vanity and sink

Before you purchase a radiant system, sketch the room it will be heating. Mats or piping are not required under closets, major appliances, and vanities. In bathrooms, about 50 percent of the floor area should be heated; in kitchens and living areas, about 60 percent.

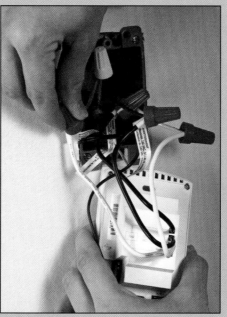

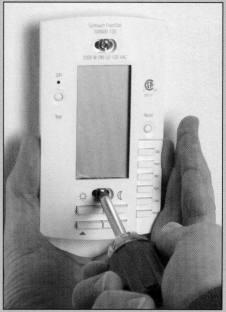

9 The control shown above has built-in GFCI protection. Using a jeweler's screwdriver, attach the two sensor wires to the screw terminals on one side of the control. Connect the ground from the mat power lead directly to the house ground.

10 Attach the black control lead marked "LINE" to the incoming black wire. Connect the white control lead "LINE" to the incoming white wire. Attach the black and white control leads marked "LOAD" to the black and white wires connecting to the mat. Fold the wires into the box.

11 Attach the faceplate. Connect to the power source or connect the line to a new breaker. Turn on the power and follow the manufacturer's instructions for setting the temperature and timer.

ADDING A TIMER

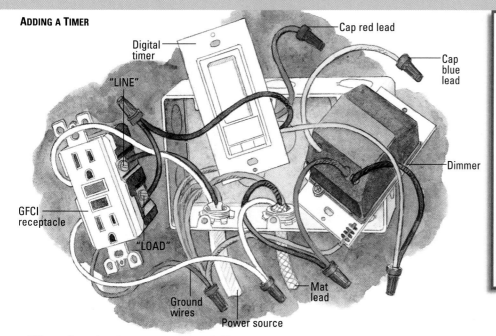

Digital timer

"LINE"

GFCI receptacle

"LOAD"

Ground wires

Power source

Cap red lead

Cap blue lead

Dimmer

Mat lead

This configuration draws power from a GFCI receptacle and combines a timer and dimmer to control the heat level. The result: A warm bathroom floor greets morning bathers. A sensor bulb and line is not needed with this approach.

SAFETY FIRST
Don't overload circuit or components

Checking the amperage demanded by a new installation will tell you if an existing circuit can carry the load or if you'll have to install a new circuit. Each square foot of electric radiant heating mat draws 0.1 amp. That means adding radiant heating mats to the work area of an average-size bath will add only 5 or 6 amps to the circuit (50–60 square feet of mat). But each component included in the system also has to be up to that amperage. Check dimmers and timers to make sure they are rated to take the amperage.

INSTALLING CERAMIC FLOOR TILE

Before you begin installing a ceramic tile floor, make sure the floor is up to the job required for ceramic substrates. Prepare the surface using the methods described on *pages 114–115.* If your bathroom remodel is in a basement, you won't need cement backerboard. You will, however, need a waterproofing membrane—not to keep water from migrating down through the tile and grout, but to keep the slab from wicking moisture up into the floor.

Figure out how many tiles you need in each layout section and stack them around the room. That way you won't have to go back and forth to get more tiles when you start a section.

Sort through all the tile boxes to make sure the dye lots match, and take out any chipped tiles. Use them for cut pieces.

If you are installing saltillo or handmade tile, its color may vary from box to box. Mix some from each box. Doing so spreads the colors evenly in the room.

PRESTART CHECKLIST

☐ **TIME**
About an hour to trowel and set 4 to 6 square feet (varies with tile size)

☐ **TOOLS**
Tape measure, chalk line, mortar mixing paddle, ½-inch electric drill, notched trowel, 4-foot level, utility knife, grout float, sponge, beater block, hammer or rubber mallet

☐ **SKILLS**
Measuring accurately, mixing with power drill, troweling

☐ **PREP**
Install backerboard, clean surface, snap layout lines

☐ **MATERIALS**
Five-gallon bucket, thinset, spacers, ¾-inch plywood squares, tile

Marking layout lines on floors

1 Dry-lay your tile with spacers on each axis, (see "Laying Out a Tile Floor," *page 121).* When the layout is square and even, mark the floor at several junctures of the grout lines. Take up the tile and snap a chalk line at the center-most pair of marks.

2 Continue to snap chalk lines across the surface of the floor at points that represent the edges of the tile. These layout lines will serve as guides to help you keep each course straight and square with the room.

CHECKING A FLOOR FOR SQUARE

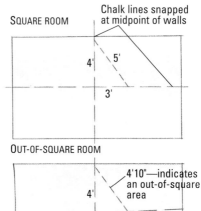

SQUARE ROOM
Chalk lines snapped at midpoint of walls
4' 5' 3'

OUT-OF-SQUARE ROOM
4'10"—indicates an out-of-square area
4' 3'

Original chalk line at midpoint was not square

Chalk line adjusted until hypotenuse is 5 feet; use this line to dry-lay tile

One of the most common problems in planning a tiled floor is out-of-square walls. Walls seldom define a room squarely, but you need some perpendicular reference to square your tile layout with the room. To determine if a floor is square, use a 3-4-5 triangle.

Snap a chalk line on the floor at the midpoints of opposite walls. From the intersection measure out on one line a distance of 3 feet. Tape the chalk line at that point and measure and tape a distance of 4 feet on the other line. Now measure the distance between the tapes. If it's 5 feet exactly, the floor is square. Adjust the lines, if necessary, until they are perpendicular.

Make a sketch of the layout of the tile on your floor. Even a rough drawing will help you organize the job.

Wavy walls can mean you will need to cut some of the edge tiles at different widths. Check the walls with a 4-foot level and mark wavy sections on the drawing as accurately as possible.

Setting the tile

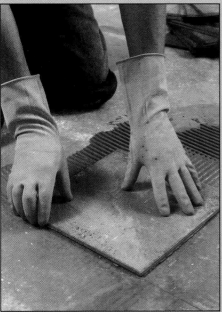

1 Pour the water in a bucket, then add about half the dry thinset. Mix the thinset with a ½-inch drill and a mortar paddle. Keep the speed below 300 rpm to avoid introducing air. Add thinset a little at a time. When the thinset is evenly mixed, let it set for 10 minutes before applying.

2 Dump mortar at the edge of a section of the room. Holding the straight edge of a trowel at about a 30-degree angle, spread the mortar evenly, about as thick as the depth of a trowel notch. Spread the mortar to the layout line; comb it with the notched edge at about a 45- to 75-degree angle.

3 Starting in the center of the room, set the first full tile at the intersection of your layout lines, positioning it with a slight twist as you embed it in the mortar. Do not slide the tile—sliding can thin out the thinset and push mortar into the joints. Keep the edges of the tile on the layout lines.

LAYING OUT A TILE FLOOR

1. Snap perpendicular lines at the midpoints of the walls and square them (see *page 120*).

2. Dry-lay tile in both directions to center the layout and leave tiles of equal width at both edges.

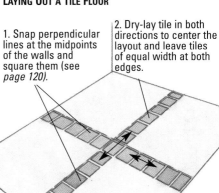

4 Using the layout pattern you have chosen, lay the next tile in place with the same twisting motion, keeping the tile aligned on your layout line. Insert spacers between the tiles and adjust the tiles to fit.

5 Continue laying tiles along both legs of the layout lines (a jack-on-jack design is shown above) or in the order of your design, spacing the tiles as you go.

Squaring and leveling the tile

1 Periodically check the tile in both directions. Lay a 4-foot level on the edge of the tile—all the edges should line up along the level. Adjust the tiles to straighten the joints, if necessary. Don't kneel or walk on set tiles. Support your weight on a 2-foot square of ¾-inch plywood.

2 When you have finished laying one section of tile, set a 4-foot carpenter's level on the surface and check for tiles that are higher or lower than the overall surface. Using a beater block, tap high tiles in place with a rubber mallet.

2×4 beater block covered with carpet

3 Pry up low tiles with a utility knife and spread more adhesive on the back. Set the tile back in place and level it with the beater block. Clean excess mortar from the joints while the mortar is still wet. Run a spacer in the joint, pulling out the excess. Let the thinset cure at least overnight.

Making straight cuts

Scoring wheel

Snap cutter: Insert the tile in the cutter, aligning the scoring wheel on the cut line. Pull or push the scoring wheel across the cut line, using firm pressure throughout the stroke. Score the tile in one pass. Hold the tile firmly in place and strike the handle with the heel of your hand.

Wet saw: Set the tile securely against the fence with the cut line at the blade. Turn on the saw and feed the tile into the blade with light pressure. Increase the pressure as the saw cuts the tile and ease off as the blade approaches the rear of the cut. Keep the tile on the table at all times.

STANLEY PRO TIP

Don't wash away the line

The blade of a wet saw is cooled with water, which will wash away a cut line made with a felt-tip marker. When marking tiles that will be cut with a wet saw, use a china marker so the line won't wash away.

Marking tile for cuts

Straight cut: Place the tile to be cut flush to the wall or obstruction, lined up on top of an installed tile. Place another tile over the tile to be cut, with its edge against the wall. Trace the edge with a marker. Draw the cutting line parallel to the mark but shorter by the width of two grout lines.

L-shape cut: Place the tile to be trimmed first on one corner, then the other, marking the cut lines with a full tile as you would for a single straight cut. Cut each side shorter than the mark by the width of two grout lines.

Curved cuts: Set the tile to be cut against the obstruction, lining up its edges with tile already laid. Mark the width of the cut by setting a tape measure on each edge of the obstruction. Move the tile to one side of the obstruction and use the tape to mark the depth of the cut.

Making curved cuts

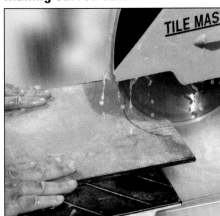

1 Using a wet saw, make several relief cuts from the edge of the tile to the curved cut line. Relief cuts do not have to be exactly parallel to each other, but make sure they stop just short of the curved line.

2 Place the jaws of tile nippers about an inch away from the curved line and carefully snap out the waste at the relief cuts.

3 Working the nippers on the cut line, snap away the remaining excess. Don't try to "bite" through the tile with the nippers. Instead grasp the tile tightly with the tool and use a prying motion.

GROUTING, CAULKING, AND SEALING

Grouting, caulking, and sealing are not difficult tasks, but they do take time. Don't rush these activities—they affect both the final appearance of your tiling project and its longevity.

Bring all materials into the room to acclimate them to its temperature, preferably between 65–75°F. Prepare the surface by removing spacers and cleaning excess mortar from the joints and surface. Lightly mist the edges of nonvitreous tile with water so they won't take too much moisture from the grout. Vitreous tiles do not require misting.

Use a margin trowel to mix grout in clean containers, following the manufacturer's instructions, adding powder to liquid a little at a time. Let it set for 10 minutes and restir it to loosen its texture. Grout should be wet enough to spread, but not runny.

PRESTART CHECKLIST

☐ **TIME**
From 15 to 30 minutes to mix, float, and clean a 4-foot-square section (varies with tile size); about five minutes to caulk a 10-foot joint, 45 minutes to seal a 15×20-foot floor, longer if applying sealer to joints only

☐ **TOOLS**
Utility knife or grout knife, grout float, nylon scrubber, margin trowel, grout bag (optional), applicator or mop for sealer, caulk gun

☐ **SKILLS**
Spreading grout with float; using caulk gun

☐ **PREP**
Install all tile and let mortar cure

☐ **MATERIALS**
Grout, bucket and water, rags, sponge, sealer, caulk

Grouting tile

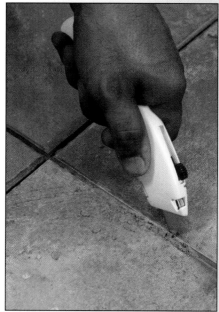

1 Remove spacers if you have not done so already. Inspect the joints for any remaining adhesive and scrape it out with a utility knife or grout knife. Remove any remaining hardened mortar from the tile surface with a nylon (not metal) scrubber.

2 Mix the grout to the consistency recommended by the manufacturer; dump or scoop out a small pile with a margin trowel. Working in 10-square-foot sections, pack the grout into the joints with a grout float. Hold the float at about a 30- to 45-degree angle; work it in both directions.

WHAT IF...
The grout joints are wide?

Irregular tiles look best with wide grout joints, but wide joints may be hard to fill with a grout float. Use a grout bag for these tiles and for rough tiles whose surfaces will be difficult to clean.

Fit a metal spout onto the bag equal to the width of the joint. Fill the bag with grout. Working down the length of a joint, squeeze the bag, overfilling the joint slightly. Compact the excess and sweep loose grout with a stiff broom when dry.

STANLEY PRO TIP

Avoid voids when power mixing grout

Power mixing can introduce air bubbles in grout and leave voids in it. Mix grout by hand with a margin trowel, adding the powder to the water. Let the mix set for 10 minutes, then remix before applying.

Tips for grouting stone

Use the grout recommended by the manufacturer. Nonsanded grout tends to recede when curing, so you may need to apply it twice if the joints in your stone installation are set at $1/16$ inch. Seal stone before grouting to ease cleaning and again after grouting.

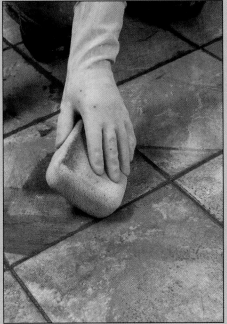

3 Once you have grouted a section, hold the float almost perpendicular to the tile and scrape the excess off the tile surface. Work the float diagonally to the joints to avoid lifting the grout. If you remove grout, replace it in the joint and reclean the surface. Let the grout set.

4 When a just-damp sponge won't lift grout from the joint, you can start cleaning. Wring out all excess water from a damp sponge and rub the surface in a circular motion. Rinse and wring out the sponge often. Repeat parallel to the joints to make them neat, and once more to finish cleaning.

5 Let the surface dry about 15 minutes, then remove the grout haze from the surface with a dry, clean rag. Avoid terrycloth material; it can lift out uncured grout. Tile with a matte finish may require another cleaning with fresh water and a clean sponge.

Sealing grout and tiles

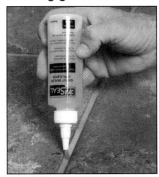

Although latex or polymer-modified grouts resist staining, you'll get the best stain protection by sealing the grout.

On glazed and other impervious tiles, apply the sealer only to the joint using an applicator designed for this purpose.

To protect saltillo and other soft-bodied tiles, seal the entire surface with a mop or applicator as recommended by the manufacturer.

Different sealers can leave stone in its natural color or enhance its tone.

Caulking the joints

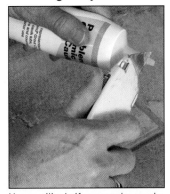

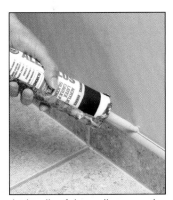

Use a utility knife to cut the nozzle to the width of the joint and at a 45-degree angle. Cut through the nozzle in one pass. Before you apply the caulk, you may want to practice the techniques on scrap.

Starting in one corner, squeeze

the handle of the caulk gun gently and apply the caulk to the joint. Keep the caulk gun moving as you squeeze so the caulk won't overrun the joint. Finish the surface of the caulk with a wet finger or sponge. Light pressure will avoid gouging.

INSTALLING MOSAIC TILE

Not long ago setting mosaic tile meant embedding each small piece in a mortar bed. Later developments, notably sheets of mosaic held together by paper adhered to their face, helped reduce installation time. These early face-mounted sheets, however, were difficult to line up.

Modern mosaics have taken improvements a step further. Each small mosaic tile is bonded to the sheet with plastic dots or on a plastic mesh, paper, or threaded backing.

You'll find mosaics in many colors and in squares, rectangles, random designs, and all forms of geometric figures. Most mosaic tiles are glass or high-fired porcelain, so they're impervious to moisture. Porcelains come with glazed surfaces for walls and with nonslip surfaces for floors.

If the style you've chosen is available only in dot-mounted sheets, make sure the dots are free of any residual manufacturing oil. This oil interferes with adhesive bonding. Check two or three sheets in each carton, wiping them with a paper towel.

If replacing a carton is not an alternative, either change your design or wash the back of each sheet with a mild detergent.

PRESTART CHECKLIST

☐ **TIME**
About 5 to 6 hours (not including grouting) for an 8×10-foot room

☐ **TOOLS**
Chalk line, tape measure, carpenter's pencil, power drill, mixing paddle, notched trowel, beater block, rubber mallet, 4-foot metal straightedge

☐ **SKILLS**
Measuring, setting tile

☐ **PREP**
Remove existing flooring; repair or replace underlayment

☐ **MATERIALS**
Epoxy mortar, mosaic tile sheets

1 Lay out perpendicular lines in the center of the room *(page 120)*, and snap grid lines at intervals of the same dimensions as the mosaic sheet. Mix the epoxy adhesive, and using a ¼-inch notched trowel, spread and comb it on a small area, just inside the layout lines.

2 Set the corner of the first sheet just inside the corner of the layout lines. Square the sheet to the lines and embed the tiles firmly into the mortar with a beater block and rubber mallet. Make sure the entire surface of the sheet is level in the mortar—mosaics show depressions dramatically.

Arranging random patterns

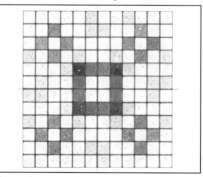

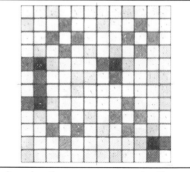

A mosaic pattern that features randomly placed colored tiles is more difficult to set than one that has regular geometric patterns—you have to make sure the color schemes throughout the design balance each other.

Lay the sheets on the surface in a dry run, changing their positions until you get the arrangement right. Then take up the sheets and number them so you can mortar them in the same order.

Such experimentation produced the balanced pattern, left, but this pattern with its centered square is not the only balanced design possible with these tiles. Avoid patterns like the one shown, right. Although it is composed of the same tiles, the pattern appears unbalanced and chaotic.

3 Pull the sheet up and check it for full coverage. If some of the tiles show bare spots, apply more mortar. Lay the sheet face down on a clean surface and skim more mortar on the back. Recomb the mortar bed with a larger notched trowel and reset the sheet with the beater block.

4 Set the next sheet using the same techniques. After four or five sheets, you should have a feel for the proper amount of mortar. As you embed the tiles with the beater block, make sure the edges of each sheet are level with its neighbors; then line up all the joints.

5 Continue setting the tiles using a metal straightedge to keep the joints straight. Wipe excess mortar from the surface of the tile with a damp (not wet) sponge. Make sure you remove all of the excess—dried mortar is very difficult to remove. Let the mortar set, then grout and clean the tiles.

STANLEY PRO TIP

Keep colors consistent

It's impossible to set mosaics without some of the mortar creeping up into the grout joints. To keep your work from looking blotchy when you apply the grout, use the same product for both the mortar bed and the grout—100 percent solid epoxy of the same color. Alternatively you might be able to color the mortar to match the grout, but such attempts often result in noticeably different shades.

Embedding the mosaic sheets into the mortar will inevitably force some mortar onto the surface of the tiles. Before you set the next section, use a synthetic scrubbing pad to clean the tile, then wipe it with a dampened sponge. Don't use too much water—it will wash out the epoxy from the joint and weaken it.

WHAT IF…
Mosaic tiles need to be cut?

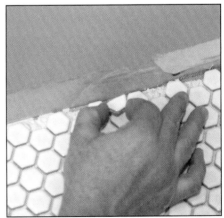

One advantage of mosaics is that the small individual tiles can often fit around obstacles without being cut. Use a utility knife to cut the backing in the contour of the obstacle and strip away the tiles.

If you need to cut an individual tile, remove it from the backing and cut it with a snap cutter. Then back-butter the cut piece and set it in the mortar.

INSTALLING STONE TILE

Stone tile requires the same firm and level setting bed as ceramic tile—only more so. Because stone is brittle and the minerals that make up its pattern are not perfectly "cemented" to each other, it is subject to fracture along the grain lines.

Stone also suffers from the normal physical inconsistencies found in any natural material. Some pieces might not be exactly as wide or thick as the others. Adjust length and width by cutting the tile with a wet saw and accommodate differences in thickness by adjusting the amount of mortar you spread.

When set, the top edges of all tiles should be flush. Back-butter each tile before you set it in the mortar bed and test it to make sure its edges are flush with its neighbors.

Most stone tile comes from the factory with beveled edges, so cutting a tile will leave it with an unbeveled edge. Hone the edge of the cut tile with a rubbing stone or with sandpaper wrapped around a block of wood. To polish a tile to a high sheen, use progressively finer grits of carbide sandpaper (from 120 to 600).

PRESTART CHECKLIST

☐ **TIME**
About 10 hours for an 8×10-foot room. Allow 3 to 4 hours for grouting and cleanup on the next day.

☐ **TOOLS**
Chalk line, tape measure, carpenter's pencil, power drill with mixing paddle, notched trowel, beater block, rubber mallet, grout float, 4-foot metal straightedge, wet saw, dry-cutting saw

☐ **SKILLS**
Marking, setting, and cutting tile

☐ **PREP**
Remove existing flooring, repair or replace underlayment

☐ **MATERIALS**
Thinset mortar, stone tile

1 Stone tile often has a dusty residue on its back, which weakens the adhesive bond. Wipe your finger across the back of the tile and if it comes up dusty, clean the backs of the tiles with a sponge and water. Let the tiles dry before bedding them.

2 Lay out a dry run so the edge tiles are the same size *(pages 120–121)*. Then snap chalk lines as guides. Using white thinset for light-colored tiles, trowel thinset onto the subfloor and back-butter the tile. Set and level the tiles, adding mortar to the back as needed. Line up tiles with a straightedge.

WHAT IF...
You have to cut a hole in the stone?

Cutting holes for obstacles such as electrical outlets becomes a relatively easy task with a dry-cutting saw equipped with a diamond blade. The saw allows you to get almost all the way into the corners to make a clean cut.

Mark the outline with a china marker (not a felt-tip, which may bleed). While a helper steadies the tile, lower the saw into the middle of the line. Work the saw forward to one end of the line, then back to the other corner. Knock out the cut piece with tile nippers and trim the corners square. Don't worry if the cut line is slightly errant; it will be hidden under the wall plate.

3 When the mortar for the field tiles has set sufficiently (usually overnight), cut the edge tiles with a wet saw and lay them in a mortar bed, back-buttering each tile as you go. Measure for each individual edge tile—it's unlikely that the room will be square and all the tiles the same size.

4 Let the mortar for the edge tiles cure for 24 hours. Then mix a batch of unsanded grout, just enough to cover a small section. To keep the stone tiles from absorbing too much water from the grout, mist them with a spray bottle. Apply the grout with a float. Remove excess grout from the surface of the stone. When the grout has set for about 15 minutes, wipe the haze with a damp sponge. Finish grouting the entire installation, working in sections so you can clean the excess before it hardens. When the grout has completely cured, seal the tiles as necessary.

WHAT IF…
Edge tiles are not available?

Some manufacturers produce stone bullnose, but if your selection doesn't come with them, you can make your own by rounding the edges with a rubbing stone. As an alternative, start with coarse carbide sandpaper wrapped around a wood block and polish with finer grades.

STANLEY PRO TIP: **Use adhesive alternatives for stone**

Granite tiles make an attractive substitute for a granite slab on a vanity countertop. If your tiles are cut to a consistent thickness, you can use silicone adhesive instead of thinset. Lay the tiles in a dry run. Then lift one at a time, apply silicone to the substrate, and press the tiles in place. Line up the tiles with a straightedge.

For some stone tiles, expensive epoxy mortar is the preferred adhesive, but you might be able to get around the cost by sealing the back of the tile with a nonporous epoxy sealer. Once the coating has cured, you can set the tiles in regular thinset mortar.

INSTALLING DRY-BACKED RESILIENT TILE

When choosing an adhesive for dry-backed tile, be sure to read labels carefully. Picking an adhesive requires a bit of science—you'll find latex-based solutions, asphalt emulsions, alcohol resins, rubber cements, and epoxies. Ask your supplier to match the qualities of the adhesive to your job site.

Most vinyl adhesives are solvent-based, which means they don't handle like thinset and other cement-based mortars. They tend to "grab" the trowel and are difficult to spread evenly. If you need to, practice spreading adhesive on a piece of scrap plywood before applying it to the floor. When you work with solvent-based adhesives, you must properly ventilate the room: Open the windows and exhaust the fumes with a window fan. Wear a respirator for full protection.

Work as much as possible from untiled sections of the floor. If you have to kneel on the tile, distribute your weight on 2×2 plywood squares. Cut two pieces so you can move them alternately as you work across the floor.

PRESTART CHECKLIST

☐ **TIME**
About 4 hours for an 8×10-foot floor

☐ **TOOLS**
Trowel, utility knife, hair dryer, chalk line, straightedge, carpenter's pencil, 100-pound floor roller

☐ **SKILLS**
Setting and cutting tile

☐ **PREP**
Repair subfloor and snap layout lines

☐ **MATERIALS**
Tiles, adhesive

Installing resilient tile

1 Starting at an intersection of lines, spread adhesive with the smooth edge of a notched trowel. Lay the adhesive right up to—but not over—the layout lines. Then comb the adhesive with the notched edge of the trowel. Let the adhesive become tacky.

2 Line up the first tile with the intersection of the layout lines and set it on the adhesive. Then set the second tile against the first one and lower it in place. Don't slide the tiles—you'll push mastic up between the joints. Check the grain direction and set the rest of the quadrant.

SETTING SEQUENCES PERPENDICULAR LAYOUTS

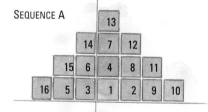

SEQUENCE A

SEQUENCE B

Use Sequence A when the adhesive has a long open time, which allows you to work more quickly because you don't have to stop as often to spread mastic. Use Sequence B when using a mastic with a short open time.

Check the grain direction

Most resilient tiles have a grain that results from the manufacturing process. The grain itself is virtually invisible but it does affect the color and perception of the pattern, depending on the angle of the light falling on the tile. Other tiles, both with and without grain, have a pattern that is directional.

Both grained and patterned tile must be laid in a certain order to achieve the ideal appearance. Look on the back of each tile before you lay it. If it has arrows imprinted on it, use the arrows as a guide. Dry-lay the tile with the arrows going in one direction, then experiment with the pattern, installing the arrows differently. Once you discover a result you like, use it consistently as you set the tile.

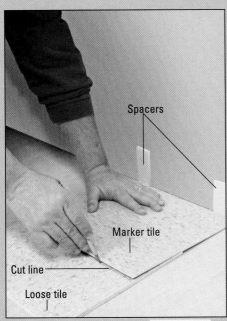

3 To mark the edge tiles for cutting vinyl tile, set a loose tile exactly on top of the last tile in a row. Then set a marker tile on top of that one, positioning it against ¼-inch spacers at the wall (resilient tile won't expand much, but the subfloor will). Run a pencil along the edge of the marker tile to mark the cut line.

4 At outside corners position a loose tile and a marker tile as if you were cutting an edge tile. Mark the loose tile as you did in step 3, and reposition the loose tile and marker tile to the other corner. Mark the loose tile for the corner cutout.

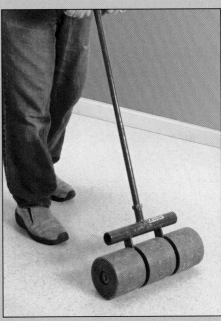

5 When you have set one quadrant, clean off excess or spilled adhesive with the solvent recommended by the manufacturer (usually detergent and water). Don't wet the floor—excess liquid weakens the adhesive. Set the remaining quadrants. Roll the floor when finished.

Cutting vinyl tile

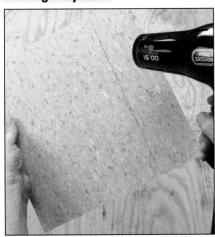

Brittle resilient tiles cut more easily if you warm them slightly with a hair dryer. Use a carpenter's pencil to mark the cut line and a utility knife to make the cut.

Score the surface of the tile with the knife, then make several passes until you have cut through the tile. If the cut edge will not be visible, you can snap the tile after a few passes with the knife.

Mix the lots

Tiles are manufactured in groups called "lots," and the color of the tile may vary from lot to lot. When you're purchasing tile, ask the dealer to supply you with tiles from the same lot. If you can't get the entire order from a single lot, mix the tiles from different cartons as you lay them. Doing so will spread any color variations randomly throughout the floor.

The easiest way to mix the tiles is to open three cartons and reassemble the tiles from each in a single batch.

INSTALLING SHEET VINYL FLOORING

One of the great advantages of sheet vinyl flooring is that it has fewer seams than other materials—fewer places where water can seep through. That makes it an excellent choice for bathroom floors. In fact, because it comes in rolls that are 12 feet wide, you can install it in smaller bathrooms with no seams at all.

Resilient sheet vinyl comes in two types. **Full-spread vinyl** has a felt-paper backing and requires an adhesive spread over the entire floor surface. That makes its installation a little more difficult and time-consuming. In return it pays you back for this extra effort by rarely coming loose from the floor. It demands, however, an almost flawlessly smooth underlayment—even small particles under the sheet will show up as bumps when the sheet is glued down.

Perimeter-bond sheet vinyl requires adhesive only around the edges of the room, making it easier and quicker to lay. It is more forgiving of minor underlayment flaws, but is also more prone to coming loose.

1 Cover the perimeter ¼ inch from the walls with butcher's paper or kraft paper. Heavier paper will move less. Cut small triangles and tape the sheet to the floor through the holes. Overlap all edges at least 2 inches and duct tape them. Roll up the template and take it to the room where you'll cut the sheet.

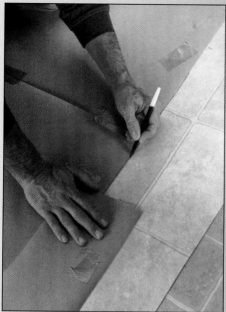

2 Unroll the vinyl sheet face up. Overlap seam edges by 3 inches and tape the seam. Unroll the paper template on the sheet, lining up the edges of the template with pattern lines. Tape the template to the sheet and mark its edge on the sheet with a washable marker.

PRESTART CHECKLIST

☐ **TIME**
About 4 hours for full-spread vinyl on a 10×12-foot bathroom floor

☐ **TOOLS**
Linoleum knife, utility knife, compass, scissors, floor roller, seam roller, straightedge

☐ **SKILLS**
Measuring and cutting template accurately, lifting and unrolling sheet goods, seaming vinyl

☐ **PREP**
Install or repair underlayment without surface defects

☐ **MATERIALS**
Butcher paper or kraft paper, masking tape, duct tape, adhesive, vinyl sheet goods, seaming solvent

Shopping for quality

Vinyl long ago replaced the mix of linseed oil, cork, and wood that was called linoleum, which graced many midcentury homes. (But special-order linoleum is available.)

All vinyl floor goods, however, are not created equal. The adage "You get what you pay for" applies here with certainty. The quality, and therefore, the durability of the material, varies widely and depends almost entirely on how much vinyl it contains.

Solid vinyl is tough, longest lasting, and most expensive. Its color and pattern are formed by embedded colored vinyl chips in the vinyl base material. Solid vinyl products also boast more choices of colors and patterns. Because the color and pattern go clear through the sheet, you won't find it wearing off easily.

The same goes for **vinyl composition** products whose pattern and color are ingrained, but composed of both vinyl and non-vinyl ingredients. The reduced vinyl content makes this product less expensive.

Rotogravure vinyl sheets get their pattern from a printing process, and the printed layer has no vinyl content at all. It is protected by a urethane wear layer, but once this layer wears to expose the printed pattern, you'll find your pretty floor slowly disappearing.

You can tell a lot about the quality of vinyl sheet goods by their thickness. Thicker materials contain more vinyl and will last longer. What kind of material you use may come down to what kind of bathroom it will go in. For example it might make sense to install a less expensive sheet in an infrequently used guest bath.

3 With a straightedge along the marks on the sheet, cut it with a utility knife. Roll up the sheet with the pattern side in and carry it to the bathroom floor. Unroll the sheet, sliding it under door casings, and tug and shift it into place.

4 For a full-spread floor, lift up one half of the sheet and fold it back. For perimeter-bond lift up the edges. Spread adhesive from the corners to the center with a ¼-inch notched trowel. Refold the sheet back into place. Adhere the second sheet (or the other half if not seaming the sheet vinyl).

5 Roll the entire surface from the center to the edges with a rented 100-pound floor roller. Use a damp rag to wipe up any adhesive around the edges of the vinyl. Replace the trim, then install baseboards and shoe molding or vinyl cove base. Install thresholds and rehang the doors.

Seaming the sheet vinyl

1 To cut a straight seam, overlap the edges 3 inches and snap a chalk line where you want the seam. Using a straightedge and utility knife, cut through both sheets in one pass. Pull back the edges and apply adhesive under them. Push seam edges down into the adhesive.

2 Roll the seam with a seam roller (called a J-roller). Use moderate pressure to avoid pushing adhesive up through the seam. Wipe off excess adhesive and let it cure. Then apply seaming solvent to fuse the edges.

STANLEY Pro Tip

Easy seams

The best location for seams is obviously on an inconspicuous, low-traffic section of the floor. Symmetry is not necessarily your goal here—a seam running down the center of your bathroom floor is likely to be distracting. Put it perpendicular to the room and close to a far wall. Find your best seam location before you start cutting the sheet to fit.

After you've laid your floor, protect it until both adhesive and seams have set.

■ If possible, don't walk on the seams for at least eight hours.

■ Keep the temperature at 65 degrees or above for 48 hours to let the adhesive cure properly.

■ Don't wash the floor for five days.

PLUMBING

One look at the tangle of pipes and valves under a kitchen sink is usually enough to make a homeowner reach for the phone book to find a professional plumber. At first glance plumbing seems difficult and messy. However, because the plumbing associated with a bathroom remodel is mostly new work, you'll find it homeowner-friendly and rewarding—especially when you consider your do-it-yourself savings. Installing your own plumbing for a new bathroom saves a sizable chunk of cash.

Learning the basics

Even if you've never lifted a pipe wrench before or fixed a faucet, you can learn how to add a new sink, toilet, or tub. But like every home improvement project, these installations rely on a firm grasp of some basic techniques. That's what you'll find in this chapter—the rudiments of plumbing systems, pipes, and fittings, and how to work with them. Step-by-step instructions bring these techniques within the reach of any do-it-yourselfer.

Building codes

Even if you're armed with experience and confidence, it doesn't mean you can work through your bathroom project as if it were a world of its own. Anytime you install a plumbing fixture where there was none before—in other words, whenever you need to run new pipes—you've entered a whole new arena. New plumbing must conform to strict codes and must be inspected by your local building department.

Building departments can get understandably fussy about plumbing installations. You'll probably have to take out a building permit, file plans, and arrange for inspections. Don't take chances—consult your building department before you start the work.

Working safely and comfortably

Before attempting any project, turn off the water and turn on a faucet to make sure the water supply is off. Take care not to touch nearby electrical outlets, especially if you are wet.

Plumbing is sometimes physically challenging, not because of heavy lifting, but because you often have to work in cramped conditions. Take a break to relieve cramped muscles and strained joints.

Use kneepads and even an old pillow to make the work area more comfortable.

Spread drop cloths around and keep a bucket and some old towels handy to catch the small amounts of water that may dribble out of pipes.

Position a flashlight or work light so you can see clearly.

Practical planning

Plan your time carefully; your family will not be able to use the bathroom until most if not all of the work is complete. Even a well-planned project can run into unforeseen problems and delays. A separate bathroom can relieve much of the stress of a remodeling project, but if you don't have one, you may need to make contingency arrangements with family or friends.

Before tackling a project, understand plumbing in general and your system in particular.

CHAPTER PREVIEW

Understanding the systems
page 136

Pipes and fittings
page 138

Working with copper pipe
page 140

Installing plastic drainpipe
page 142

Working with PEX tubing
page 144

Running pipes through walls and floors
page 146

Connecting new to old
page 148

Installing a stop valve
page 150

UNDERSTANDING THE SYSTEMS

The maze of pipes running through your walls and floors have two basic but different functions—the **supply system** brings water into the house, and the **drain-waste-vent system** carries wastewater and gases out of the house.

Supply system

In a typical system, a single ¾- to 1¼-inch supply pipe brings water into the house. This water is supplied by a utility company, which is responsible for its purity.

Soon after entering the house, most supply pipes run through a water meter, which records the amount of water you use. If your water bill is the same from month to month, your water is probably unmetered.

The supply pipe then travels toward the water heater. There the pipe splits into two branches. One supplies cold water to the house and the other fills the water heater. The pipe that emerges from the water heater supplies hot water to the house.

These two pipes run in pairs to supply hot and cold water to various rooms and fixtures. Vertical pipes are sometimes called risers. Older supply pipes are typically made of galvanized steel, while newer homes have pipes made of copper or plastic—PVC or CPVC.

Somewhere near the water heater, pipes usually reduce in size to ¾ inch. Farther on, as they turn into branch lines, pipes typically reduce to ½ inch. If water pressure is low, the problem may be calcium buildup or supply pipes that are too small.

The flow of water can be shut off before the water enters the house, at a main shutoff just inside the house, at branch lines, and near the individual plumbing appliances.

Drain-waste-vent system

Carrying water out of a house smoothly is the job of the drain-waste-vent (DWV) system. These pipes must be installed according to precise specifications found in national and local plumbing codes. Never install a DWV pipe until you check with your building department and are sure you comply with local codes.

Drain water for every fixture must run through a trap made of plastic or chromed brass. The walls of such traps are thinner than supply and DWV pipe, and the trap is made to be dismantled easily.

Traps are shaped like a P or an S. This shape traps water so fumes and gases cannot back up into the house. A toilet has its own built-in trap. A trap usually connects to a branch drainpipe, typically 1½ or 2 inches in diameter. A branch drain carries water to the main stack.

Drainpipes must be correctly sloped so that water can run freely through them. Plumbing codes require special fittings that make sweeping rather than abrupt turns so that waste matter does not get stuck.

The centerpiece of a DWV system is the main stack, a fat pipe usually 4 to 6 inches in diameter, which runs straight up through the roof. It carries wastewater out to the local sanitary sewer system or septic tank, keeps water flowing smoothly, and also carries noxious fumes out of the house. Often a home has one or more secondary stacks, perhaps 2 or 3 inches in diameter, that serve the kitchen or another part of the system.

Older homes have stacks made of cast iron, while newer homes use plastic ABS or PVC pipe. Drain lines and stacks often have cleanouts, which are elbowed pipes with a plug that can be temporarily removed to allow a clog to be augered out.

The drain for every fixture must be connected in some way to a vent pipe, which usually extends up through the roof. In the most common arrangement, a stack extends upward so that its upper portion acts as a vent, while its lower portion is a drain. Sometimes a separate pipe called a revent is used to vent a section of a system. A revent reaches up and over its appliance to tie into a stack.

Vent pipes need not be as large as drainpipes, but they must be kept clear. A vent may become clogged by a bird's nest or debris from reroofing. If so be sure to clear it out with an auger.

Whenever you install new service, it is very important to have the venting installed and operating correctly (pages 252–255).

A bathtub access panel

Bathtub plumbing is complicated, so many homes have an access panel to allow you to reach it. To find an access panel, look in the adjacent room or closet, on the wall directly behind the tub faucet.

FIXTURE TRAPS

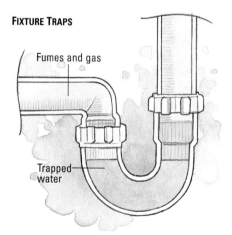

Fumes and gas

Trapped water

The drain water for every fixture must run through a trap—a section of pipe shaped like a sideways P or S. Because of its shape, it holds water, creating a seal that keeps fumes and gases from entering the house. A toilet has a built-in trap. Sink traps are made of chrome-plated brass or plastic, with joints that can be taken apart easily.

HOUSEHOLD SUPPLY LINES, VENTS, AND DRAINS

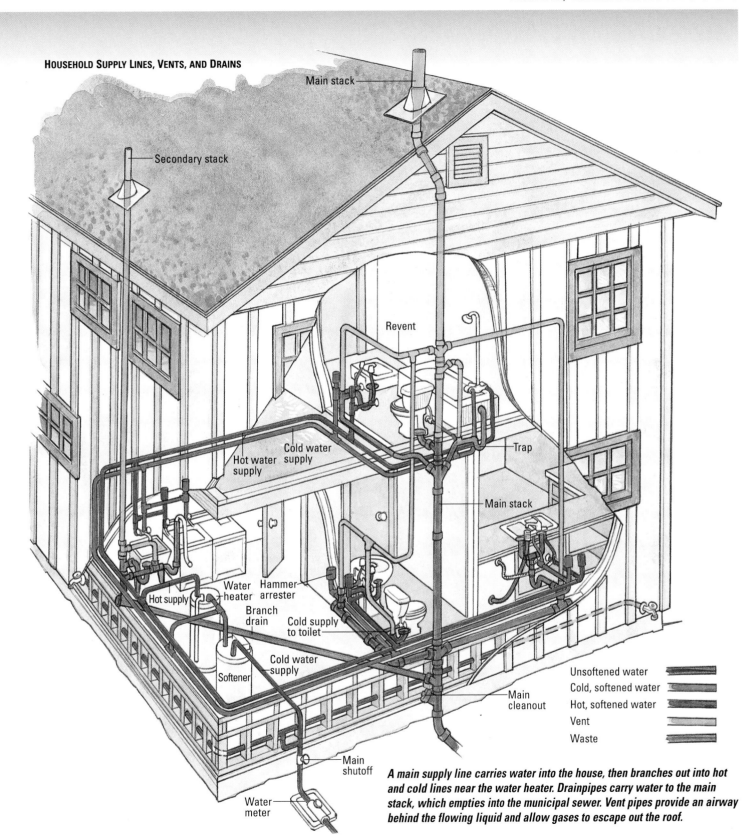

Main stack

Secondary stack

Revent

Cold water supply

Hot water supply

Trap

Main stack

Water heater

Hammer arrester

Hot supply

Branch drain

Cold supply to toilet

Cold water supply

Softener

Main cleanout

Unsoftened water
Cold, softened water
Hot, softened water
Vent
Waste

Main shutoff

Water meter

A main supply line carries water into the house, then branches out into hot and cold lines near the water heater. Drainpipes carry water to the main stack, which empties into the municipal sewer. Vent pipes provide an airway behind the flowing liquid and allow gases to escape out the roof.

PIPES AND FITTINGS

When you install new fixtures, you'll need to know what kind of pipe to use and what size it is. Newer homes usually have drainpipes made of some kind of plastic and supply pipes made of copper; a pre-1950 home may have cast-iron drainpipes and galvanized steel water supply pipes.

Plastic

Plastic pipe is inexpensive and easy to work with, making it popular among installers. Joints are glued together using a primer that cleans the surfaces and a cement that bonds them securely *(pages 142–143)*. There are four different kinds of plastic used in residential plumbing.

White or cream-color **PVC (polyvinyl chloride)** pipe is the most common choice for drainpipes. It's strong, lasts nearly forever, and is almost completely impervious to chemicals. PVC is sometimes used for supply pipes, but codes in most communities no longer allow it for hot water lines. That's because heat shrinks it and weakens the joints. To find out the strength (or "schedule") of a PVC pipe, look for stamped printing on it. In most localities schedule 40 is considered strong enough for residential purposes.

CPVC (chlorinated polyvinyl chloride) pipe has the strength of PVC and is also heat-resistant, so many (but not all) codes allow its use for interior supply lines.

Black **ABS (acrylonitrile butadiene styrene)** drainpipe was the first plastic pipe to be used in homes. Most localities no longer permit its use because it deteriorates rapidly. PVC is considered a superior material.

Flexible **PE (polyethylene)** supply pipe is the newest kind of plastic pipe, but many codes restrict its use. **PEX (cross-linked polyethylene)** is stronger and can handle hot as well as cold water.

Copper

Copper pipe is long-lasting and resists corrosion, making it ideal for water supply pipes. It is more expensive than plastic but still reasonably priced.

Rigid copper pipe comes in three thicknesses. The thinnest, rated "M," is considered by most local codes to be strong enough for residential purposes. Thicker pipes, rated "L" or "K," are used outdoors. To join rigid copper pipe, you "sweat" the joint—heat it with a propane torch until molten solder flows freely into the joint *(pages 140–141)*.

Flexible copper tubing is used primarily to supply water to appliances. You'll find small-diameter tubing carrying water to an ice

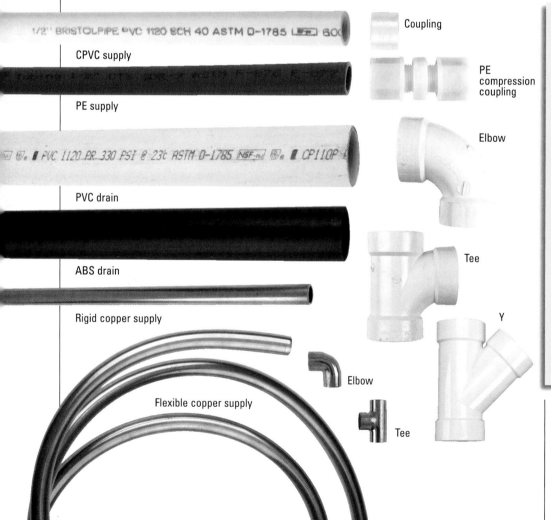

CPVC supply

PE supply

PVC drain

ABS drain

Rigid copper supply

Flexible copper supply

Coupling

PE compression coupling

Elbow

Tee

Y

Elbow

Tee

Measuring pipe

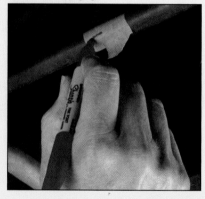

To determine the size of a pipe, wrap a piece of tape or a strip of paper—something that will not stretch—around it. Make a mark to indicate the outside circumference of the pipe. Consult the chart opposite to find the inside diameter of the pipe.

Standard diameters
Supply pipes usually have an inside diameter of ½ inch, ¾ inch, or 1 inch. Drainpipe generally ranges in size from 1½ inches to 4 inches.

maker. Larger tubing supplies a dishwasher. The tubing is easily bent to make fairly tight turns. If it gets kinked, however, there's no way to fix it; the piece must be replaced. It is joined to fittings and valves using compression fittings *(pages 144–145)*.

Steel

Many older homes have **galvanized steel pipes** for supply lines, and sometimes for branch drain lines as well. It has a dull gray color. Galvanized pipe is strong—a nail has a hard time piercing it—but its useful life is only 50 years or so. Joints develop rust and, more importantly, the galvanized surfaces attract minerals and cause them to build up in the pipe. The minerals clog the pipe, restricting the flow of water. Galvanized drainpipe rarely gets clogged enough to stop water from flowing, but the joints may rust and leak.

Black steel pipe is used for gas lines only. It should not be used for water supply lines because it rusts quickly. (An exception: In some areas black steel is allowed for lines that supply a boiler that heats the house.) Yellow-coated black pipe is used for underground gas lines.

To join steel pipe you must first wrap the threads with white teflon tape (yellow for gas pipes) or brush them with pipe dope (a thick sealant that may be gray, white, or yellow), then tighten it. The joints must be very tight so they cannot be loosened without a long pipe wrench. Inadequately tightened joints will leak eventually.

Cast iron

Used only for drain lines and vents, **cast-iron pipe** is heavy and strong. Many people prefer it over plastic drainpipe because cast iron deadens the sound of running water, while plastic seems to amplify it.

Cast iron can last for more than a hundred years. However, it's not unusual for one or two sections to rust through while the rest of the pipe remains in good shape.

Traditionally cast-iron pipe is joined by first stuffing oakum (a loose rope of greasy fiber) into the recess of one pipe, fitting in the end of the next pipe, then pouring molten lead into the recess. Newer "no-hub" fittings employ a neoprene sleeve whose edges are sealed tight against the pipe with clamps.

Fittings

Whenever pipe turns a corner or branches off, a fitting is required. **Elbows** (or "els") make 90- or 45-degree turns. **Tees** and **Ys** are used where pipes branch off. **Couplings** join two pipes together.

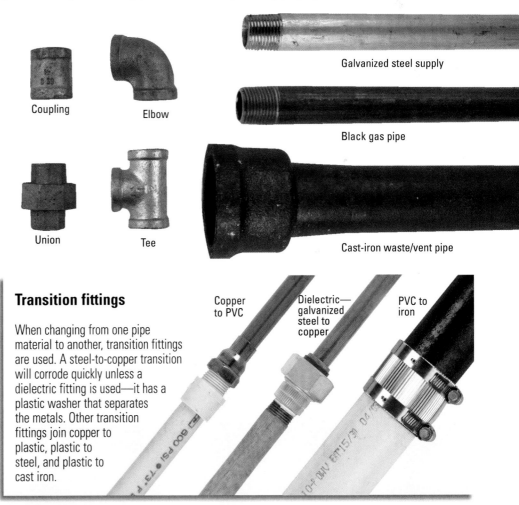

Coupling

Elbow

Union

Tee

Galvanized steel supply

Black gas pipe

Cast-iron waste/vent pipe

PIPE SIZES

Material	Outside Circumference	Inside Diameter
Copper	2"	1/2"
	2¾"	¾"
	3½"	1"
Steel (galvanized or black)	2"	⅜"
	2⅜"	½"
	3⅛"	¾"
	4"	1"
	4¾"	1¼"
	5½"	1½"
	7"	2"
Plastic (PVC, CPVC, or ABS)	2¾"	½"
	3½"	¾"
	4¼"	1"
	5⅛"	1¼"
	6"	1½"
	7½"	2"
	10½"	3"
	14"	4"
Cast Iron	7"	2"
	10⅛"	3"
	13⅜"	4"

Transition fittings

When changing from one pipe material to another, transition fittings are used. A steel-to-copper transition will corrode quickly unless a dielectric fitting is used—it has a plastic washer that separates the metals. Other transition fittings join copper to plastic, plastic to steel, and plastic to cast iron.

Copper to PVC

Dielectric— galvanized steel to copper

PVC to iron

WORKING WITH COPPER PIPE

A properly soldered (or "sweated") pipe joint is as strong as the pipe itself. A poorly soldered joint will leak. It might not leak until the next day, or in a year or two, but it will leak.

The key to making a strong joint is to work systematically. You must cut the pipe square and remove all the burrs. The inside of the fitting and the outside of the pipe must be sanded to a shine. Flux must be applied to both surfaces or the solder won't adhere. Then you must heat the pipe evenly so the solder will be fully drawn into the joint. Even wiping is essential—a droplet of solder can weaken a joint.

Keep it round

Pipe ends and fittings must be perfectly round. If it's dented even slightly you can't restore it to its original shape. Cut the pipe again or buy a new fitting.

Cutting with a tubing cutter ensures roundness. If space is tight and you must cut with a hacksaw, do it slowly and gently. If you must bend a pipe to move it away from a wall, work carefully.

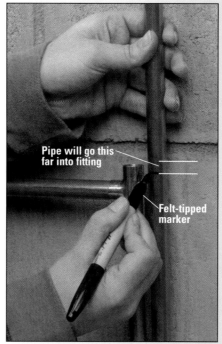

Pipe will go this far into fitting

Felt-tipped marker

1 Hold the pipe against the fitting to mark the cut or measure its length with a tape measure. Be sure to include the distance the pipe will travel into the fitting. Mark the cut with a felt-tipped marker.

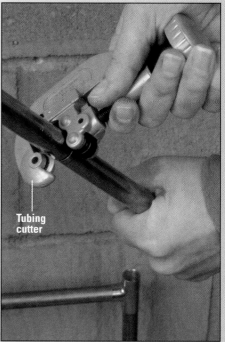

Tubing cutter

2 Use as large a tubing cutter as space permits. Line up the cutting wheel on your mark. Twist the knob until the wheel starts to bite into the pipe. Rotate the cutter once around the pipe, tighten a half turn or so, and repeat until the pipe is cut. Assemble all the parts of a joint in a dry run.

PRESTART CHECKLIST

☐ **TIME**
About 15 minutes to cut a pipe and join a fitting

☐ **TOOLS**
Tubing cutter or hacksaw, multiuse wire brush, propane torch (preferably with a trigger igniter), flux brush, groove-joint pliers, flame guard

☐ **SKILLS**
Cutting pipe, soldering

☐ **PREP**
Protect any flammable surfaces with a fiber shield or a cookie sheet

☐ **MATERIALS**
Copper pipe and fittings, flux, solder (95 percent tin for drinking water supply), damp rag

Sweating a brass valve

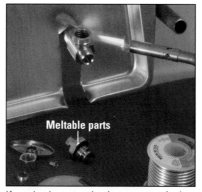

Meltable parts

If a valve has any plastic parts—as is the case with most stop valves—disassemble the valve and remove all the meltable parts. Heat the brass valve body as you would a fitting. It may take a bit longer to heat than a fitting. After sweating the joint, wait for the valve to cool before replacing the plastic parts.

STANLEY PRO TIP

Protect walls and framing from the torch flame

While caught up sweating a copper joint, you may not notice that the flame is charring a joist or wall surface. Protect flammable surfaces with a fiber shield *(page 54)* or use an old cookie sheet. **Keep a home fire extinguisher handy.**

If you can't pull a pipe more than a half inch away from a wall or framing member, don't worry about heating all around the fitting. As long as you heat two opposite sides, the solder will draw evenly around the joint.

Avoid MAPP gas, an alternative to propane fuel. It produces an extremely hot flame and is not recommended for most residential work.

After the job is complete, **check the area an hour later to be sure no flammable surfaces are smoldering.**

3 Using a wire brush equal to the size of the fitting, ream out every inside opening until it is shiny. Even oil from your hand may weaken the joint. If you accidentally touch a brushed opening, ream it again.

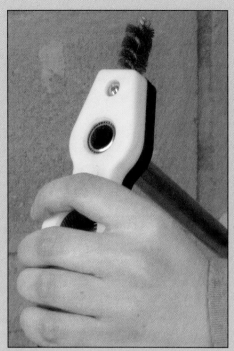

4 Insert the pipe in the multiuse brush and spin the brush a few times until the pipe's outside surface shines. As an alternative brighten the surface with emery cloth or a flexible sanding material. Rebrush or resand if you touch the shiny area.

5 Using a flux brush (available with the flux or sold separately at your home center), apply flux to all inside openings of the fitting and to the outside of the pipe. Take care to keep the flux brush away from any debris; clean it if any particles stick to it.

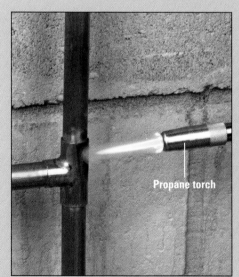

6 Light your propane torch and point the flame at the fitting—not at the pipe and not on the joint itself. The tip of the blue portion of the flame should just touch the fitting. Move the flame back and forth so you heat two opposite sides of the fitting.

7 When the fitting starts to smoke, remove the flame and touch the tip of the solder to the joint. If it does not melt, heat again. Once the fitting is hot enough, the solder will be drawn into the joint. Move the solder around so the entire joint fills with solder.

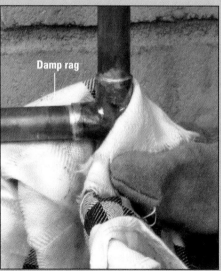

8 Immediately repeat the process for any other joints in the fitting. This will go quickly because the fitting is already hot. Once all the joints are soldered, quickly wipe all the joints with a damp rag. Avoid bumping the fitting for 10 to 15 minutes.

INSTALLING PLASTIC DRAINPIPE

Plastic PVC pipe and fittings are inexpensive and easy to install. However, a good PVC joint takes a little planning. Once glued, a joint is rock-hard and cannot be adjusted. If you make a mistake, you'll have to cut out the section and start all over again.

Making a dry run

To prevent a mistake, cut the pipes and assemble them without glue to make sure everything fits correctly and points in the right direction. When joining multiple sections, cut and assemble all of them to make sure that the last pipe in the run is facing the right direction. Mark and number the pipes with a felt pen so you can reassemble them correctly. Disassemble them, apply primer to each end and fitting, apply the cement, and join each pipe in order.

PRESTART CHECKLIST

☐ **TIME**
About one hour to cut and assemble five or six pipes and fittings

☐ **TOOLS**
PVC saw or backsaw, miter box or power mitersaw, deburring tool, felt-tipped marker

☐ **SKILLS**
Sawing, measuring, working methodically

☐ **PREP**
Make a drawing of the drain/vent assembly; clear a path for the pipes

☐ **MATERIALS**
Primer and cement for your type and size of pipe *(page 143)*

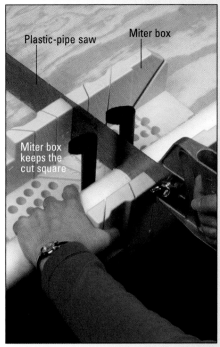

1 Mark the cut with a felt-tipped marker—include the length of the pipe inside the fitting. You can use a hacksaw or backsaw, but a plastic-pipe saw is made specifically for this work. A power mitersaw with a fine-cutting blade will produce the most accurate cuts.

2 Remove all the burrs from the cut pipe end. You can do this by scraping with a knife, but a deburring tool does a better job and is easier to use. Assemble cut pipes and fittings in a dry run (below).

DRY RUN FOR DRAINPIPE

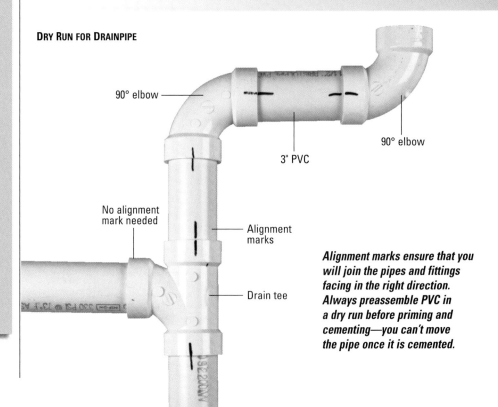

90° elbow

90° elbow

3" PVC

No alignment mark needed

Alignment marks

Drain tee

Alignment marks ensure that you will join the pipes and fittings facing in the right direction. Always preassemble PVC in a dry run before priming and cementing—you can't move the pipe once it is cemented.

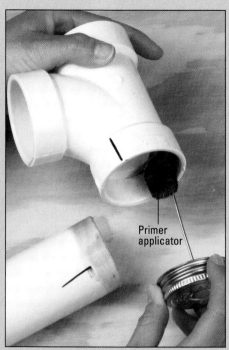

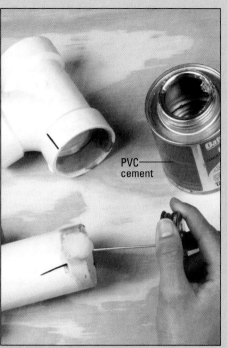

PVC cement

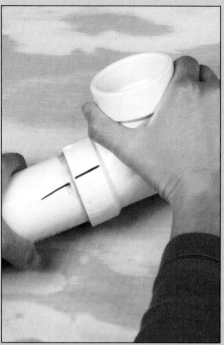

3 Apply primer to the inside of the fitting and to the pipe ends. The applicator should be wet enough to produce a fairly dark line, but not so wet that the primer drips. Place the pieces where they will not get dirty. If debris sticks to the primer, it will be difficult to join the pipes.

Primer applicator

4 Apply cement to the inside of one fitting opening and to the end of one pipe. Work quickly—the cement starts to set in a few seconds.

5 Push the pipe into the fitting and twist so the alignment marks line up. Hold for a few seconds, then wipe with a damp cloth. In a minute the joint will be strong enough so you can assemble the next piece. After 15 minutes you can run unpressurized wastewater through the pipes.

WHAT IF...
You are connecting ABS pipe?

Most codes require PVC for drain lines, but if you already have black ABS pipe in your home, local codes may allow you to add the same material to your system instead of replacing it with PVC.

Cut and assemble the black ABS pipe in the same way as you would PVC pipe. Use a plastic-pipe saw or backsaw with a miter box, remove the burrs, and put pipe and fittings together in a dry run. Use a sharpened, light-color crayon to make alignment marks.

Instead of primer apply ABS cleaner to pipe ends and fitting openings. Use special ABS cement to glue the pieces together. Push the pieces together and twist.

To connect PVC pipe to existing ABS pipe, use a no-hub fitting (page 148).

ABS cleaner applicator

Use the right products

Check the label on a can of primer or cement to make sure it's made for your type of pipe. Local inspectors may or may not approve of "all-purpose" cement. The larger the pipe diameter, the bigger the applicator should be so you won't have to dip it more than once. As a rule, an applicator should be about half the diameter of the pipe to be joined.

WORKING WITH PEX TUBING

The supply pipe of the future may already be here. Older PE (polyethylene) tubing has long been used for irrigation systems, but it must be buried for protection and can carry only cold water. Cross-linked polyethylene (PEX) is stronger and can handle hot as well as cold water. It is approved for use in many areas of the country—especially the South—and is gaining acceptance elsewhere.

PEX is an installer's dream. It's easy to cut, and it is flexible enough to make gentle bends around corners. Joints in the run are made with compression fittings that require no special tools or materials—just a pair of pliers or an adjustable wrench. Rigid fittings require a special crimping tool (see Steps 2 and 3). Where approved by local codes, PEX is an ideal material if you want to replace old galvanized pipes—you can snake it through walls.

Another advantage of PEX is that it offers a manifold fitting (Step 2), which allows you to pull one water supply line to a location and then add branch lines to various fixtures.

Flexible tubing cutter

1 Holes for PEX tubing need not be carefully laid out in a straight line. PEX can be bent around corners, but don't make the bend too sharp or kink the tubing. In most cases you can run the pipe through the holes and then cut it in place. Drill 1-inch holes for ½-inch tubing.

Manifold fitting

Crimping tool

Crimp ring

2 Make sure the tubing end is cut square and that the cut is free of burrs. To make a crimped connection, slide the crimp ring onto the tube, then slip the tube onto the fitting.

PRESTART CHECKLIST

☐ **TIME**
About an hour to run and install about 50 feet of pipe with five fittings

☐ **TOOLS**
Plastic tubing cutter or plastic-pipe cutter, crimping tool, groove-joint pliers, adjustable wrench, reaming tool, drill

☐ **SKILLS**
Understanding of supply pipes

☐ **PREP**
Bore holes for running pipe through joists or studs

☐ **MATERIALS**
PEX tubing, compression fittings, crimp rings

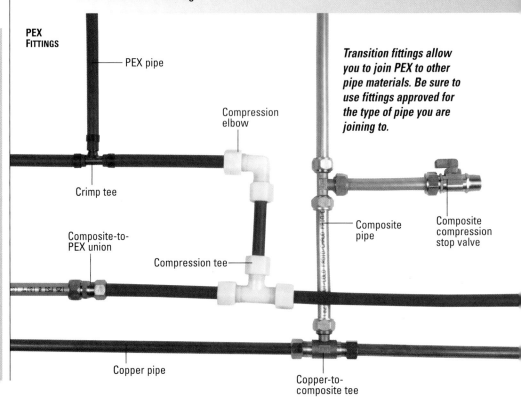

PEX FITTINGS

PEX pipe

Crimp tee

Composite-to-PEX union

Copper pipe

Compression elbow

Compression tee

Copper-to-composite tee

Transition fittings allow you to join PEX to other pipe materials. Be sure to use fittings approved for the type of pipe you are joining to.

Composite pipe

Composite compression stop valve

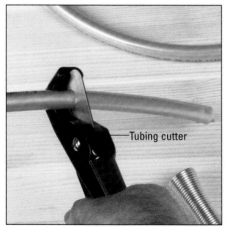

3 Grasp the ring with the crimping tool and squeeze until you feel the ring compress. Tug on the connection to make sure it is rock-solid.

4 To install a stubout, temporarily screw the drop-ear elbows, mark the tubing for cutting, and cut with a tubing cutter.

5 Remove the elbow, attach it to the tubing using the crimping tool, and reattach the elbow. To prevent rattling when the water is turned on and off, clamp the pipe firmly every couple of feet. Where pipe runs through a hole, gently tap in a wooden shim.

Installing composite pipe

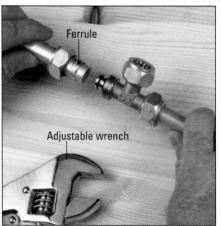

In addition to straight polyethylene pipe, composite pipe, with an aluminum core sheathed in plastic, is approved in some areas for water supply and for gas lines. Cut it with a tubing cutter.

Use a reaming tool to true the tubing into round and to clean out the inside of the cut end. Insert the tool and give it a couple of twists. Make sure no scrapings are left inside the tube.

Slip a nut and a ferrule onto the tube end, then slip the tube onto the fitting. Finger-tighten, taking care not to cross-thread. Then tighten the nut with one full turn (no more), using an adjustable wrench or pliers.

RUNNING PIPES THROUGH WALLS AND FLOORS

Once you've drawn a plan for your new plumbing and have had it approved, develop a strategy for running the pipes. This should be fairly easy in a bathroom remodel where all the framing is exposed. But be prepared for a few surprises and slight changes in your plans once you've removed the wallcovering and flooring.

Removing wall and floor surfaces prior to plumbing takes about half a day of hard work. But replacing finished surfaces after plumbing (especially patching walls) usually takes several days. A large wall patch—even replacing an entire wall—takes little more time than a small patch, so open up plenty of working space.

If you need to run a new stack because running a revent to an existing stack is impossible, you may have to remove and replace the existing wall entirely. A toilet must have a 3-inch drain, and 3-inch pipe can be installed only in a 2×6 wall. (Two-inch pipe can be run through a 2×4 wall.)

PRESTART CHECKLIST

☐ **TIME**
For a modest bathroom, two or three days to cut into walls and flooring and run pipes through framing

☐ **TOOLS**
Demolition tools, drill with various bits and hole saws, reciprocating saw, level, tools for installing pipe

☐ **SKILLS**
Carpentry, knowledge of your home's structure, installing pipe

☐ **PREP**
Have your plan approved by the local building department

☐ **MATERIALS**
Pipes, fittings, clamps, and assembly materials listed on your plan

1 Remove the wall surface up to the ceiling. You'll probably need a new sheet of drywall when you resurface the wall, but save the cutout for patching other places.

2 Cut a hole with some wiggle room for the new pipe. For a 3-inch pipe, use a drill and reciprocating saw to cut a hole about 4¼ inches by 10 inches through both the bottom plate of the room you are working in and the top plate of the room below. Cut away a 10-inch by 2-foot section of flooring.

Stabilizing and protecting pipes

Whenever possible run pipes through holes in the center of framing members. To keep pipes from rattling, line the holes with felt or use wood shims. Slip a shim under the pipe and tap in until it is firmly in place, but not tight, to allow for expansion. If notches are needed, make them as small as possible; they weaken the framing member. Protect pipes from nails by attaching metal plates.

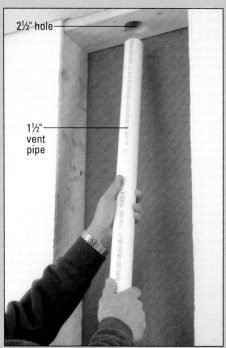

3 Assemble the approved fittings on the top of the drainpipe. Take special care that they face the right direction. The drainpipe should be longer than needed—you can cut it to size from below later. Slip the pipe down through the hole.

4 You may need to cut a hole in the wall of the room above or below to guide the vent pipe up or the drainpipe down. In the attic you may be able to run the vent over to tie into an existing vent. If not, drill a hole in the attic ceiling and have a roofer install a roof jack for the vent pipe.

Right-angle drill

Hole-cutting saw

5 Anchor the drainpipe with straps. Cut a smaller opening in the ceiling for the vent pipe. For a 1½-inch vent pipe, a 2½-inch hole is sufficient. Guide the vent pipe up through the hole and into the attic or room above and slip its lower end into the fitting at the floor.

2½" hole

1½" vent pipe

Running pipe through a floor

This hole is ⅜ inch lower than hole in previous joist

Running drainpipe through joists calls for meticulous work. The holes must follow a straight line across the floor and must ascend or descend so the pipe will be sloped ¼ inch per foot. (If joists are 16 inches on center and pipes run across them at a right angle, holes should differ in height by about ⅜ inch.)

Running pipe through walls

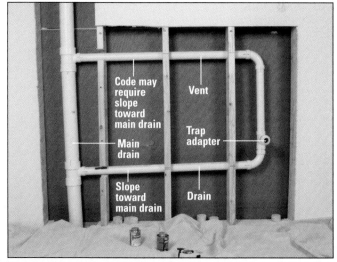

Code may require slope toward main drain

Vent

Main drain

Trap adapter

Slope toward main drain

Drain

Vent pipes may run level, though some codes may call for a slight slope toward the main drain. All drain lines must be sloped. For a precise slope, strike a level line on the studs and measure down ¼ inch per running foot. Codes may call for fireproof caulking in walls.

CONNECTING NEW TO OLD

Whether installing a new drain, vent, or supply line, the most common way to tie into an existing line is to cut the old line and install a tee fitting. If you happen to find a pipe that is capped at its end, simply install an elbow or coupling there instead.

Shut off water to existing supply pipes and drain the lines. Flush all toilets and caution others not to use drains. After opening a drain line, make sure no one uses a sink or faucet that drains into it. Seal any open drain lines with a large rag to protect against fumes.

If joining different materials, make sure the fitting conforms to local code. Dielectric unions are made for this purpose.

Typically it doesn't matter exactly where you join to an existing pipe, but the new service must be precisely located. So it's usually easier to start pipe runs at the new location and travel toward the existing pipes rather than vice versa.

PRESTART CHECKLIST

☐ **TIME**
Once pipes are run, usually less than two hours to connect new to old

☐ **TOOLS**
Cutting and fitting tools for any type of pipe you will be working with, carpentry tools, reciprocating saw, hex-head driver

☐ **SKILLS**
Cutting and joining the type of pipe you will be using in the project

☐ **PREP**
Run new pipes from the new service location to the existing pipe; install the last pipe a little longer than it needs to be so you can cut it to length when you make the connection to the old pipe

☐ **MATERIALS**
Joining materials for the pipe you will be working on, transition fittings

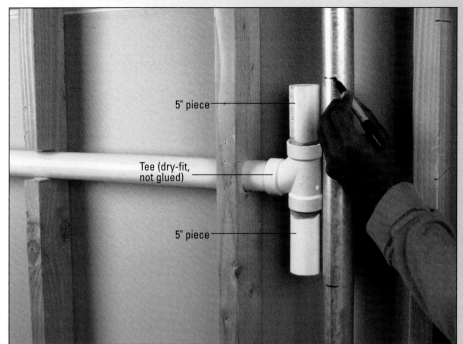

5" piece

Tee (dry-fit, not glued)

5" piece

1 To join a new plastic drainpipe to an old steel pipe, run new pipe into the room. Prime and glue two 5-inch pieces of pipe to a tee fitting. Temporarily run pipe—longer than it needs to be—so it comes near the old pipe. (When running pipe across a stud wall, you may need to notch-cut some of the holes using a reciprocating saw.) Dry-fit the tee assembly onto the new pipe and hold it next to the existing pipe. Mark the existing pipe for cutting. You may need to cut out a section slightly longer than the tee assembly to accommodate the neoprene sleeves on the no-hub couplings.

WHAT IF...
You need to connect new PVC to old ABS?

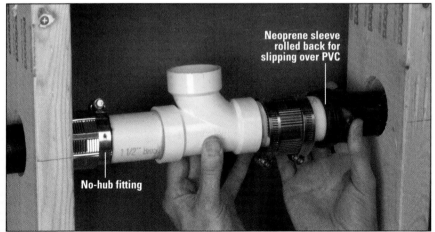

Neoprene sleeve rolled back for slipping over PVC

No-hub fitting

Even though there are specialty primers and cements intended for joining PVC pipe to an old ABS line, local codes may not permit connecting in this manner. Instead use a no-hub fitting, which has a neoprene sleeve and metal clamps, to hold it firm. Some municipalities may require that the fitting be accessible for future repairs.

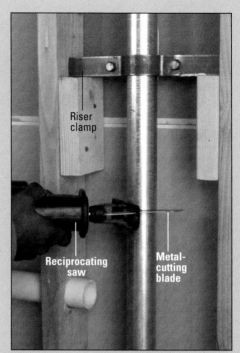

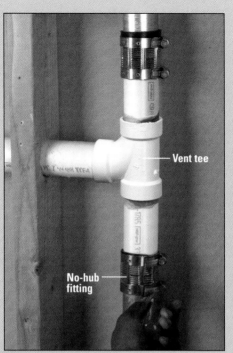

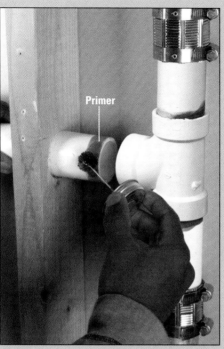

2 Support the pipe above and below with riser clamps so it cannot drop or sway as you work, and so the PVC fitting will not have to bear the weight of the drain. You will probably need to install a new stud or two as well as blocking for the upper clamp.

3 Slide a no-hub fitting onto each end of the old pipe, slide back the banded coupling, and fold up the neoprene sleeves. Position the tee assembly. Fold the neoprene sleeves over the assembly and slide the metal bands over the sleeves. Tighten the nuts with a hex-head driver.

4 Cut the new pipe to exact length and test that it fits into the tee fitting; you may need to loosen the nuts and rotate the fitting slightly. Prime and glue the pipe to the fitting *(pages 142–143)*.

Tapping into supply lines

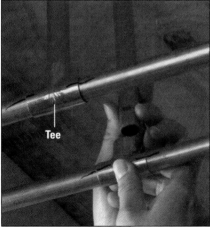

To tap into existing copper lines, **shut off the water.** With a tubing cutter, cut an opening in each pipe that is about an inch shorter than a tee fitting. Dry-fit the tees. If the pipes are rigidly installed, remove a clamp or two so you can pull the pieces apart slightly.

Dry-fit the pipes that will be inserted into the tees and draw alignment marks. Disassemble, wire-brush the fittings and pipe ends, brush on flux, and sweat the joints *(pages 140–141)*.

Joining copper to existing galvanized pipe

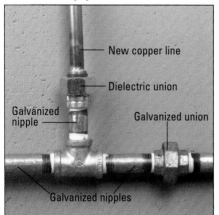

To tie a new copper line into an old galvanized line, install a new galvanized tee fitting by cutting the line and bridging it with unions and nipples. Screw a galvanized nipple into the tee and connect the copper line to the nipple using a dielectric union.

INSTALLING A STOP VALVE

Every faucet and toilet in a home should have its own stop valve so you can easily make repairs. Installing one is usually not difficult, though you may find yourself working in cramped quarters.

Take care to buy the correct valve. Its inlet must accommodate the size of pipe coming from the wall (usually ½ inch but sometimes ¾ or ⅜ inch). Its threaded spout must match the size of the supply tube—either ½ or ⅜ inch. You can install either a compression or sweatable valve.

If the pipes are plastic, make cuts with a close-work hacksaw and cement the valve in place.

To shut off the water where there is no existing stop valve, find the main shutoff valve to the house and close it. Some water will remain in the pipes and tubes after water has stopped flowing out the faucet, so place a bucket and towel underneath.

PRESTART CHECKLIST

☐ **TIME**
One or two hours to install a new stop valve in copper pipe

☐ **TOOLS**
Close-work hacksaw, two adjustable wrenches, propane torch

☐ **SKILLS**
Cutting and joining copper pipe

☐ **PREP**
Shut off the water; drain the line; place a bucket or towel below the pipe to be cut to catch debris

☐ **MATERIALS**
New compression or sweatable stop valve, flux, solder, possibly a new supply tube, pipe-thread tape

Installing a valve on copper pipe

1 **Shut off the water** and drain the line by turning on a faucet at a lower location. Cut the copper pipe with a tubing cutter or close-work hacksaw. Shine the end of the pipe with an emery cloth. Slide a nut and ferrule onto the pipe.

2 Slide the stop valve all the way onto the pipe. Hold the valve with one adjustable wrench while you tighten the nut with the other.

WHAT IF...
You use a plastic supply tube?

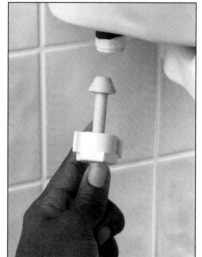

A plastic supply tube seals using a ball-shaped end held firmly by a nylon nut. Some have a rubber ferrule as well.

Replacing a solid supply tube

1 Bend a chrome-plated copper or plain copper supply tube carefully by hand or use a tubing bender.

Installing a valve on steel pipe

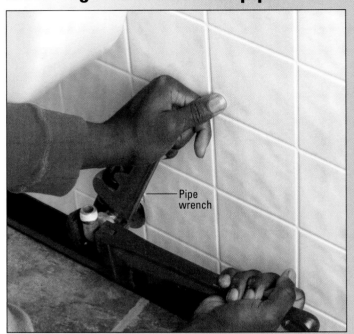

1 **Shut off the water** and drain the line by turning on a faucet at a lower location. Hold the steel pipe still with one pipe wrench while you remove the elbow with another wrench. If you can't budge the elbow, slip a length of 1¼-inch steel pipe on the wrench handle for more leverage.

2 Clean the pipe threads and wrap pipe-thread tape clockwise around the threads several times. Screw the stop valve onto the pipe and tighten with an adjustable wrench. (Don't crank hard with a pipe wrench or the valve might crack.)

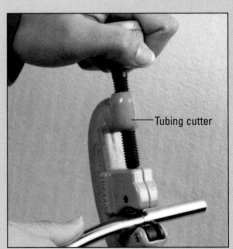

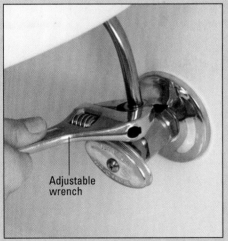

2 Insert one end of the tube into the faucet inlet, hold the other end near the stop valve, and mark it for a cut. Make the cut with a tubing cutter (*pages 140–141*).

3 At the upper end, slip on the mounting nut and a ferrule. Poke the tube into the faucet inlet, slide the ferrule up to the inlet, and tighten the nut. Slip a nut and ferrule onto the lower end of the tube and attach to the stop valve in the same way.

4 Use an adjustable wrench to tighten the nut that connects the supply tube to the valve. If the valve moves, brace it with another wrench.

WIRING

Although many homeowners fear working with electricity, wiring a new bathroom is an amateur-friendly trade. A handy person carefully following instructions can produce safe and reliable electrical installations. Attention to detail is the key.

Approach household electricity with caution and respect. Professional electricians take steps to ensure themselves double and even triple protection against shocks. You need to be just as careful while doing the work.

Insulate yourself

The effect of a shock varies according to how much power is present, your physical constitution, and how well insulated you are. Of these three variables, you have control over the latter. Wear rubber-soled shoes. Remove jewelry. Keep yourself dry. If the floor of your work area is damp or wet, put down some dry boards and stand on them. Use rubber-gripped tools.

If you are wearing dry clothes and rubber-soled shoes, receiving a 120-volt shock will grab your attention, but it probably will not harm you. However, if you have a heart condition or are particularly sensitive to shock, the effects could be more serious. If you haven't taken proper precautions, chances are greater that a shock will cause injury.

If you are working with 240-volt current, the danger is much greater. Maintain a healthy respect for electrical power. Even if you have survived one shock, the next one could be more serious.

Shut off the power

Before starting any electrical project, always shut off power to the circuit. Then test to make sure there is no power present in the electrical box or wires.

You may be tempted to skip this step and save a trip to the service panel. Or you may think you can change a receptacle or light without touching any wires. Don't risk it. It takes only a few minutes to provide yourself with the necessary protection against shock.

Put your plans on paper

Before you tackle the wiring for your project, make rough drawings showing the lighting and electrical service you want to achieve. Start planning cable runs that can be routed with minimal damage to the walls.

Next figure out whether your existing service can support new electrical lines. You may be able to connect to existing circuits. Or you may need to add a circuit or two to your existing service panel, or install a subpanel or a new service panel.

Why codes count

The importance of building codes can't be overemphasized. First, codes protect you and everyone in your home from shock and fire. Second, they provide common ground for everyone who works on electrical systems. Someone who works on your home's wiring after you will be able to understand the system.

CHAPTER PREVIEW

Cable and wire
page 154

Electrical boxes
page 155

Fasteners and clamps
page 156

Wire nuts
page 157

Receptacles and switches
page 158

Wiring a bathroom
page 159

Stripping and clamping cable
page 160

Metal and PVC conduit
page 162

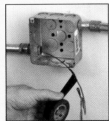

Pulling wires through conduit
page 165

Running cable in framing
page 166

Running cable through finished rooms
page 168

Installing receptacles and switches
page 172

CABLE AND WIRE

Most house wires—the wires that run from the service panel through walls to receptacle and switch boxes—are **solid-core**, meaning they are made of a single, solid strand. Light fixtures and some switches come with **leads**—wires made of many strands of thin wire, which are more flexible. The thicker a wire, the lower its number; for instance, #12 wire is thicker than #14.

Cable refers to two or more wires encased in a protective sheathing. Cable packaging indicates the gauge and number of wires. For example "12/2" means two (black and white) 12-gauge wires, plus a ground wire.

Nonmetallic (NM) cable, sometimes called Romex, has two or three insulated wires, plus a bare ground wire, wrapped in plastic sheathing. Many local codes permit NM cable inside walls or ceilings, and some codes allow it to be exposed in basements and garages. **Underground feed (UF) cable** has wires wrapped in solid plastic for watertight protection. Use it for outdoor projects.

Armored cable encases insulated wires in metal sheathing for added protection. **Metal-clad (MC)** has a green-insulated ground wire. **BX (also called AC)** has no ground wire, only a thin aluminum wire unsuitable as a ground; the metal sheathing provides the path for grounding. Some local codes require armored cable or conduit (below) wherever wiring is exposed.

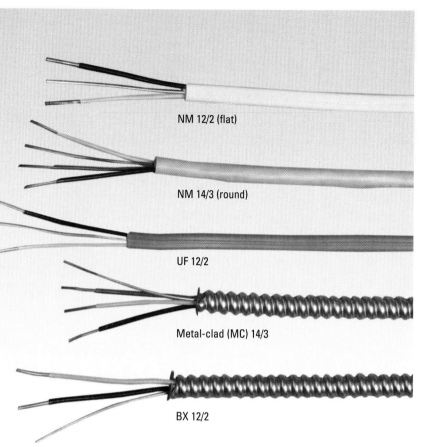

NM 12/2 (flat)

NM 14/3 (round)

UF 12/2

Metal-clad (MC) 14/3

BX 12/2

Conduit types

EMT rigid metal conduit

PVC ½" conduit

Greenfield

EMT ½"

Conduit—pipe that wires run through—offers the best protection against damage to wires. It also makes it easy to change or install new wires in the future: Pull the wires through the conduit rather than cutting into walls to run new cable.

Metal conduit once was used as a path for grounding; recent codes require a green-insulated ground wire. **PVC (plastic) conduit** is cheaper but not quite as strong. Metal **Greenfield** and plastic **EMT tubing** are flexible types of conduit. They are expensive but useful when working in tight spots.

Wire colors and sizes

The thicker a wire, the more amperage (amps) it can carry without overheating. A #14 wire carries up to 15 amps; a #12 wire up to 20 amps; and a #10 wire up to 30 amps. Never overload a wire; for instance, never place a #14 wire on a 20-amp circuit.

Wires coated with insulation that is black, red, or another color are hot wires, carrying power from the service panel to the receptacle or switch box. (White wires are neutral, meaning they carry power back to the service panel.) Green or bare wires are ground wires. **Be aware, however, that electrical work might not have been done correctly, so the wires in your house could be the wrong color.**

HOT WIRES

#14 red

#12 blue

#10 brown

#12 black

GROUND WIRES

#12 green

#12 copper

ELECTRICAL BOXES

Wiring installations in a remodeling project usually begin by adding a box. All connections—whether splices or connections to terminals—must be made inside a code-approved box. (Some fixtures, such as fluorescent and recessed lights, have self-contained electrical boxes approved by most building departments.)

Plastic or metal?

Check with your building department to see whether plastic boxes are acceptable. Some municipalities require metal boxes, which are more expensive but usually no more trouble to install.

In older systems that use conduit or armored-cable sheathing as a grounding path, the boxes must be metal because they are part of the grounding system. Homes with NM or MC cable use green-insulated or bare copper wires for grounding and don't require metal boxes. However, some local codes call for metal boxes, which provide a more secure connection for the ground wire.

Remodel and new-work boxes

A remodel box has fittings that secure it to a finished wall. Plastic boxes have "wings." Metal boxes feature expandable clips or bendable ears that hold them in the wall. Remodel boxes all have internal clamps that clasp the cable to the box.

New-work boxes install quickly in framing that has not been covered with drywall or plaster. To install most models, hold the box in place (the box should extend beyond the framing by the thickness of the wall material) and drive in two nails.

Octagonal box with
nailing bracket

Single-gang box

Two-gang box with stud catcher

Remodel box with wings

Ceiling remodel box

Gangable
switch box

Remodel
ceiling fan box
with brace

STANLEY PRO TIP: **Buy boxes that are big enough**

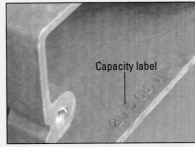

Capacity label

To make sure a box will not be overcrowded, always buy as big a box as will fit the space available. The cubic-inch capacity of electrical boxes should be listed by the store selling them.

To calculate whether a box will be crowded, use these figures: A #14 wire takes up 2 cubic inches; a #12 wire takes up 2¼ cubic inches. Count the fixture or device as one wire. For instance this box contains eight #12 "wires"—two blacks, two whites, three grounds, and one receptacle—for a total of 18 cubic inches.

FASTENERS AND CLAMPS

In addition to cable and boxes, electrical jobs call for a few other supplies: tape, staples—or straps to secure cable to framing members—and clamps that hold cable to boxes.

Light fixtures usually come with all the necessary hardware for fastening to a ceiling box. If you have old boxes, you may need to buy extra hardware.

Cable fasteners

Codes require that all exposed cable be tightly stapled to the wall, ceiling, or a framing member. Also use staples when running cable in unfinished framing. For NM cable buy plastic-insulated staples that are the right size for the cable.

To anchor metal conduit, hammer in drive straps every few feet. For PVC conduit or armored cable, use one- or two-hole straps; make sure they fit snugly around the cable or conduit.

Avoid the black drywall (or all-purpose) screws because they break easily. Bugle-head woodscrews cost more but are more reliable and easier to drive.

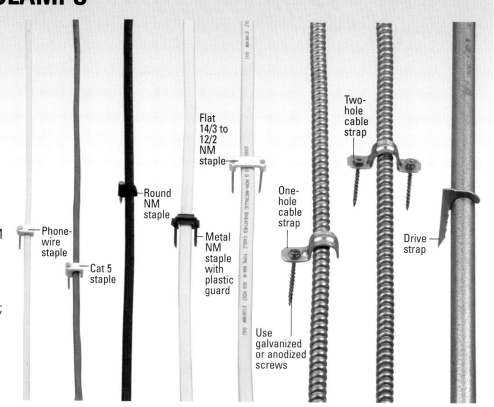

Phone-wire staple

Cat 5 staple

Round NM staple

Metal NM staple with plastic guard

Flat 14/3 to 12/2 NM staple

One-hole cable strap

Use galvanized or anodized screws

Two-hole cable strap

Drive strap

Clamp types

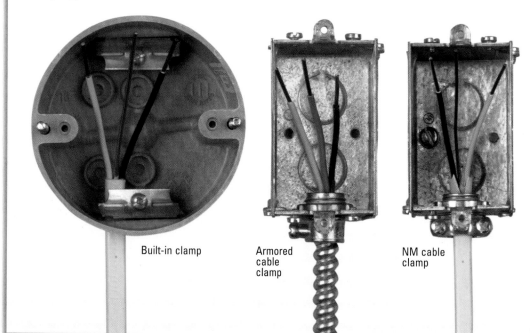

Built-in clamp

Armored cable clamp

NM cable clamp

New-work plastic boxes have holes with plastic flaps that lightly grab NM cable. With that type of box, you must staple the cable to a framing member near the box. Use these only in unfinished framing. When installing a remodel box or a box that will be exposed, the cable or conduit must be firmly clamped directly to the box.

A cable clamp comes in two parts: the clamp and the locknut. An NM clamp holds the cable using a strap with two screws; an armored-cable clamp holds the cable using a single setscrew.

For instructions on how to clamp cable to a box, see *pages 160–161*.

WIRE NUTS

In old installations wire splices often were covered with thick electrician's tape. That is not only a slow way to cover a splice, but it is also a code violation. Cover every splice with an approved wire nut.

Assemble a collection of various size nuts so you will be ready for any splice. Wire nuts are color-coded according to size. The colors and sizes may vary according to manufacturer. Read the containers to make sure the nuts you buy will fit over your splices. The most common arrangement is like this:

■ The smallest wire nuts—which usually come with a light fixture—are often white, ivory, or blue. If these have plastic rather than metal threads inside, throw them away and get orange connectors with metal threads for a secure connection.
■ Orange nuts are the next size up and can handle splices of up to two #14 wires.
■ Midsize yellow wire nuts are the most common. Use them for splices as small as two #14s or as large as three #12s.
■ Red connectors are usually the largest wire nuts and can handle a splice of up to four #12s.
■ Green wire nuts are used for ground wires. They have a hole in the top, which allows one ground wire to poke through and run directly to a device or box.
■ Gray "twister" wire nuts are designed to be all-purpose—they can handle the smallest to the largest splices. However, they are bulky and expensive.
■ "B-cap" wire nuts are slim, which makes them useful if a box is crowded with wires.

Two #16 stranded wires

Two #14 solid wires

Two #14 solid ground wires

Three #12 wires

Four #12 wires

All-purpose "twister" wire nuts

Space-saving "B-cap" wire nuts

STANLEY PRO TIP: **Use high-quality tape**

Professional-quality electrician's tape costs more than bargain-bin tape, but it sticks better and is easier to work with.

You should cut pieces of tape rather than ripping them off the roll; ripped pieces have rippled ends that do not stick. Cutting with a utility knife is often awkward and time-consuming, so buy tape in a dispenser—just pull out and down to make a clean cut.

Grounding pigtail

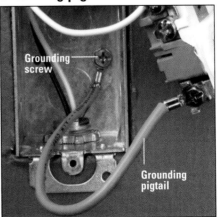

Grounding screw

Grounding pigtail

If codes require you to attach grounds to metal boxes, save time and work by buying grounding pigtails. If your boxes do not already have them, buy green-tinted grounding screws that fit into threaded holes in the boxes.

RECEPTACLES AND SWITCHES

The 120-volt duplex receptacle (a receptacle with two outlets) is the workhorse of any residential electrical system. Because household wiring has remained standardized almost from the time it was first introduced, the duplex receptacle accepts even the oldest tools and appliances.

Receptacles are easy to replace, so install new ones if your old receptacles are damaged, paint-encrusted, or unsightly. (See *pages 172–173* for more on how to install them.) However, do not replace an older, ungrounded receptacle with a three-hole receptacle unless you can be sure it will be grounded. (See *page 55* for how to test grounding.)

If the wires connecting to a receptacle are 12 gauge or thicker, and it is protected by a 20-amp circuit breaker or fuse, you can safely install a 20-amp receptacle. Otherwise install a standard 15-amp receptacle. Amp ratings are printed or stamped on the side of the receptacle.

Some people prefer to mount the receptacle in the box with the ground hole on top; others prefer it on the bottom. In terms of safety, it does not matter. For appearance, be consistent.

Bargain-bin receptacles are fine for most purposes. But if a receptacle will receive a lot of use—as it is likely to in your new bathroom—purchase a "spec-rated" or "commercial" receptacle, which is stronger and more resistant to damage.

Essential switches
The most common household switch, a single-pole, has two terminals and simply turns power on or off.

A three-way switch has three terminals; a four-way has four. These are used to control a light from two or three locations, such as at both doors of a multiple-entry bathroom.

A dimmer switch (or rheostat) controls a light's intensity. Usually you can replace any single-pole switch with a dimmer. However, buy a special dimmer switch to control either a fan or a fluorescent light—a standard dimmer will overheat and can burn out a fan motor or a fluorescent tube.

Special switches
In addition to the familiar toggle and rotary switches, specialty switches can do everything from turning on when you walk into a room to varying the speed of an exhaust fan. Decorative switches include styles that rock back and forth or slide up and down rather than toggling.

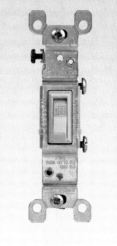

A **GFCI** (ground fault circuit interrupter) receptacle provides extra protection against shocks and is required by code in damp areas such as bathrooms.

A **single-pole** switch has two terminals and a toggle labeled ON and OFF. Always connect two hot wires to it, not two neutrals.

A **three-way** switch has three terminals; its toggle is not marked for on or off.

A **rotary dimmer** switch is the most common type. Some styles look like toggle switches.

A **sliding dimmer** with an on/off toggle "remembers" how bright you left the light the last time it was on.

WIRING A BATHROOM

Even a relatively large bathroom tends to be damp. Light fixtures must be watertight, ventilation must be effective, and all receptacles should be ground fault circuit interrupters (GFCI).

Circuits
The lights and fan must be on a different circuit from the receptacle(s). Some codes require that bathrooms have their own circuits; others permit bathrooms to share circuits with receptacles or lights in other rooms. In some localities all bathroom wiring—including the lights—must be GFCI-protected.

The vent fan
To satisfy codes and for your comfort, a bathroom needs a fan that effectively pulls moist air out and sends it outside. *Pages 252–255* show how to install one. Some local codes require that the fan always comes on when the light is on; others allow you to put the fan on its own switch.

Usually there is a vent/light fixture in the middle of the ceiling, which may be controlled by one or two switches. Some fixtures also include a heating unit or a night-light. A bathroom heater—whether it is a separate unit or part of a fan/light—may use so much electricity that it requires its own circuit.

Lights
In addition to a light or fan/light in the middle of the ceiling, plan to put lights over the sink, where they can shine on a person standing at the mirror. A strip of lights above the mirror is a common arrangement, but most people find that two lights, one on each side of the mirror, illuminate a face more clearly. The switch may be by the entry door or near the sink.

A tub or shower does not need to be brightly lit, but people shouldn't have to shower in the dark. Install a recessed canister light with a waterproof lens made for shower areas.

Receptacles
Install at least one 20-amp GFCI receptacle within a foot or so of the sink. Position the receptacle so a cord does not have to drape over the sink when someone is using a hair dryer.

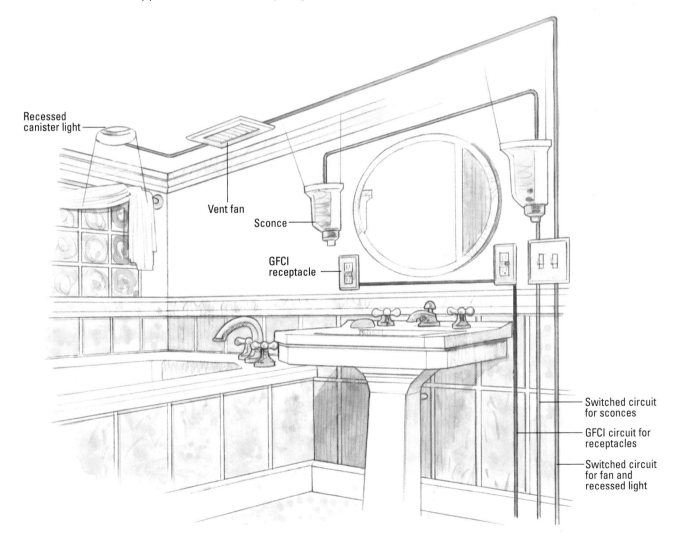

Recessed canister light

Vent fan

Sconce

GFCI receptacle

Switched circuit for sconces

GFCI circuit for receptacles

Switched circuit for fan and recessed light

STRIPPING AND CLAMPING CABLE

Nonmetallic (NM) cable is easy to work with and inexpensive, so it's not surprising that it is the most common type of cable used in household wiring.

NM cable is usually sold in 25-, 50-, or 100-foot lengths or more. When in doubt buy the larger package—it doesn't cost much more and it may come in handy later.

NM's plastic sheathing does not offer much protection to the wires, so keep it out of harm's way. Codes call for running NM through the center of studs so that drywall nails cannot damage it. If the cable is less than 1¼ inches from the edge of a framing member, install a protective nailing plate *(page 167)*. Some codes require metal plates even if the cable is in the center of a stud.

Take care not to damage the wire insulation when working with NM cable. Slit the sheathing right down the middle with a sharp utility knife. To avoid slicing the wire insulation, don't cut too deep. Or use a sheathing stripper.

When cutting cable leave yourself an extra foot or two. If you make a mistake while stripping, you can recut the cable and try again.

Armored cable

Some municipalities require armored cable or conduit rather than NM. The coiled metal sheathing protects the wires from nails (unless a nail hits it dead center).

Wherever cable will be exposed—for example where you've run a new bathroom circuit through a basement—many local codes call for armored cable or conduit.

You may want to run armored cable behind moldings where it comes near nails. Armored cable costs more than NM, takes longer to strip and clamp, and can't make tight turns. However, with practice you can install armored cable nearly as quickly as NM.

BX cable has no ground wire *(page 154)*, is common in older homes, and is still available in some areas. Local code may limit use of BX to no more than 6 feet; then ground wire must be used. MC cable has a green-insulated ground wire used like the bare ground wire in NM cable.

Stripping NM cable

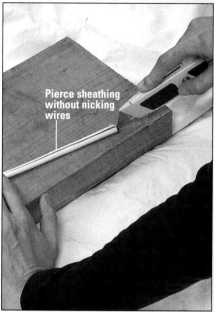

Pierce sheathing without nicking wires

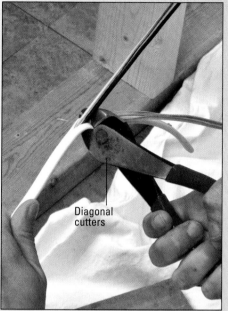

Diagonal cutters

1 Lay the cable on a flat work surface, such as a small sheet of plywood. Starting 8–10 inches from the end, insert the tip of a utility knife blade into the center of the cable, pushing just hard enough to cut through the sheathing. Slice the sheathing, exerting even pressure.

2 Pull back the plastic sheathing, as well as the paper that wraps the wires, exposing 6–8 inches of wire. Use a pair of diagonal cutters to snip back the sheathing and paper. If you use a utility knife, cut away from the wires to avoid cutting or nicking the insulation.

Grounding NM cable

If the box is metal, code requires it to be grounded. The surest method is to connect both the device and the box to the ground wire using pigtails.

If the box is plastic, simply connect the ground wire to the device's grounding terminal.

Clamping NM cable

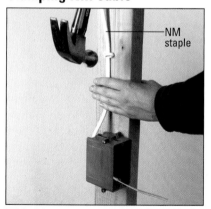

NM staple

With this type of box, push the wires through the hole and the tab will grab the cable. About ½ inch of sheathing should show inside the box. Staple NM to framing so it's out of reach of nails—within 8 inches of the box and every 2–4 feet thereafter.

Stripping armored cable

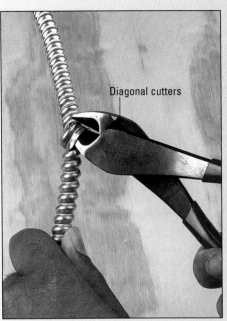

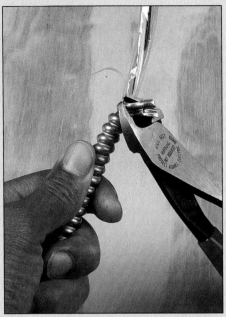

1 Bend the cable about 10 inches from its end and squeeze with your hand until the coils of the armor come apart. If you can't do this by hand, use a pair of pliers. Firmly grip the cable on each side of the cut and twist until the split-armor coil pops out, away from the wires.

2 Using diagonal cutters, cut the exposed coil of sheathing. You may have to grab the coil with the cutters and work it back and forth to open and make the cut.

3 If you are cutting a piece to length, slide back the sheathing and cut through the wires. Otherwise slide the waste piece off and throw it away. Cut off any sharp points of sheathing. Remove the paper wrapping and any thin plastic strips. If the cable is BX, cut the thin metal bonding strip to 2 inches.

Grounding MC cable

MC cable has a ground wire. Attach it the same way you would the ground wire in NM cable *(page 160)* except strip the green insulation first.

STANLEY PRO TIP: **Clamp armored cable**

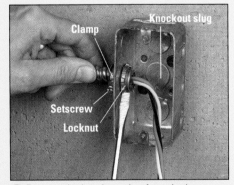

1 If the cable did not come with a bag of little bushings, purchase some. Slip a bushing over the wires and slide it down into the sheathing so it protects wires from the cut end of the armor. Remove the locknut from the armored-cable clamp and slide the clamp over the wires and down onto the bushing. Then tighten the setscrew.

2 Remove the knockout slug from the box. Guide the wires and the clamp through the hole. Slip the locknut over the wires and screw it onto the clamp. Tighten the nut by levering it with a screwdriver or tapping it with a screwdriver and hammer.

METAL CONDUIT

Conduit offers superior protection and safety for wires. Even if local codes permit NM for basement and crawlspace runs, consider installing conduit to protect the wiring.

Choosing conduit

Metal conduit comes in several thicknesses. For most interior home installations, EMT (also called "thinwall") is strong enough. In some areas PVC conduit conforms to local codes for indoor use.

Metal conduit may serve as the path for grounding, or local codes may require you to run a green-insulated ground wire. If you use PVC conduit, you definitely need a ground wire, either a green-insulated or bare copper wire. **For metal conduit without a ground wire, take extra care that all the connections are firm; one loose joint could break the grounding path.**

Conduit fittings

A conduit bender, used by professional electricians, is a fairly expensive tool that takes time to master. Unless you will be running lots of metal conduit, you'll save time by buying prebent fittings. A **coupling** joins two pieces of conduit end to end. A **sweep** makes a slow turn through which wires can slide easily. A **pulling elbow** makes a sharper turn.

The setscrew fittings shown here (right) are commonly used with EMT conduit; they provide joints that are firm but not waterproof.

Flexible metal conduit

Flexible metal conduit, also called Greenfield, is like armored cable without the wires. It's not cheap, so it is typically used only in places where it would be difficult to run conduit.

When installing a hardwired appliance, such as an electric water heater, buy an electrical "whip," which is a section of armored cable equipped with the correct fittings for attaching to that specific appliance.

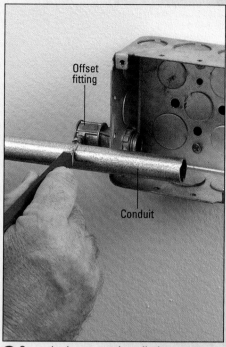

1 Anchor metal boxes to the wall with screws. For exposed wiring use "handy boxes," which have rounded edges and metal covers. An offset fitting allows the conduit to run tight up against the wall.

2 Once the boxes are installed, measure the conduit for cutting. The surest method is to hold a piece in place and mark it rather than using a tape measure. Remember that the conduit will slide about an inch into each fitting.

Metal conduit

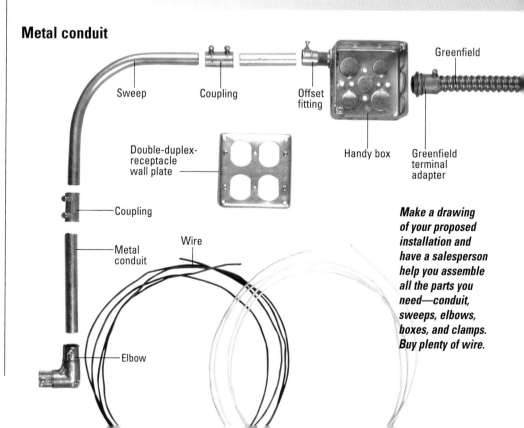

Make a drawing of your proposed installation and have a salesperson help you assemble all the parts you need—conduit, sweeps, elbows, boxes, and clamps. Buy plenty of wire.

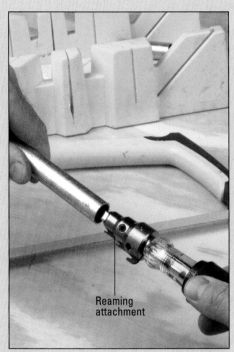

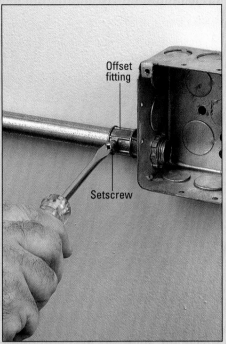

Offset fitting

Setscrew

One-hole strap

Reaming attachment

3 Cut the conduit to fit with a hacksaw. Do not use a tubing cutter, which creates sharp edges inside the conduit that could damage wire insulation. Remove the burrs inside and out. A conduit-reaming attachment on a screwdriver makes this easy.

4 Slide the conduit all the way into the fitting and tighten the setscrew. Test to make sure the connection is tight. (If you will not be installing a ground wire, these connections are critical for grounding.)

5 Anchor the conduit with a one- or two-hole strap at least every 6 feet and within 2 feet of each box. The larger the conduit, the closer the straps need to be. Check with local codes. Screws should be driven into joists or studs, not just into drywall.

Conduit that's large enough

Make sure the wires have ample room inside the conduit to slide through easily. Local codes have detailed regulations regarding conduit size, but in general, ½-inch conduit is large enough for five or fewer wires; ¾-inch conduit is used for more than five wires. When in doubt, or if you might run more wire in the future, buy the larger size—it doesn't cost much more than the smaller size.

Anchoring conduit
Anchor conduit with one- or two-hole straps every 6 feet and within 2 feet of each box.

A pulling elbow every fourth turn

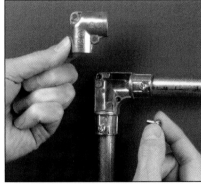

Every time you make a turn, it gets harder for the wires to slide through. If the conduit will make more than three turns before entering a box, install a pulling elbow so you can access the wires. Never make a splice here, just use it as an access point when pulling wires.

STANLEY PRO TIP: **Anchor to masonry**

To attach boxes and straps to concrete, block, or brick, buy masonry screws and the correct masonry bit. Level the box and drill pilot holes.

Drive a masonry screw into the pilot hole, being careful not to overtighten it. The combination of proper hole and screw provides a much more secure attachment than a plastic anchor.

PVC CONDUIT

Plastic conduit is nearly as durable as metal conduit and it costs less. Some local codes permit it for exposed indoor wiring.

When installing PVC conduit, connect four or five pieces in a dry run, then dismantle and glue the pieces together. When making a turn, take care that the elbow or sweep is facing in exactly the right direction when you glue it. Once the glue sets, there's no way to make adjustments. Work in a well-ventilated area when using PVC primer and cement—the fumes are powerful and dangerous.

Consult local codes for the correct PVC cement. You may be required to apply purple-color primer to every piece before you apply the cement. **Always run a green-insulated ground wire through PVC pipe.**

1 Install PVC boxes, then measure and mark the conduit for a cut. Cut with a backsaw and miter box, or a hacksaw, or a circular saw equipped with a blade for cutting plywood.

Backsaw

Miter box

2 Use alignment marks to ensure that the pieces will face in the right direction. Apply PVC primer (if needed) and cement to the outside of the conduit and to the inside of the fitting.

Alignment mark

Primer

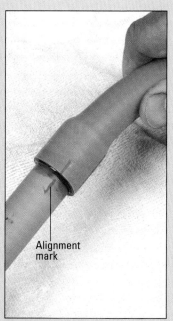

3 Immediately push the conduit into the fitting, twisting slightly to align the marks. Hold the pieces together for about 10 seconds; wipe away excess cement.

Alignment mark

Flexible nonmetallic conduit

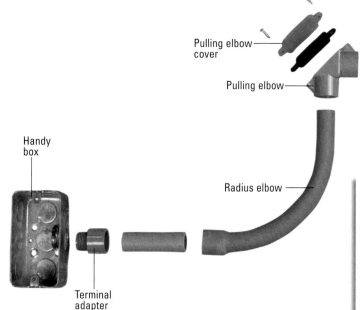

Pulling elbow cover

Pulling elbow

Handy box

Terminal adapter

Radius elbow

Coupling

PVC box

Have a salesperson help you assemble all the parts you need: conduit, couplings, elbows, sweeps, and PVC boxes. Connect to a metal box using a terminal adapter.

Flexible nonmetallic conduit

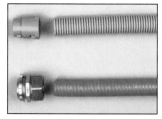

Flexible plastic tubing is a convenient way to channel wiring. Blue corrugated EMT tubing is used for indoor installations; moisture-impermeable tubing is used outdoors. Both come in long coils. Check to see whether these products are allowed by your local codes.

PULLING WIRES THROUGH CONDUIT

If wires travel less than 6 feet through conduit and make only one or two turns, you may be able to just push them through. For longer runs use a fish tape.

If wires become kinked while you work, they will get stuck. So have a helper feed the wire carefully from one end of the conduit while you pull at the other end. If you must work alone, precut the wires (leave yourself an extra 2 feet or so) and unroll them so that they can slide smoothly through the conduit.

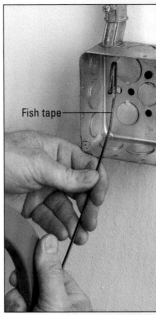

Fish tape

1 At a box or pulling elbow, push the fish tape into the conduit and thread it back to the point of entry.

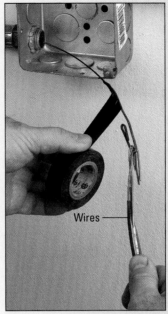

Wires

2 Strip 6 inches of insulation from one wire, 8 inches from another wire, 10 inches from a third wire, and so on. Fold the wires over the fish tape as shown and wrap tightly with electrician's tape.

3 Pull smoothly, using long strokes to avoid stopping and starting. If the wires get stuck, back up a foot or so and start again.

TEAM UP TO PULL WIRE THROUGH CONDUIT

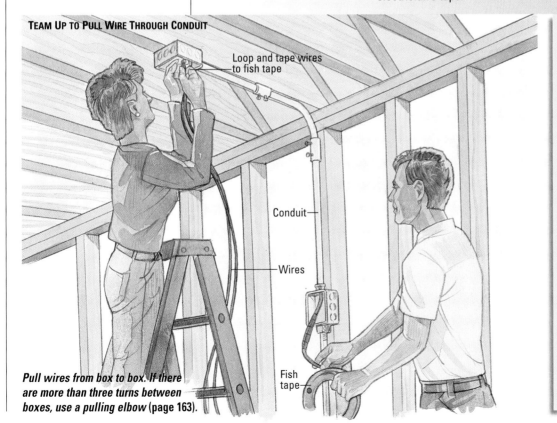

Loop and tape wires to fish tape

Conduit

Wires

Fish tape

Pull wires from box to box. If there are more than three turns between boxes, use a pulling elbow (page 163).

STANLEY PRO TIP

Use pulling lubricant

If the pulling gets tough, try squirting some pulling lubricant on the wires. Don't use soap, detergent, oil, or grease, which can damage wire insulation.

RUNNING CABLE IN FRAMING

Under most building codes, nonmetallic (NM) cable is acceptable for framing runs, but some localities require armored cable or conduit. Armored cable is run much like the NM cable shown, though you may need to drill larger holes and you'll have more difficulty turning corners. To run conduit through framing, use a level or a chalk line to make sure the holes are aligned for straight runs.

If a wayward nail pierces NM cable, the result could be disastrous. Place holes in the framing out of reach of drywall nails and attach protective plates at every hole.

PRESTART CHECKLIST

☐ **TIME**
About 3 hours to run cable and attach to seven or eight wall or ceiling boxes

☐ **TOOLS**
Drill, ¾-inch spade bits, screwdriver, wire stripper, lineman's pliers, hammer, tape measure, level

☐ **SKILLS**
Drilling; stripping cable sheathing and wire insulation; attaching staples

☐ **PREP**
Double-check that all the boxes are correctly positioned; clear the room of all obstructions

☐ **MATERIALS**
Correct cable (page 154), staples, nailing plates

1 Set the box as shown, about a hammer length from the floor and extended beyond the stud by the drywall thickness. Drive the box nails into the stud or joist. Drive screws or nails to anchor a flanged box.

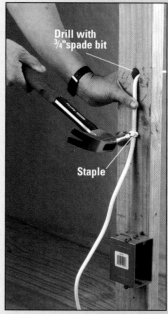

Drill with ¾" spade bit

Staple

2 Mark and drill level holes in the studs about 12 inches above the box. Uncoil the cable and pull it through the holes. Staple the cable within 8 inches of a plastic box, 12 inches of a metal box, then every 2 feet.

3 Mark where you will strip sheathing and cut the cable. About ½ inch of sheathing should enter the box, and the wires inside the box should be 8–12 inches long (you can always trim them later).

INSTALLING NM CABLE

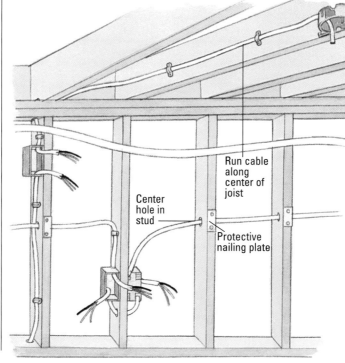

Run cable along center of joist

Center hole in stud

Protective nailing plate

NM cable should be routed where it cannot be reached by nails later pounded into the wall. Where possible add protective nailing plates. When working with engineered joists, check the manufacturer's information before cutting, drilling, or nailing. You could void the warranty for the joists.

Placing receptacles: Most codes call for receptacle boxes 12 inches from the floor and switch boxes 46 inches high. Run cable about a foot above the boxes where possible.

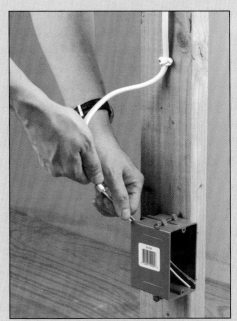

4 With a hammer and screwdriver, open the knockout. On some plastic boxes, you remove the knockout entirely. For the one shown, crack open one end of the tab so it can grab the cable. A metal box may have a built-in clamp, or you may have to add a clamp before sliding in the cable.

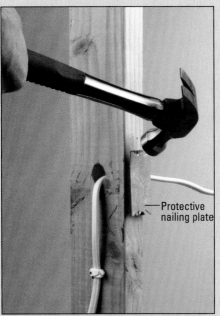

Protective nailing plate

5 Wherever a nail might accidentally pierce the cable, attach a protective nailing plate. Tap the plate in place and hammer it in. Attach a plate on both sides of the stud, if needed.

Turning a corner

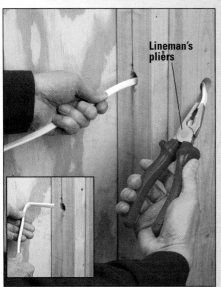

Lineman's pliers

When you reach a corner, drill a hole in each stud. Bend the cable into an L shape. Poke the cable through the first hole and wiggle it into the next hole. When the cable starts to stick out the second hole, grab it with pliers and pull.

STANLEY PRO TIP: **Mount a ceiling light fixture box**

Decide where you want a ceiling light fixture to go (usually the center of a room). Attach a flanged box directly to a ceiling joist (left). For more precise placement, install a box attached to a hanger bar; the box slides along the bar. Note: A hanger bar cannot support a ceiling fan; you must use a fan-rated box.

Using a mud ring

Mud ring

Adapter rings, also called mud rings, are typically ½ inch or ⅝ inch thick. Choose a ring that matches the thickness of the drywall or paneling you will install. Attach the box flush with the front edge of the framing member, then add the ring.

RUNNING CABLE THROUGH FINISHED ROOMS

When running new electrical service for your bathroom through rooms that are finished with drywall or plaster, plan carefully to minimize damage to walls and ceilings. Sometimes you can go through a basement or attic to get at the finished wall or ceiling. Removing a large section of drywall often means less work than repairing many smaller holes.

Use remodel boxes—they clamp to the drywall or plaster rather than attaching to a framing member *(page 155)*.

Use a stud finder to locate the studs and joists and make a drawing of the room showing their locations. Plan the easiest—not necessarily the shortest—routes for cables to the boxes in your bathroom. Sometimes moving a box over a few inches makes the run easier.

Once you have a plan, cut the holes for the remodel boxes, run the cable, and install the boxes.

PRESTART CHECKLIST

☐ **TIME**
About half a day to run cable through a wall and a ceiling and install boxes

☐ **TOOLS**
Stud finder, fish tapes, wire stripper, screwdriver, hammer, drill, fishing drill bit, pry bar, drywall saw or jigsaw, torpedo level

☐ **SKILLS**
Measuring; cutting through drywall or plaster; using fish tapes

☐ **PREP**
Carefully plan the cable routes and box locations; spread a drop cloth on the floor

☐ **MATERIALS**
Electrical cable, protective nailing plates, electrician's tape, remodel boxes

Running cable behind base molding

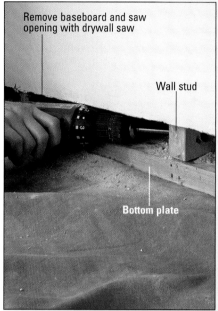

Remove baseboard and saw opening with drywall saw

Wall stud

Bottom plate

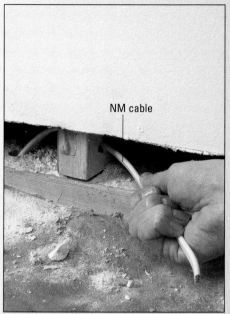

NM cable

1 Cut out a strip of drywall or plaster to expose the bottom plate and studs. If possible cut low enough so you can replace the base molding to cover your work. If the molding is less than 3 inches wide, see the tip on *page 169*. Drill ¾-inch holes near the bottom of the studs.

2 Thread cable through the holes and pull it fairly tight. Once the cable is run, install a nail plate to protect each hole. Replace the drywall and the molding. You may need to attach the drywall with adhesive and reposition some nails to avoid hitting the protective plates.

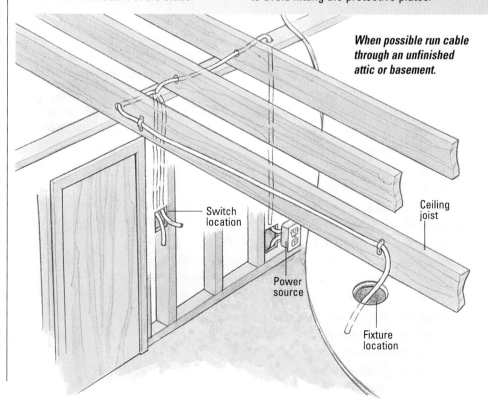

When possible run cable through an unfinished attic or basement.

Switch location

Power source

Fixture location

Ceiling joist

Running cable through a basement

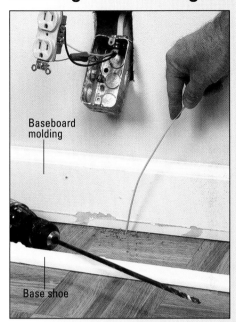

1 If the basement below is unfinished, remove the base shoe and drill a locator hole. Poke a wire down through the hole.

2 In the basement find the locator wire. Drill a hole up through the middle of the bottom plate.

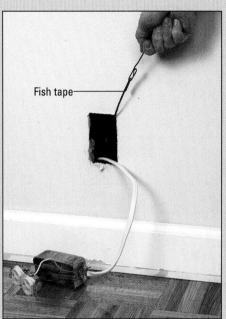

3 To run cable remove the box. Thread one fish tape down through the knockout while a helper threads another fish tape up through the basement hole. Hook the tapes and pull up. If the box is difficult to remove, punch out a knockout slug and pull the cable through the hole in the box.

Run cable behind a door casing

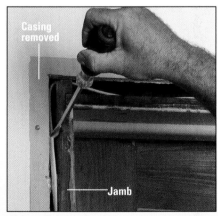

1 Pry off the casing. Where there is a gap between the jamb and framing, thread the cable. Where the jamb is tight against a stud, drill a hole so you can run cable through the wall. Door frames are attached to a double stud so the hole will be 3 inches long.

2 Install a protective plate wherever cable is at risk of being pierced by a nail. Use a chisel to cut a notch for the plate in the jamb so the casing sits snug up against the jamb.

STANLEY PRO TIP

Base cap when the base is not wide enough

If you need to cut a hole too high for the base molding to cover, either replace the old molding with a wider base or install a base cap to add width to the base molding.

Running cable through ceilings and walls

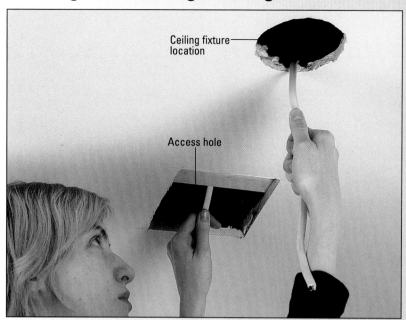

Middle of ceiling: If you need to run cable across the middle of a ceiling or wall, find the joists or studs and cut holes that are large enough for your hand to fit into. (Save drywall pieces and use them to patch the holes later.) Drill holes and thread the cable through. Once the cable is run, install protective nailing plates.

Fire blocks: Some homes have fire blocks—horizontal 2×4s between the studs, usually 4 or 5 feet above the floor. Use a stud finder to locate one. Cut a hole in the wall and drill a hole through the fire block.

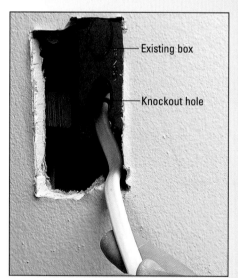

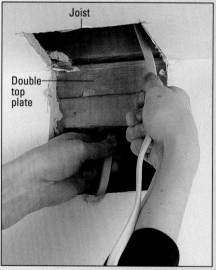

Behind a box: If the hole for a new box is behind an existing box, punch out a knockout slug in the existing box. Run fish tapes from both directions, hook them together, and pull through the box. Now you can pull cable through the box to the hole.

No attic access: To run cable up the wall and across the ceiling, cut holes in the wall and the ceiling. Drill a hole up through the top plate. If there is a joist in the way, drill a hole through it as well. Bend the cable and thread it through the holes.

Using a fishing drill bit

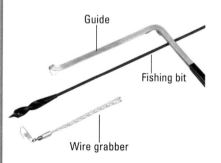

A fishing bit reduces the number of holes in walls and ceilings. Drill a hole through a joist or stud, using the guide to aim the bit. Fasten a wire to the bit and pull it back through the hole.

Installing the boxes

1 Hold the face of the box against the wall, straighten it with a torpedo level, and trace its outline. Cut the outline line through the paper. Cut the hole with a drywall saw. Cut to the inside of the knife cut to prevent fraying the paper. Slip the box into the hole to make sure it fits.

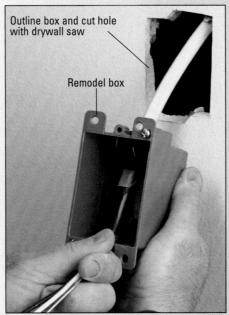

2 Run cable through the box hole. Strip 12 inches of sheathing and run the cable into the box. Whichever clamping method the box uses, make sure ½ inch of sheathing shows inside the box. Tug to make sure the cable is clamped tight.

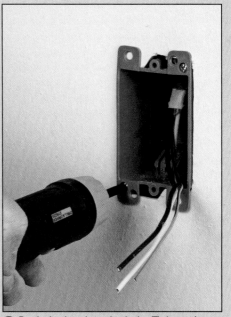

3 Push the box into the hole. Tighten the screw until you feel resistance and the box is firmly attached.

STANLEY PRO TIP: **Fish into the attic**

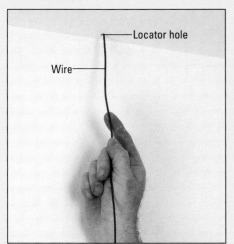

1 Drill a locator hole directly above the hole or box in the wall. Poke a wire through the hole. The wire may have to push through fiberglass or loose-fill insulation.

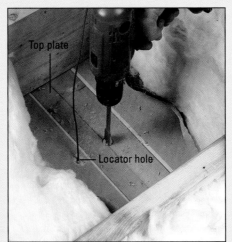

2 Near the locator hole, drill a ¾-inch hole through the center of the top plate. If your house has fire blocking, cut a hole in the wall and drill a hole through the blocking.

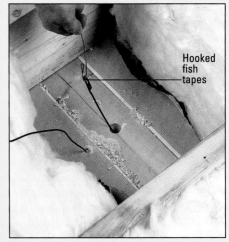

3 Thread a fish tape down through the attic hole while a helper threads a fish tape up through a box or hole in the wall. Once the tapes hook together, pull up.

INSTALLING RECEPTACLES AND SWITCHES

Bathrooms require GFCI receptacles, and installing them is a simple matter. Check GFCIs at least once a month by pushing the "test" button.

A single-pole switch is the most common type of switch. It has two terminals (not counting the ground), and its toggle is marked with ON and OFF. If three wires attach to it (not counting the ground), it's a three-way switch.

PRESTART CHECKLIST

☐ **TIME**
About 2 hours to run cable and make connections (not including cutting a pathway for the cable and patching the walls)

☐ **TOOLS**
Voltage tester, drill, saw, hammer, fish tape, screwdriver, wire stripper, long-nose pliers, lineman's pliers, utility knife, stud finder, torpedo level, tape measure, pry bar, perhaps a drywall saw or jigsaw

☐ **SKILLS**
Stripping and connecting wires to terminals; installing boxes; running cable through walls and ceilings

☐ **PREP**
Lay a drop cloth on the floor

☐ **MATERIALS**
New receptacle or switch, cable, remodel box and clamps, wire nuts, electrician's tape, protective nailing plates, cable staples

1 Cut a hole for a remodel box and cable access, if necessary. Run cable to the hole, clamp the cable to the box, and install the new box.

2 A GFCI wired in the middle of a circuit will protect all receptacles down the line. Connect the wires that bring power to the box to the LINE terminals and those that go to receptacles to LOAD terminals.

3 Wrap the receptacle with tape and push it back into the box. Because a GFCI is bulkier than a standard receptacle, take extra care folding the wires into the box behind it.

Stripping and attaching wires

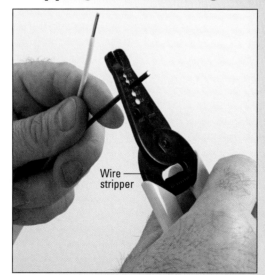

1 Open the stripper, place the wire in the correct hole, and squeeze it shut. Give a slight twist, then slide the insulation off.

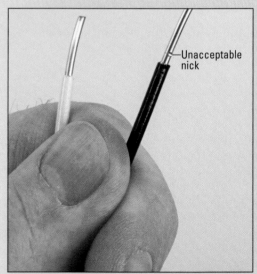

2 If you have to pull hard or the stripper leaves a nick, check that you are using the right hole. If the problem persists, buy a new wire stripper.

Using wire nuts

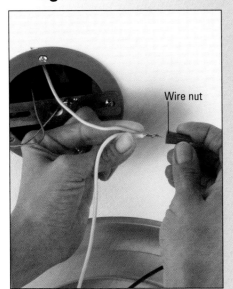

Wire nut

Strip 1¼ inches of insulation from the wires and twist them tightly. Poke the wires into a wire nut as far as possible. Twist the nut tight. Tug on the wire to check the connection. Wrap the bottom of the nut with electrician's tape.

Installing switches

1 If you're replacing a switch, check the wires and terminals. Cut and restrip damaged wire. Loosen the terminal screws and pull off the wires. If you're installing a new switch, run cable and install the box.

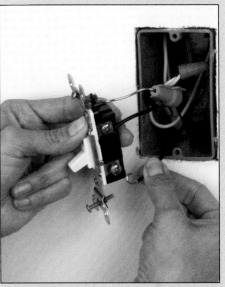

2 Form loops in the wire ends with a long-nose pliers, wrap them clockwise around terminals, and tighten screws. Wrap the switch with electrician's tape to cover terminal screws and any bare wire. Install the switch and cover plate.

Loop

3 With the tip of a pair of long-nose pliers, grab the bare wire just past the insulation and twist it to the left. Slide the pliers up a little and bend to the right, forming a partial circle.

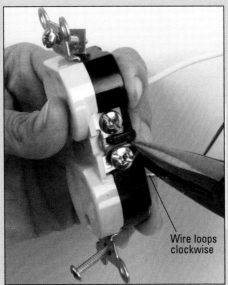

Wire loops clockwise

4 Unscrew the terminal screw until it becomes hard to turn. Slip the looped wire end over the screw threads. Grab the wire on either side of the screw with long-nose pliers and tighten around the terminal screw.

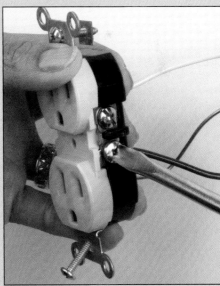

5 Check that the loop is on the terminal screw clockwise. Tug to make sure the wire cannot come loose. Tighten the terminal screw until the wire is snug between the screw head and the surface of the terminal.

INSTALLING NEW BATHROOM FIXTURES

Installing a new bathroom with a toilet, sink, and tub may well be the most challenging do-it-yourself project you'll ever tackle. You'll need a thorough understanding of plumbing systems and techniques, a good helper, and the patience to keep at it until you get everything right.

Getting a handle on the plumbing

The following pages show how to install eight major bathroom improvements using conventional techniques applied in a common residential structure. There are, however, quite a few variations on this basic arrangement. Your situation may call for pipe runs that differ from those shown, so you may need to develop a custom plan that suits your home.

You'll need a good understanding of the basic skills and techniques of plumbing. If you're new to such installations, you might find it helpful to practice some of the rudiments of working with pipe before you start. Develop a general plan for hooking the new plumbing to the old. Pay special attention to the drain vents and make sure you use pipe types and sizes that conform to code. If possible hire a professional plumber to spend an hour or two giving you advice. This modest investment could save you time and money later on.

A look at the entire project

Whether you are remodeling an existing bathroom or installing one in a new addition, you will need carpentry skills.

Modifying the framing sometimes can make the plumbing work easier. Plan and install the plumbing so it damages joists and studs as little as possible; reinforce any framing members that have been compromised. It's usually best to run any electrical lines after the plumbing has been installed.

Working safely

Working with bathroom fixtures can be heavy and tiring work. Safe working habits should be just that—habits—and should not require you to pay special attention to them. Wear gloves and safety equipment as appropriate, masks or a respirator when doing anything that raises dust, and take frequent breaks to keep your mind and body fresh.

A complete bath installation calls for thorough planning, advanced plumbing skills, and patience.

CHAPTER PREVIEW

Preparing the site
page 176

Running drain and vent lines
page 178

Running copper supply lines
page 184

Installing a tub
page 186

Installing a flex-line shower unit
page 189

Installing a prefab tub surround
page 190

Building a shower enclosure
page 192

Installing a whirlpool tub
page 206

Installing a toilet
page 212

Installing a sink faucet
page 216

PREPARING THE SITE

Adding new DWV lines typically requires an extra-wide 2×6 "wet wall" or two side-by-side 2×4 walls. If you're only adding drain lines for a vanity sink (or pair of them), only 2-inch pipe runs through the walls. For this installation many codes permit a standard 2×4 wall. Unless you live in an area with a warm climate, avoid running pipes in an exterior wall.

To expand a bathroom, you may need to build a new wall. (For more information on building walls, see *pages 80–99).* Before removing a wall, make sure it's not load-bearing; check with a carpenter or structural engineer if you are not sure.

Whether you are framing a new space or remodeling an existing space, make sure the framing accommodates the tub.

Remove drywall or plaster from the areas where you will run plumbing. Clear out all cabinets, fixtures, and other obstructions.

If wiring is in the path of plumbing, shut off power to the circuit and test to make sure. You may want to remove cables and reinstall them after the plumbing is in place.

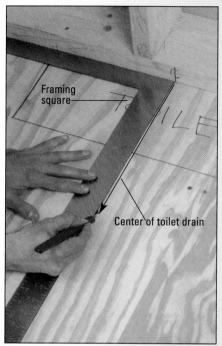

1 Determine the exact center of the toilet drain. For most toilets this is 12 inches from the finished wall surface. If you will install ½-inch drywall, measure 12½ inches out from the framing. (Toilets with drains that set 10 and 14 inches from the wall are available, though usually in white only.)

Framing square

Center of toilet drain

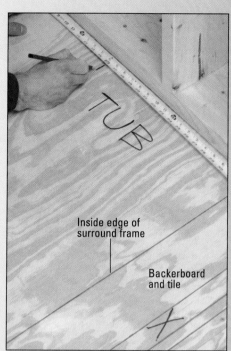

2 Study the instructions that come with the tub and the waste-and-overflow assembly to determine exactly where the tub drain needs to be *(pages 206–209).* Mark the tub outline on the floor. In this case the framing, backerboard, and tiling for a whirlpool tub must be added.

Inside edge of surround frame

Backerboard and tile

PRESTART CHECKLIST

☐ **TIME**
A day or more to remove wallcoverings; about half a day to mark positions of fixtures

☐ **TOOLS**
Hammer, pry bar, level, framing square, drill, hole saw, jigsaw, circular saw, reciprocating saw

☐ **SKILLS**
Basic carpentry skills, planning for plumbing runs, careful measuring

☐ **PREP**
Preapproved plumbing plans by your building department

☐ **MATERIALS**
Lumber for any framing that's needed

PLAN FOR FINISHING THE ROOM BELOW

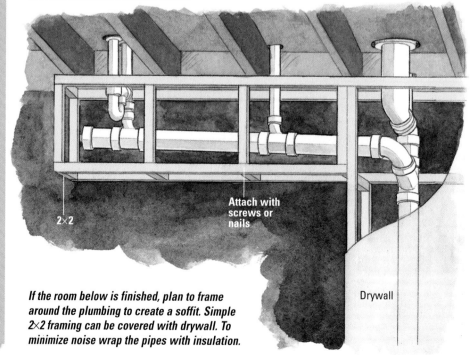

2×2

Attach with screws or nails

Drywall

If the room below is finished, plan to frame around the plumbing to create a soffit. Simple 2×2 framing can be covered with drywall. To minimize noise wrap the pipes with insulation.

Tub supply location

Sink drain, marked for cutting with hole saw

Notch marked for drain/vent fitting

Circular saw

Hole for toilet drain

Reciprocating saw

3 Mark the bottom plate for the location of the vent and drainpipes. Position the tub/shower vent so it will not interfere with the installation of the faucet *(pages 210–211)*. You may need to move or add a stud or two to accommodate the tub/shower faucet. Also mark where the supply lines will enter the room. Check all your measurements twice.

4 Use a hole saw or jigsaw to cut a hole in the floor for the toilet drain. Use a circular saw and a reciprocating saw to cut a section of flooring large enough to allow you to run the plumbing. Wherever you need to run pipes through joists, give yourself plenty of room to work.

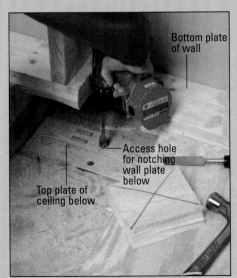

Bottom plate of wall

Access hole for notching wall plate below

Top plate of ceiling below

Hole saw

5 Drill holes or cut notches as needed. To make room for the toilet drain *(pages 212–213)*, cut a large notch in the bottom plate of the wall and the top plate of the ceiling below.

6 Using a hole saw, cut 2¼-inch holes for the tub and sink drains. Remove a 12×14-inch section of flooring for the tub/shower drain—cut a larger opening if you don't have access from behind or below.

STANLEY. PRO TIP

Run pipe through an intervening story

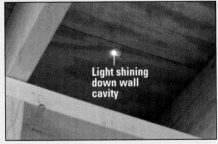

Light shining down wall cavity

If the new bathroom is on the second story, you will need to run a drainpipe down the wall of a first-story room. Don't tear into the wall to confirm the drain location. Instead cut the bathroom drain hole and position a bright light over it. Take measurements and drill a test hole in the basement. If the location is right, you'll see the light.

RUNNING DRAIN AND VENT LINES

Because they are complicated and in some cases must be positioned precisely, drain and vent lines should be installed before the supply pipes. However, sometimes it may be possible to make room for supply runs by moving a vent pipe over a few inches.

If you must run drainpipes across a floor, carefully calculate the altitude—the amount of vertical room available—so you can pitch the drainpipe at 1/8 to 1/4 inch per running foot.

Sometimes it's difficult to visualize just how drainpipes will travel through walls and floors. Once you start assembling the pieces and testing them for fit, you may need to modify your plans.

Some inspectors want horizontal vent pipes to be sloped so moisture caused by condensation can run back to the drain; others don't consider this important. Err on the safe side and slope the vents.

PRESTART CHECKLIST

☐ **TIME**
Working with a helper, about two days to install drain and vent lines for a simple bathroom

☐ **TOOLS**
PVC saw or power saw, level, reciprocating saw, drill, carpentry tools

☐ **SKILLS**
Cutting and joining PVC pipe, running pipes through walls, connecting new pipe to old

☐ **PREP**
Have your plans approved by an inspector; prepare the room (pages 176–177)

☐ **MATERIALS**
PVC pipe and fittings to meet codes, fittings to join to existing drainpipe, PVC primer and cement, pipe strap

A. Running the main drain line

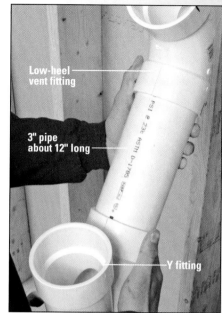

Low-heel vent fitting

3" pipe about 12" long

Y fitting

Low-heel vent fitting

Y fitting

1 Start with a length of 3-inch pipe long enough to reach the basement or crawlspace (see step 5, *page 180*). You may be able to cut it to exact length after it has been installed. Dry-fit a Y fitting, a length of pipe, and a low-heel vent fitting as shown, lining them up precisely.

2 Insert the assembly down through the wall plates and temporarily anchor it. Make sure the Y fitting is low enough to allow for installation of the other drain lines (Step 2, *page 181*). Once you are sure of the configuration, pull up the assembly and prime and glue the pieces.

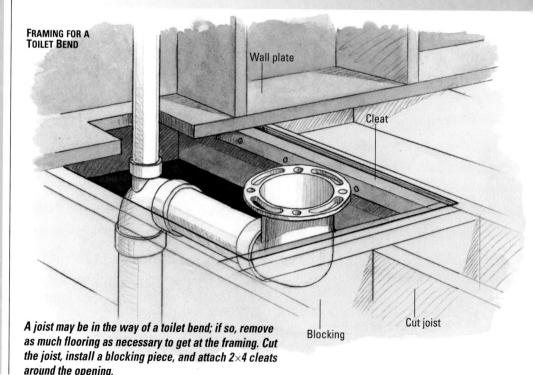

FRAMING FOR A TOILET BEND

Wall plate

Cleat

Blocking

Cut joist

A joist may be in the way of a toilet bend; if so, remove as much flooring as necessary to get at the framing. Cut the joist, install a blocking piece, and attach 2×4 cleats around the opening.

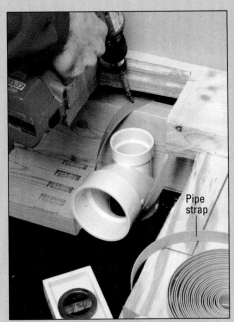

Pipe strap

4×3 reducing closet bend

3" pipe section

3 Place the assembly back into the hole. Secure the low-heel vent fitting to the framing with pipe strap. Secure the pipe from below as well.

4 Dry-fit a length of 3-inch pipe and a 4×3 reducing closet bend to the vent fitting. Check that the center of the closet-bend hole is the correct distance from the wall—in most cases 12½ inches from the framing to allow for ½-inch drywall. Check that the pipe slopes ⅛ to ¼ inch down to the fitting. (If necessary you can trim the top of the closet bend after the flooring has been replaced.) Once you are sure the toilet drain setup is correct, mark the alignment of the fittings and disassemble. Glue the pieces together.

TOILET VENT OPTIONS

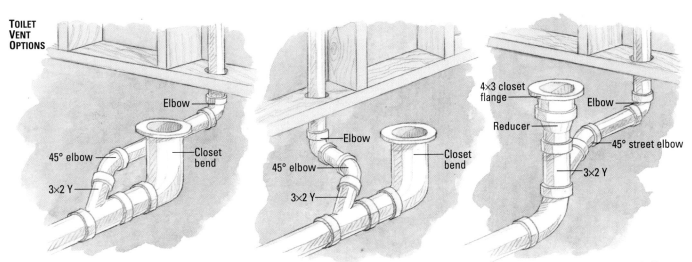

Elbow

45° elbow

3×2 Y

Closet bend

Elbow

45° elbow

3×2 Y

Closet bend

4×3 closet flange

Elbow

Reducer

45° street elbow

3×2 Y

If the toilet drain does not connect directly to a vent, you must find another way to vent it. If the drain line runs away from the wall where you want the vent, use a reducing Y and a 45-degree street elbow to point the vent line toward the wall. The horizontal vent pipe runs right next to the closet bend.

If the vent wall is parallel to the drain pipe, install a reducing Y and a 45-degree street elbow to point toward the wall. You may need another elbow (of any degree) to position the vertical vent where you want it.

If the vent wall is opposite the drain line, use a reducing Y and a 45-degree street elbow. The fittings can be pointed straight at the wall or at an angle, as needed.

Running the main drain line (continued)

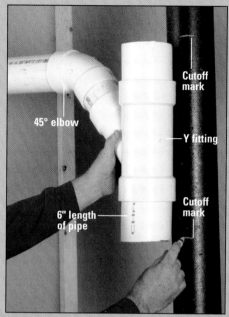

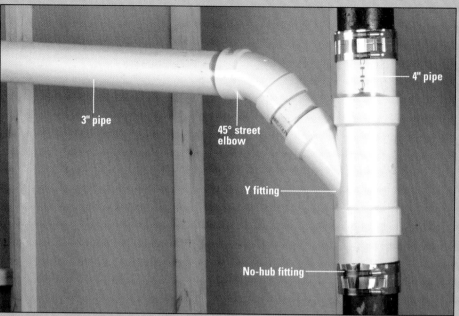

5 Run a horizontal pipe to the existing stack and assemble the parts needed for tying into it. All fittings should be Ys or drain elbows so wastewater can flow easily. Hold the horizontal pipe so it's sloped at ⅛ to ¼ inch per foot and mark the existing pipe for cutting *(pages 148–149).*

6 If the existing pipe is cast iron, take care to support it securely before cutting. In the setup shown, a 4×3 Y connects to the house drain using no-hub fittings (which should be used to connect to either cast iron or ABS). Once you are sure the fittings are correct and the horizontal pipe slopes correctly, make alignment marks. Disassemble the parts, apply primer, and reassemble the pieces in order, starting at the existing drain.

OTHER DRAIN CONFIGURATIONS

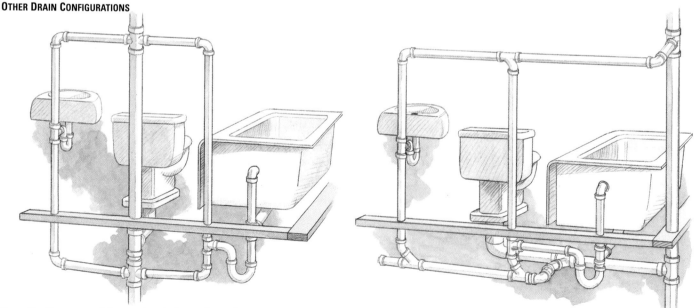

Your situation may call for another drain configuration. This example shows a single-floor home in which all the fixtures tie into horizontal pipes, which in turn run to the stack.

In this example for a two-story home, first-floor vent pipes run up to join the second-floor vents at the top of their runs. All the vents tie in at a point well above the second-floor fixtures.

B. Running individual drain lines

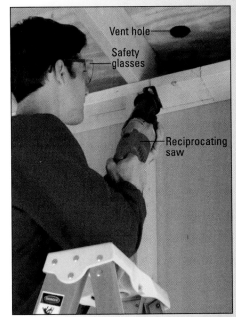

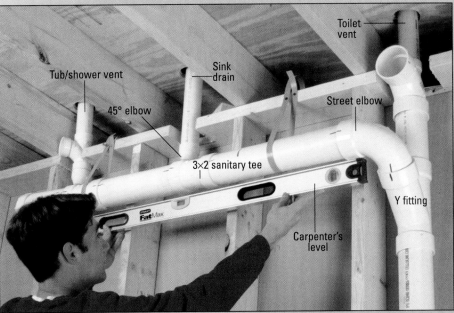

1 Slip lengths of 2-inch pipe down through the holes drilled in the floor plate for the tub and sink vents. Have a helper hold the pipes plumb as you mark the plate below for notching. Cut notches about an inch wider than the pipe to accommodate a fitting.

2 Cut and dry-fit the horizontal drainpipe and the fittings to connect the tub and sink drains. (A 3-inch horizontal pipe is shown, but your inspector may permit a 2-inch pipe.) Insert a street elbow into the Y and hold the other pieces in place to mark for cutting. Make sure the horizontal pipe slopes at a rate of ⅛ to ¼ inch per running foot. Install a reducing tee and a 45-degree elbow (or street elbow if you need to save room) for both joints. If the pipe will be accessible, install a cleanout on the fitting for the tub; otherwise install a drain elbow instead of a tee.

WHAT IF...
You need to run a drain for a shower only?

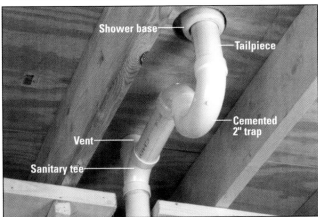

A 1½-inch drain trap is often permitted for a shower, but a 2-inch trap will ensure quick flow of water and will be less likely to clog. A shower has no waste-and-overflow assembly, so the rough plumbing consists of a cemented trap that rises to the correct height for the shower base *(page 193)*.

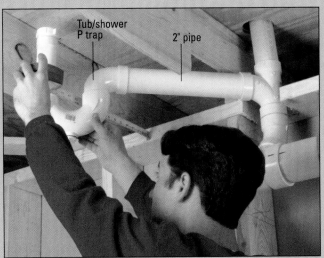

3 To plumb the drain for the tub, dry-fit a 2-inch trap onto a length of 2-inch pipe that is longer than it needs to be. Study the directions for the tub to determine precisely where the trap should be located. Hold the trap-and-pipe assembly in place and mark it for a cut. Dry-fit and check that the horizontal pipe slopes correctly. Once all the parts are accurately assembled, draw alignment marks and prime and glue the pieces together.

C. Installing the vents

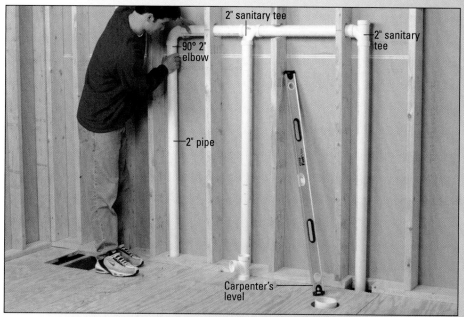

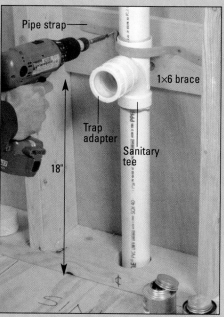

1 Your codes may require the horizontal revent lines to be as high as 54 inches above the finished floor, or at least 6 inches above the fixture flood level (the point where water will start to spill out). Use a carpenter's level to mark the studs for drilling holes. Run the horizontal vent lines sloped downward toward the fixtures at a rate of ⅛ to ¼ inch per running foot. Drill holes, cut pipes, and connect them in a dry run using drain fittings.

2 Install a sanitary tee facing into the room for the sink trap. The ideal height is usually 18 inches above the finished floor, but check your sink instructions to be sure. Cement a 1¼-inch trap adapter into the tee. Install a piece of 1×6 blocking and anchor the pipe with a strap.

RUNNING A VENT AROUND AN OBSTRUCTION

If a medicine cabinet, window, or other obstruction prevents you from running a vent straight up, you'll have to turn a corner for a short distance, then turn again to head upwards. Horizontal runs should be at least 6 inches above the fixture flood level—the rim of a sink, for example.

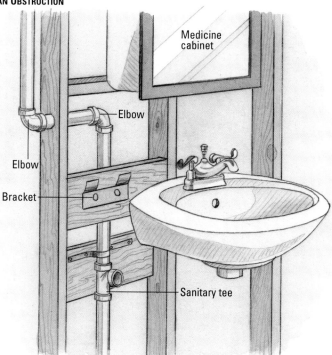

Running up through the ceiling

To run a vent pipe through the ceiling, first drill a test hole to make sure you won't bump into any joists in the attic. You may need to move the hole over a few inches. The top plate may be doubled, meaning you have to drill through 3 inches. You may need to drill with a hole saw first from below (shown), then from above.

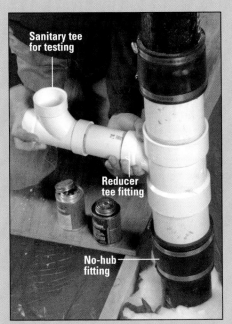

3 In the attic, tap into a conveniently located vent pipe. Following the steps shown on *pages 178–182*, cut the pipe and connect a reducer tee fitting. Use no-hub fittings to connect a PVC fitting to cast-iron or ABS pipe.

4 Run the new vent line over to the tee fitting. The pipes should slope gently away from the existing vent pipe so water can travel downward. Your inspector may want you to include a tee fitting to be used for testing. Once the drain system is assembled and cemented, plug the drainpipe at the lower end. Pour water into it until all the drain and vent pipes are filled with water. Allow the water to sit for a day to make sure there are no leaks.

INSTALLING A ROOF JACK

Check local codes for the correct way to install a roof jack. In most areas you will need to install a 4-inch pipe. Some areas allow for a plastic pipe to extend out the roof (shown); in other areas a metal pipe is required. Purchase a roof jack with a rubber flange that will seal a 4-inch pipe.

Cut the 4-inch pipe to roughly the same angle as the roof slope and hold it plumb, its top touching the attic ceiling. Mark for the hole, which will be oval. Cut the hole using a drill and a reciprocating saw.

You may need to cut some roofing shingles back. Slip the jack under the roof shingles at its upper half; the lower half of the jack rests on top of shingles. Poke the vent pipe up through the rubber flange. To anchor the jack, lift up some shingles and drive in roofing nails. If any nails are not covered by shingles, cover the heads with roofing cement.

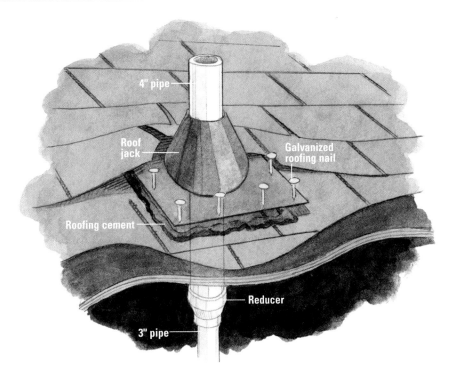

RUNNING COPPER SUPPLY LINES

Rigid copper is the material of choice for supply lines in most localities, although flexible or rigid plastic is permitted in some areas. An hour or two of practice will prepare you to cut copper pipe and sweat joints quickly and securely *(pages 140–141)*.

Supply lines can be routed along almost any path, although extending a pipe run and adding bends will lower water pressure slightly. This plan shows running pipes so that they do not cross drainpipes or vents. In most cases it's easier to make the horizontal runs below the room in the crawlspace or basement. If you need to run pipes horizontally in the room, see *page 185*.

Installing hammer arresters (Step 3) eliminates the banging noise when you turn a faucet on or off.

Copper pipe can last for many decades. However, it is easily punctured or dented. Position it out of harm's way and install nailing plates to the studs to protect pipes against errant nails.

Hot water is always on the left, cold water on the right.

PRESTART CHECKLIST

☐ **TIME**
About half a day to run supply lines for a sink and toilet

☐ **TOOLS**
Drill, bit and bit extender, propane torch, tubing cutter, multiuse wire brush, flame guard, groove-joint pliers, carpentry tools for installing braces, flux brush

☐ **SKILLS**
Accurate measuring and drilling, working with copper pipe

☐ **PREP**
Install all or most of the drain and vent pipes; determine the supply routes

☐ **MATERIALS**
Copper pipe and fittings, flux, solder, damp rag

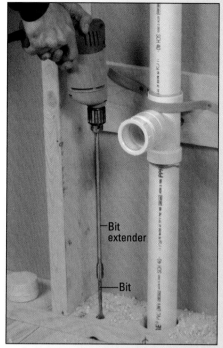

1 Consult the manufacturer's instructions to position pipes for the shower faucet, sink, and toilet. For example the shower faucet in this plan calls for vertical pipes 10 inches apart. Use a spade bit attached to a bit extender to drill holes in the center of the wall plate, if possible.

2 Install cross braces so you can anchor the pipes firmly. Cut pieces of 2×4 or 1×4 to fit snugly between studs and attach them by drilling pilot holes and driving screws. If you plan to install a pedestal sink *(pages 214–215)*, attach a 2×6 or a ¾-inch plywood brace (shown) to support its bracket.

Running and securing supply pipes

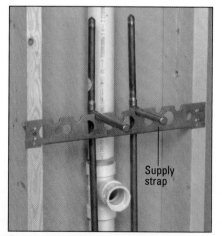

A copper supply strap attaches to the face of the studs. Pipes fit into notches or holes, sized and spaced for correct placement. The pipes can be soldered onto the strap using the same techniques as for sweating fittings.

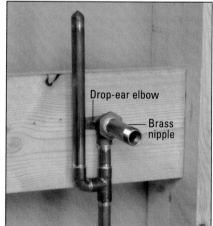

A drop-ear elbow makes the most secure attachment. If you use one, the hammer arrester must be connected to a tee and an elbow just below the drop-ear elbow. Insert a brass threaded nipple into the elbow.

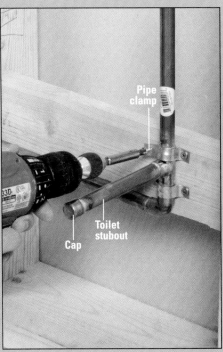

3 Tie into existing supply lines *(pages 148–149)*. Hot and cold stubouts should be 8 to 10 inches apart and 19 to 23 inches above the floor; consult the manufacturer's instructions to be sure. A toilet stubout is usually 8 inches above the floor.

Dry-fit a complete assembly for the sink and the toilet. For each stubout use a tee fitting, a 6-inch length of pipe (which you will cut off later), and a cap to protect the pipe. Install a hammer arrester to each.

4 Sweat all the parts following instructions on *pages 140–141*. Anchor the pipes with at least one—preferably two—clamps at each stubout as shown.

Tap into shower supplies

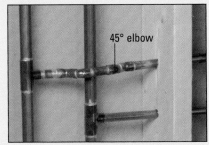

Rather than running sink supply lines from below, you may want to run them horizontally from the shower. If the shower lines are ¾ inch, use reducer tees to tap into the lines. Use 45-degree elbows to snake one line past the other (in this case the hot past the vertical cold-water line). If the sink is used at the same time as the shower, water temperature will change.

WHAT IF…
Supply lines must run past drain or vent pipes?

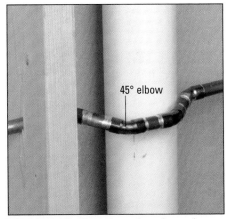

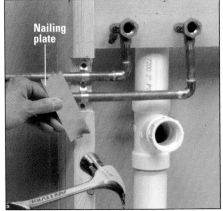

To run supply lines around an obstruction such as a drain or vent pipe, use four 45-degree elbows. This arrangement makes for smoother water flow and less loss of water pressure than using 90-degree elbows.

Another option is to cut notches rather than holes and run supply pipes in front of the vent pipes. If you do this, install protective nailing plates or the pipes could be punctured by a nail when the drywall is installed.

INSTALLING A TUB

An inexpensive tub may be narrow and may not cover the same floor space as an older tub. Many people find a narrow tub uncomfortable. Purchase a tub with ample width.

Home centers carry spa (or whirlpool) tubs that can fit in a standard tub opening. Installing one of these models is not much more work than installing a standard tub; the difference is that a spa or whirlpool needs to plug into a GFCI (ground fault circuit interrupter) electrical receptacle.

Preparing the floor and the walls

If the bead of caulk at the base of a tub has even a small gap, water that puddles on the bathroom floor will seep underneath the tub, quickly damaging any bare wood. To be safe, install protective flooring on the entire floor, including the area the tub will cover.

Most tubs fit into a 60-inch opening, but some older ones may be longer. Measure to make sure your tub will fit.

PRESTART CHECKLIST

☐ **TIME**
About a day to install a replacement tub where there is an existing drain

☐ **TOOLS**
Groove-joint pliers, pry bar, level, drill, screwdriver, strainer wrench, putty knife

☐ **SKILLS**
Making drain connections in a tight spot, basic carpentry skills

☐ **PREP**
Clear the area; cover the floor with plywood and a drop cloth

☐ **MATERIALS**
Tub, waste-and-overflow unit, plumber's putty, pipe-thread tape, caulk, cement board and tiles, or other wall-finishing material

1 Check the drain and replace any damaged parts. Consult the manufacturer's literature and measure to make sure the drain is in the correct location. Purchase a waste-and-overflow unit *(page 187)* and determine how you will connect it to the drain line (below). Screw ledger boards to the studs at the height recommended by the manufacturer.
Ideally the finish flooring material should run under the tub.

DRAIN CONNECTIONS

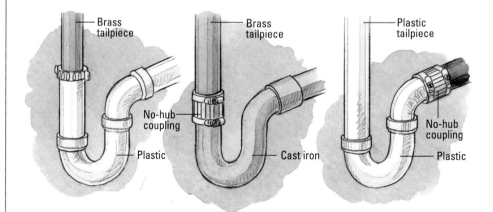

Waste-and-overflow (WO) units have been attached to drain lines in various ways over the years. Here are some of the most common methods. A rubber no-hub coupling (sometimes called a mission coupling) may be used to connect to a cast-iron or plastic drain line.

Usually the WO tailpiece connects to the drain via a slip nut. Whichever method you use, plan ahead so that you won't have a nasty surprise after the tub has been wrestled into position.

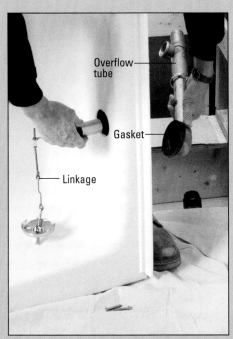

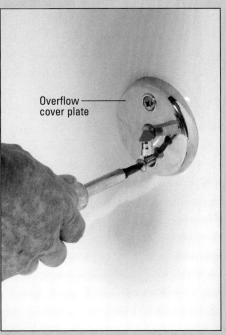

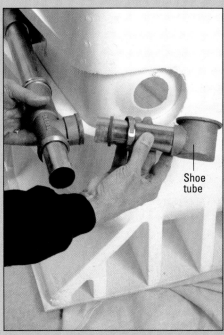

2 Working with the tub turned on its side, dry-fit the overflow tube and the shoe. Make any necessary cuts, then make permanent connections. Place the gasket on the overflow flange, position it behind the overflow hole, and insert the linkage.

3 Inside the tub slip the screws into the overflow trim. Hold the overflow flange in place and hand-tighten one of the screws. Start the second screw and tighten both with a screwdriver.

4 Insert the shoe tube into the opening in the overflow tube, and slip the other end up into the drain hole.

WHAT IF...
You have an extra-deep tub?

If the tub is deeper than usual, the opening in the overflow tube may be too high for the shoe. If so cut and install an extension for the overflow tube. In some cases an extension is included with the waste-and-overflow unit.

BATHTUB WASTE-AND-OVERFLOW ASSEMBLIES

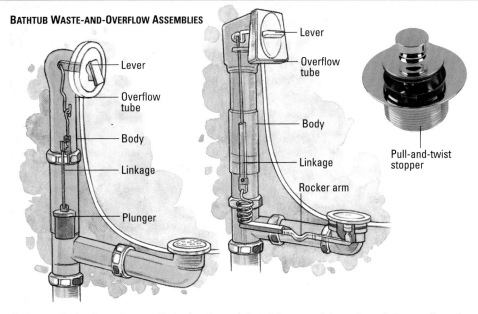

A plunger design has a brass cylinder (or plunger) that slides up and down through the overflow pipe to open or close the drain. A brass pop-up drain has a rocker arm that pivots to raise or lower the stopper. Many plastic units have no interior mechanism; instead, the stopper itself (above right) is raised and lowered by lifting. This method drains more slowly than the other two methods.

Installing a tub (continued)

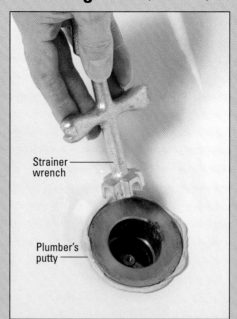

Strainer wrench

Plumber's putty

5 Inside the tube place a rope of plumber's putty under the strainer or drain flange. Hold the shoe with one hand while you screw in the flange. Finish tightening with a strainer wrench. Clean away the squeezed-out putty with a plastic putty knife.

6 Before tilting and moving the tub, plan the move so you avoid damaging the waste-and-overflow unit, which protrudes below the tub. It may work best to rest the tub on 2×4s part of the time. With a helper move the tub into position. You may have to tilt the tub as shown. Slide it into the opening and gently lower the tub in place. You might want a helper to guide the overflow tube into the drain line (see Step 8) while you do this. Slide the drop cloth or any other protective material out from under the tub. Protect the interior of the tub.

Torpedo level

Waste-and-overflow tailpiece

Backerboard

7 Check the tub for level; an out-of-level tub may not drain completely. Attach the tub to the studs according to manufacturer's directions. You will probably nail or screw through an acrylic tub flange (shown). For a metal tub, drive nails just above the flange.

8 Working from behind or below, connect the waste-and-overflow tailpiece to the drain line using one of the methods shown on *page 186*. To test for leaks, close the stopper and fill the tub. Open the stopper; watch and feel for any sign of wetness.

9 To fill in the gap above the tub, cut and install strips of cement backerboard, which is more moisture-resistant than green drywall. Install tiles to fit, allow the adhesive to set for a day, and apply grout. Apply silicone or "tub and tile" caulk where the tiles meet the tub.

INSTALLING A FLEX-LINE SHOWER UNIT

If your bathtub has a spout but no showerhead, installing one would be a big job. The demolition, wall repair, and tiling would take much more time than the plumbing. One solution is a flex-line shower unit. It installs quickly, and its removable showerhead is a handy feature.

If you want to install a flex-line shower, the surrounding walls should be covered with tile or another water-resistant material. If you have an old claw-foot tub that does not abut the walls, purchase a circular shower curtain.

PRESTART CHECKLIST

☐ **TIME**
About an hour for most units

☐ **TOOLS**
Drill with masonry bit, screwdriver, hammer, groove-joint pliers

☐ **SKILLS**
Drilling holes in tile, assembling parts

☐ **PREP**
No need to shut off the water; place a towel in the bottom of the tub to catch any parts

☐ **MATERIALS**
Flex-line shower unit, pipe tape, plastic anchors, nails, screws

1 Remove the old spout and screw on the one that comes with the shower unit.

2 Hold the showerhead bracket or template in place, and mark for mounting holes. Press the tip of a nail on a mark and tap with a hammer to make a small chip as a starter hole. Drill holes with a masonry bit.

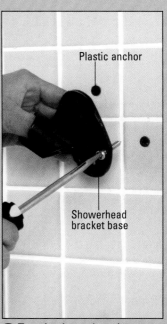

3 Tap plastic anchors into the holes and attach the showerhead bracket with the screws provided. Snap on its decorative body. Screw the flex line to the tub spout and slip the showerhead into the bracket.

FLEX-LINE SHOWER UNIT

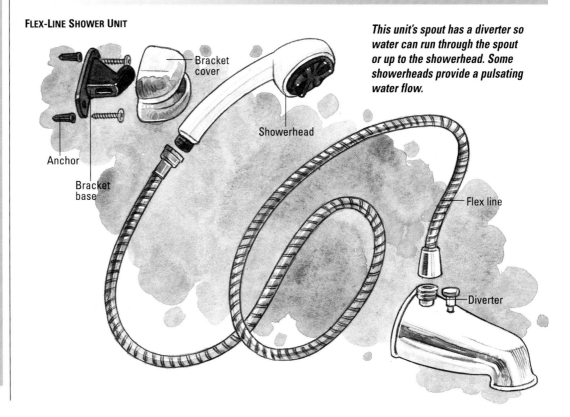

This unit's spout has a diverter so water can run through the spout or up to the showerhead. Some showerheads provide a pulsating water flow.

INSTALLING A PREFAB TUB SURROUND

A prefab tub surround is a quick way to give a tub and shower area a fresh start. High-quality units have colorful, durable finishes as well as convenient niches and towel bars.

Make sure the unit you buy has panels with flanges that overlap each other so you don't have to cut the panels to fit precisely. With a standard 60-inch-wide opening, you probably won't have to cut at all, other than making holes for the spout and the faucet control or handles.

Preparing the wall surface

The walls should be smooth and even. Scrape away any peeling paint and patch any cracks or weak spots. Apply primer paint to the walls to ensure a strong bond with the adhesive. It's possible to install over tile, but the panels will have gaps at the front edges, which must be covered with tile or acrylic.

PRESTART CHECKLIST

☐ **TIME**
Several hours to install a solid-surface tub surround

☐ **TOOLS**
Level, drill, caulk gun (or tube), notched trowel, tape measure, utility knife

☐ **SKILLS**
Measuring and drilling holes

☐ **PREP**
Clean and prime the walls, close the drain and place a drop cloth in the tub; remove the spout and the faucet control or handles

☐ **MATERIALS**
Shower surround kit, manufacturer's recommended adhesive, masking tape, cardboard for a template

Notched trowel

1 Press a corner piece into position and mark the sides and top with a pencil. Using a notched trowel or a caulk gun (depending on the manufacturer), apply adhesive to the center area inside the pencil lines. Apply evenly so the panel will not be wavy.

Center panel

2 Press the center panel in place and smooth it with your palm. Install other pieces in the same way, following the manufacturer's installation procedures.

PREFAB TUB ENCLOSURE

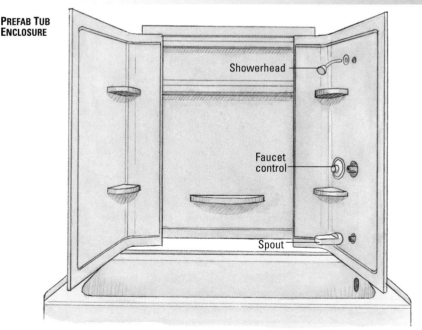

Showerhead

Faucet control

Spout

Available acrylic or polystyrene tub surrounds may have a modern, decorative, or retro look and come in various colors. While these units are less permanent than tile, they install quickly, are relatively inexpensive, and will last for many years.

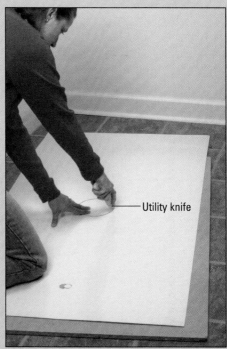

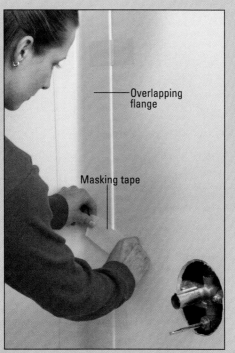

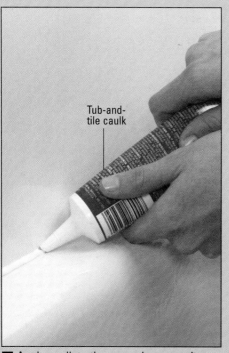

3 Place the piece that will cover the plumbing wall on a scrap piece of plywood. Make a template and cut holes using a utility knife or a drill bit and hole saw of the correct size. Install the end pieces in the same way as the back pieces.

4 The panels can be adjusted before the adhesive hardens, which usually occurs about a half hour after application. Apply pieces of masking tape to ensure that their top edges form a straight line. (The bottom edges will be caulked, so they can be slightly uneven.)

5 Apply caulk to the space between the strips and a bead where the panels meet the tub. Practice applying even pressure to the tube while drawing smoothly along the joint. After applying the caulk, smooth it with your finger. Clean up any mistakes with a damp sponge.

Make a template

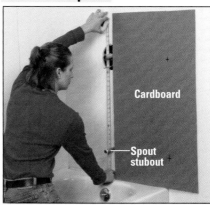

To prevent mistakes in cutting holes, cut a piece of cardboard the same width as the panel to be installed. For each hole measure up from the tub and over from the corner panel and mark the center of each hole. (If the panel will overlap the corner panel, take that into account.) Cut holes with a utility knife.

Hold the template up against the wall as a trial run. Once you are certain the holes are correct, place the template over the panel and mark it for drilling the holes.

WHAT IF...
You're installing a shower faucet?

If you need to replace the shower faucet, remove the wall surface. Follow the plumbing instructions on *pages 146–147*. Cover the wall with cement backerboard or water-resistant drywall (greenboard).

Building a Shower Enclosure

A new shower stall installed in a corner of a room will require you to build only one wall. If it's in the middle of a wall, two new walls are required. The walls may reach all the way to the ceiling, or they may stop partway up. In the latter case, the top ledge must be covered with tile or another moisture-resistant surface. The opening can have a door, or you can install a curtain rod.

For a corner installation, a one-piece unit *(page 194)* is much simpler to install, though you have a limited choice of colors.

A 32-inch shower base will feel cramped; buy a base that is at least 34 inches. Some bases must be set in thinset mortar or in a bed of sand, while others can be simply placed on the floor.

For details on how to run drain and supply lines, see *pages 178–181*.

Prestart Checklist

☐ **Time**
Two or three days to install a base, plumbing, tiled walls, and a shower door

☐ **Tools**
Carpentry tools, groove-joint pliers, drill, tools for plastic *(page 142)* and copper pipe *(page 140)*, tiling tools, steel rod

☐ **Skills**
Working with plastic and copper pipe, framing a wall, installing tile

☐ **Prep**
Install a drainpipe with trap in the center of the base, as well as supply pipes, faucet, and shower riser

☐ **Materials**
Shower base, roofing felt, PVC primer and cement, 2×4 studs, cement backerboard, backerboard screws, tiles, tile adhesive, grout, caulk, shower door

Building a Tiled Shower Enclosure

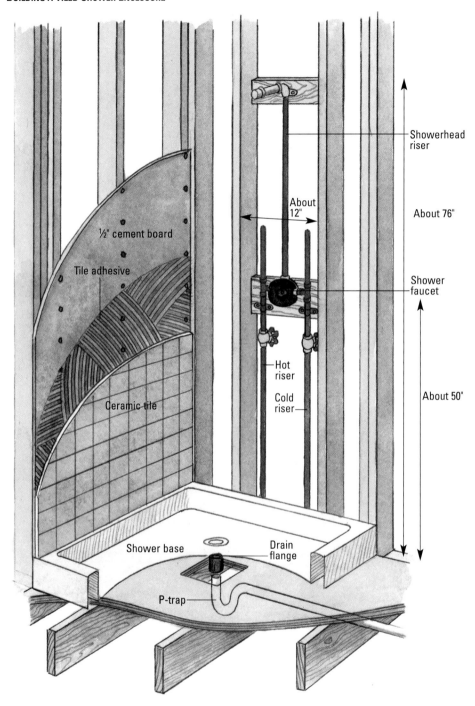

½" cement board

Tile adhesive

Ceramic tile

About 12"

Showerhead riser

About 76"

Shower faucet

Hot riser

Cold riser

About 50"

Shower base

Drain flange

P-trap

A shower drain should be installed at the center of the shower base. The flange should be level with the floor. Run the supply pipes after the framing is installed.

A. Installing the shower base

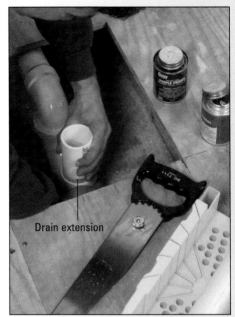

Drain extension

Carpenter's level

Roofing felt

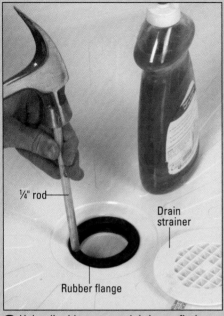

¼" rod

Drain strainer

Rubber flange

1 Set the shower base over the drain to make sure the drain is directly below the opening of the base. Remove the base, then cut and cement an extension to the drainpipe. The extension should be flush with the floor.

2 Place a layer or two of roofing felt to smooth any unevenness in the floor. (Some manufacturers may require a bed of mortar or sand.) Set the shower base over the drain to confirm that the drain is positioned where you want it. Check for level; shim with roofing felt as needed.

3 Using liquid soap as a lubricant, fit the rubber flange (provided with the shower base) over the drain extension and push it as far down as you can. Tap it all the way in place with a ¼-inch steel rod. Install the drain strainer.

REFRESHER COURSE
Installing a drain

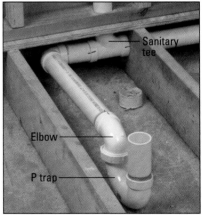

Sanitary tee

Elbow

P trap

See *pages 178–181* for instructions on running a new drain line. A shower drain should be connected directly to a trap. Drain lines must slope at a rate of ¼ inch per running foot and must be properly vented *(pages 182–183)*.

WHAT IF...
The base uses a PVC flange?

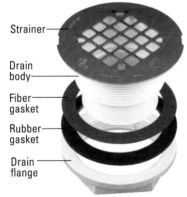

Strainer

Drain body

Fiber gasket

Rubber gasket

Drain flange

Cement the drain flange to the drainpipe; the flange should be flush with the floor. Set the gaskets on top of the flange. Place the shower base over the drain hole. Check that the gaskets are still in place. Screw the drain body through the hole in the base and into the flange. Attach the strainer.

STANLEY PRO TIP

Install a custom-mortared shower base

A custom-mortared shower base frees you from the styles, sizes, and colors available in prefab units. You can have anything you want. Constructing such a base, an endeavor once only within the reach of the pros, is an installation that is increasingly being done by do-it-yourselfers. It relies on a CPE (heavy plastic) liner set inside the frame to waterproof the surface. See *pages 200–205* to learn how to install a mortared shower pan.

B. Framing the shower

2×4 stud wall

Doubled 2×4 stud at outside corners

Protect base with a drop cloth

Cement backerboard

1 With the shower base in place, build 2×4 walls for the sides. Remember that the studs will be covered with ½-inch-thick cement board, plus the tiles (usually about ⅜ inch thick). No studs should be more than 16 inches apart. On the plumbing wall, space the studs so you can position the shower faucet—a pair of studs spaced about a foot apart will accommodate most faucets. Install horizontal braces to support the faucet and the showerhead arm. Some bases may require a ledger *(page 186)*. Install the supply pipes and faucet, following instructions on *pages 184–185, 210–211*.

2 Cut pieces of cement backerboard to fit. Cover all wood surfaces with the backerboard. Attach them to the studs with backerboard screws. Check that the wall surface is smooth and even because the tiles will follow any contours. Before tiling fill the gap at the bottom with caulk.

One-piece shower units

Corner and rectangular shower stalls—made of acrylic fiberglass or polystyrene—are much easier to install than a custom-made enclosure. One-piece units are designed for new construction only because they are too large to fit through a door. Three-piece units are quickly assembled and are ideal for remodeling.

Two or three walls of these units must be installed up against solid walls. A corner unit can be installed in any corner that is reasonably square. A rectangular or square unit requires an opening of the correct width and height.

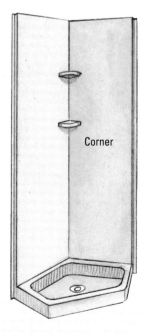

Corner

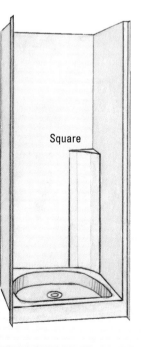

Square

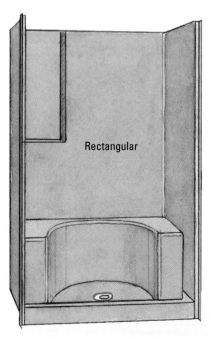

Rectangular

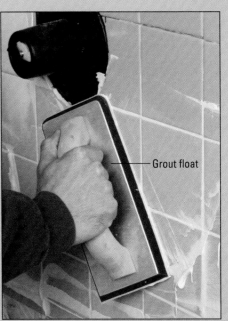

Grout float

3 Cover the backerboard with ceramic tile or with a prefab tub surround kit (pages 190–191). Consult a book on tiling for guidelines on selecting, laying out, and cutting tile. In general, tiling should be planned to minimize small pieces. Wherever a tile edge will be exposed, install a bullnose piece, which has one finished edge (see illustration below). Use a notched trowel to apply thinset mortar or organic tile adhesive, then set the tiles. Use a tile-cutting hole saw for the faucet and showerhead stubouts. Once all the tiles are applied, allow the adhesive to set overnight.

4 Mix a batch of latex-reinforced grout and use a grout float to first push the grout into the joints; then scrape away most of the excess. Wipe several times with a damp sponge, working to create consistent grout lines. Allow to dry and buff with a dry towel. Caulk all the inside corners.

CAULK THE EDGES OF THE STALL

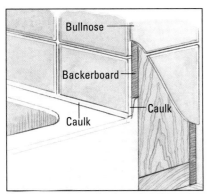

Bullnose

Backerboard

Caulk

Caulk

The bottom of a wall, where the tiles meet the shower base, must be installed correctly or water will seep behind the tiles and damage the studs. Install the backerboard to the top of the base's flange and fill the gap below with caulk. Apply tiles and apply a bead of caulk.

Installing a shower door

Jamb piece

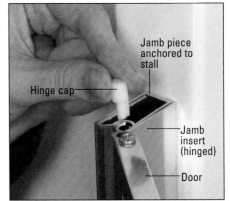

Hinge cap

Jamb piece anchored to stall

Jamb insert (hinged)

Door

Measure the opening and select a door with a frame you can adjust to fit your unit. Follow manufacturer's instructions. In general you'll begin by cutting the jamb piece to size and installing a bottom track and seal. Each jamb is made of two interlocking pieces. One attaches

to the stall with screws and anchors. When both jambs are installed, decide which way the door should swing and install the hinged insert with the clamps provided. Slide the door in place, cap, and add the door handle. Install the other jamb insert and adjust.

TILING A SHOWER ENCLOSURE OR TUB SURROUND

Because a shower enclosure is a wet installation, you must waterproof the walls and the framing. Use felt paper in combination with cement backerboard, but not with greenboard or waterproofed gypsum board.

A bathtub introduces additional challenges. If the tub is level, set a full tile at its top edge. To help hide the awkward appearance of an out-of-level tub, make the bottom row of tiles at least three-fourths of a tile high.

For a shower enclosure, extend the tile and the backerboard at least 6 inches above the showerhead. For a tub surround only, install the backerboard and tile 12 inches above the tub.

PRESTART CHECKLIST

☐ **TIME**
About 20 minutes per square yard to prepare and set tile

☐ **TOOLS**
Utility knife, stapler, hair dryer, 4-foot level, tape measure, chalk line, carbide scriber, margin trowel, notched trowel, straightedge, drill, snap cutter or wet saw, nippers, grout knife, putty knife, masonry stone, caulk gun, grout float

☐ **SKILLS**
Ability to use hand tools, cordless drill, and trowels

☐ **PREP**
Repair structural defects, remove finished wall material to studs

☐ **MATERIALS**
Asphalt roofing cement, 15-pound felt paper, staples, bucket, thinset, dimensional lumber for battens, backerboard, screws, tape, tile, spacers, caulk, grout, rags, sponge, water, tile base or bullnose, nylon wedges, accessories

A. Preparing the substrate

1 Apply asphalt roofing cement to the flange of the tub. This is the place where most tub and shower surrounds fail; water that gets into this joint will migrate upwards, and down into the floor. The asphalt cement seals the tub to the waterproofing felt or 4-mil poly sheet.

2 Cut a piece of felt paper long enough to turn all corners and cover the surface in a single run. Apply asphalt mastic to the studs, then staple the paper, warming it with a hair dryer before pressing it into the corners. Overlap top pieces on lower ones and seal overlaps with asphalt mastic.

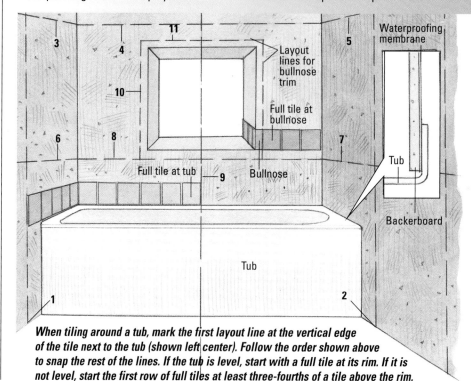

When tiling around a tub, mark the first layout line at the vertical edge of the tile next to the tub (shown left center). Follow the order shown above to snap the rest of the lines. If the tub is level, start with a full tile at its rim. If it is not level, start the first row of full tiles at least three-fourths of a tile above the rim.

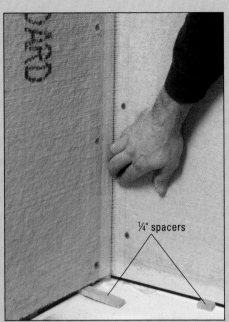

3 Cut backerboard so its edges will be centered on the studs and fasten it to the studs with backerboard screws. When fitting backerboard above a tub, leave a ¼-inch gap between the bottom edge of the board and the tub rim.

4 Reinforce the corners of the backerboard with fiberglass mesh tape. Skim-coat the tape with thinset, let it dry, and sand smooth. Repeat the process, feathering the edge of the thinset. The spacers create a ¼-inch gap for the bead of caulk.

5 Caulk the gap at the bottom of the backerboard with clear or white silicone caulk. The caulk seals the joint between the tub and backerboard, and allows for some expansion and contraction of the different materials.

Using a story pole

1 Make a story pole to mark the tile layout on walls. For square tiles set a row of tiles (and plastic spacers if they will be used) in the selected pattern on a flat surface. Mark a straight 1×2 to match the tile spacing. Include any narrow trim tiles or accent tiles. For rectangular and odd-shape tiles, make separate sticks for the horizontal and vertical layouts.

2 Use the story pole to mark the horizontal grout joints along the vertical reference line, beginning at the mark for the top row of tiles. If the cut tiles at the tub edge will be less than half the height of a full tile, move the top row up half the height of a tile. Note: If tiling to a ceiling, evenly divide the tiles to be cut at the ceiling and tub edge.

B. Installing the tile

1 Using a dimensional layout drawing, locate the point on which a horizontal and vertical grout line will fall. Hold a 4-foot level on both planes and mark reference lines. Then snap layout grids whose dimensions equal the width of the tiles and grout joints.

2 Tack a batten on the bottom of the wall, if necessary *(page 106)*, and prepare enough adhesive to cover the number of layout grids you can lay before the adhesive begins to set up. Set field tiles on the back wall first. Don't set tiles around fixtures yet.

3 When the back wall is done, set the side walls. Start from the front, leaving cut tiles for the back edge at the corner of the adjoining wall. Tape the tiles if necessary to hold them in place *(page 106)*. Remove excess adhesive from the joints; let it cure.

STANLEY Pro Tip

Cut the corners

Cut the tile at the corner of the tub carefully. This cut can be somewhat tricky, so it's best to lay out the curve on a cardboard template and transfer the line to the tile. Make relief cuts and bite out the curve with nippers.

Tack a Batten
Keeping the tiles level

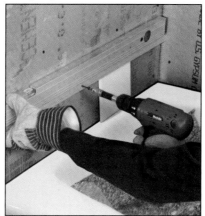

To keep the first row (and all that follow) level, tack a 1× batten to the backerboard one full tile width above the tub. Cover the tub with heavy paper to protect it from damage it might incur as you tile the wall.

Refresher Course
Measure the thread length

If you are tiling over existing wall tile or installing new tile with backerboard, the combined thickness of the new materials may exceed the length of the threads on the faucet valves. The threads of the valves need to extend beyond the new wall.

Before you install any tile, measure the depth of the threads. If they are less than the thickness of the new materials, you'll have to install new faucets—a job best left to a plumber.

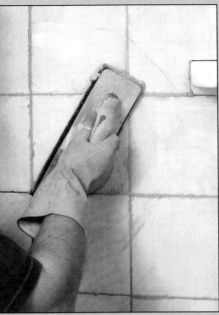

4 When the adhesive has dried overnight, cut and set the edge tiles and remove excess adhesive from the joints. Then mark, cut, and install the tile around the showerhead and faucets. Leave at least ¼ inch around the fixtures and fill that recess with silicone caulk. Let the adhesive cure.

5 When the adhesive is dry, clean the surface and joints of any remaining excess. Mix grout and apply it with a grout float, forcing it into the joints in both planes. Let the grout cure until a damp sponge won't lift the grout out of the joints.

6 To scrape excess grout off the surface, hold the float almost perpendicular to the tile and work diagonally to avoid pulling the grout from the joints. Dampen a sponge, wring it out thoroughly, and clean the surface twice, smoothing the joints. Scrub off the haze with a clean rag.

Installing a shower bench

1 Set the bench against the walls in its location and mark mounting holes. Drill mounting holes completely through substrate. Attach the bench form with screws, then remove the screws and fill the fastener holes with adhesive caulk. Refasten the bench to the wall.

2 Caulk all the edges at the wall with silicone caulk. Apply stiff mortar to completely fill the bench. Slope the mortar from the back to the front, packing it tightly.

3 Pack mortar into the bench form, filling any voids. Tile the bench before you tile the walls. Use bullnose for the edges or round the edges of field tiles with a masonry stone.

Installing surface-mounted fixtures

When you set the wall surface, leave a space for surface-mounted accessories, such as soap dishes, cutting the tile around it if necessary. Use a margin trowel to apply mortar to both the recess and the back of the accessory and press the unit into place. Keep it centered with wedges. Tape it in place until the mortar dries, then caulk the joint.

INSTALLING A MORTARED SHOWER PAN

A mortared shower pan allows you to custom-fit a shower enclosure. The key to a successful installation lies in the use of a chlorinated polyethylene (CPE) or PVC membrane—tough but flexible plastics that form the pan of the enclosure and make the floor waterproof. Over the membrane, a mortar bed floor supports the tile. Smaller tiles work best to conform to the slope.

This thick-bed installation relies on a troweled mortar mix which, when properly mixed, is like a sandy clay. Floating a thick bed takes two steps: floating the sloped subbase for the membrane and floating a reinforced top floor that follows the slope of the subbase. Because of its considerable weight, you should install it only on a slab or properly supported wood subfloor.

PRESTART CHECKLIST

☐ **TIME**
Two to three days to frame the enclosure, float the floor, and tile and grout the interior

☐ **TOOLS**
Carpenter's hammer, framing square, tape measure, 4-foot level, carbide scorer, utility knife, wrench, scissors, tinsnips, stapler, ½-inch drill, mixing paddle, notched trowel, grout float, jigsaw, marker, circular saw

☐ **SKILLS**
Basic framing skills, mixing and floating mortar, setting tile, grouting

☐ **PREP**
Strengthen and repair subfloor

☐ **MATERIALS**
Dimensional lumber, ¾-inch exterior plywood, backerboard, backerboard screws, dry mortar mix, metal lath, felt, staples, 4-mil polyethylene, thinset, CPE or PVC membrane and solvent, nails, masking tape, shower drain, tile, grout

A. Framing the stall

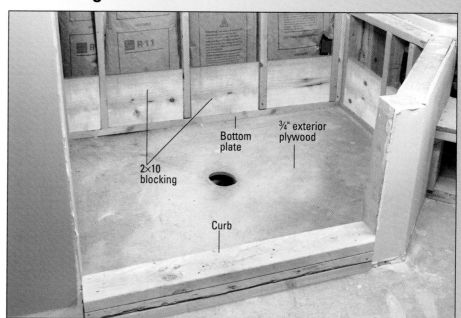

Bottom plate
¾" exterior plywood
2×10 blocking
Curb

Replace an unsound subfloor with ¾-inch exterior plywood. Cut pressure-treated bottom plates and preassemble the walls, centering the studs every 16 inches. Erect and brace the walls. Fasten the bottom plates to the floor with 3-inch decking screws and tie the top corners together. Toe-nail 2×10 blocking between the studs to support the sides of the membrane. Build the curb from three pressure-treated 2×4s. Tack ¾-inch guides around the perimeter (not necessary for stalls larger than 4 feet on both sides). Cut a hole in the center of the floor and fit the lower drain plate.

FIT THE LOWER DRAIN PLATE
Seal the drain to prevent leaks

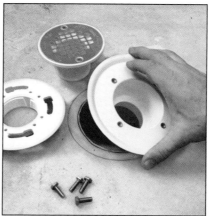 

1 Cut a hole in the floor with a hole saw or jigsaw (drilling a starter hole first). Coat the bottom of the lower drain with beads of silicone—one outside and one inside the bolt circle.

2 Coat the interior of the drain with PVC primer and cement, and twist the drain onto the waste line. Let the cement dry, then insert the drain bolts into the lower drain plate, leaving about ¾ inch exposed.

B. Building the sloped subbase

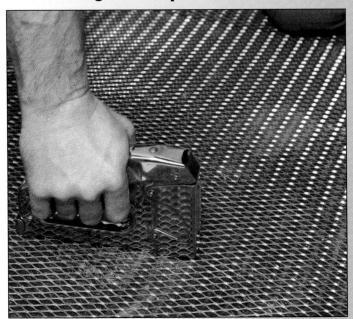

1 Cut a piece of 15-pound felt to fit the floor area between the bottom plates or the ¾-inch float guides, and staple the felt to the floor. Cut a section of metal lath to the same dimensions. The metal gives the floor a "tooth" for the mortar. Set the metal lath in place and snip out a circle about an inch wider than the circumference of the drain. Staple the entire sheet of metal lath securely to the floor, flattening any bumps that could weaken the subbase.

Plug drain hole temporarily with a towel or rag

2 Using bagged sand mix from your home center (or 4 parts sand, 1 part portland cement), mix up a batch of dry deck mud with latex additive (not water). Mix the mortar in a wheelbarrow (not a bucket). Dump the mortar onto the floor, spreading it with a wood float and sloping it from the top of the guides (or from the bottom wall plate on larger stalls) to the top of the drain flange. Compact the mortar into an even surface and let it dry overnight.

WHAT IF...
You want to install a mortared shower bench?

1 Spread mortar on the shower pan and set concrete block in the mortar. Plumb and level the block. Mortar the side pieces in place and repeat the process for the next course(s) of block. Then spread a level coat of thinset on the surfaces to be tiled.

2 Tile the bench as you would a wall, lining up the courses on the front of the bench with the courses on the walls. Finish tiling the shower and grout the entire installation. Seal the grout with the product recommended by the manufacturer.

DRY DECK MUD
The squeeze test

The mortar for a shower enclosure should be just wet enough to clump together. You'll know it's right when you squeeze it and it just holds its shape.

C. Installing the membrane and upper drain plate

1 Roll out the membrane on the surrounding floor. Mark the cut lines 9 inches larger than the shower floor on the sides and back, and 16 inches larger in the front (to cover all faces of the curb). If the stall is larger than the membrane, solvent-weld additional sections. Reinforce the drain area by solvent-welding a 10-inch circle of membrane in the center. Roll or fold the membrane so it fits easily in the enclosure.

2 Set the membrane on the floor of the enclosure and unroll it from front to back, pulling it forward until it covers the front of the curb. Working from the drain outward, smooth out the air bubbles. Then staple the top 1 inch of the sheet to the blocking. Weld the corners and cut the sheet at the bottom of the jambs. Fold the sheet over the curb and tack it only on the front. Solvent-weld a dam corner (available from the manufacturer) over the jamb cuts.

STANLEY PRO TIP

Keep the membrane flat

Shower pan membranes must lie flat on the subbase and against the sides. Wrinkles create air pockets that weaken the bed. It can be difficult to keep the membrane flat on the sloped subbase, especially in large enclosures. To keep the membrane flat as you smooth out the air bubbles, trowel a thin coat of asphalt mastic or laminating adhesive on the subbase and blocking. Make sure the adhesive you use is compatible with the membrane material.

WHAT IF...
You need to add another section of membrane?

If the shower enclosure is larger than the CPE or PVC sheet, you will need to seam an additional section. Coat both sides of the seam with the primer or sealer appropriate to the material, covering about 4 inches from the edges. Let the primer dry. Overlap the edges and roll them tightly. After 5 minutes try to separate the seam. If it comes apart, repeat the process.

WELD THE CORNERS
Make the membrane watertight

After stapling the membrane along its length, you will have excess material at the corners. Fold the corners into triangles and solvent-weld the folds in place.

3 To cut the membrane so the bolts will be exposed, feel around each raised bolt head and press the membrane down until the profile of the bolt shows clearly. Then with a sharp utility knife, cut a ⅜-inch "X" in the membrane over the bolts—just enough to allow you to push the membrane over the bolt head. Then unscrew the bolts so you can fasten the upper drain plate.

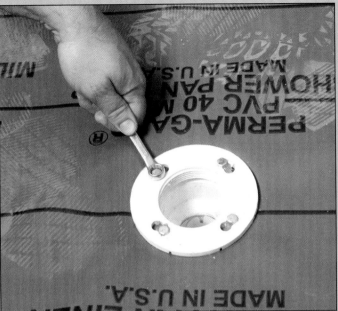

4 Position the upper drain plate so the holes are directly above the X cuts in the membrane. Don't seal the underside of this plate with silicone—it will clog the weep holes. Reinsert the bolts in the holes, turn the plate to lock it, if necessary, and tighten the bolts evenly with a wrench. Using a long sharp knife, carefully cut away the membrane in the drain hole. (Don't use a utility knife. Its blade is not long enough to make a clean cut.) Then check for leaks.

CHECK FOR LEAKS

To check for leaks in the membrane, plug the drain hole with an expandable stopper, which you can purchase at a hardware store.

Fill the pan with water to about an inch from the top of the membrane. Let the water come to rest, mark its level on the side of the pan, and let the water sit for 24 hours. Then check the level. If it's still at the mark, the pan is watertight. If the water is below the mark, the membrane has a leak somewhere.

Check the surrounding floor for water, which would have come from a leak in the side. If there's no evidence of water, pull the plug, expand its diameter a little, and repeat the test.

If the water has drained out completely, it's probably leaking at the drain flange, which is either too loose or too tight (and may have cut the membrane). Tighten the bolts if they feel too loose. If the flange has cut the membrane, remove the drain plate, let the membrane dry completely, and solvent-weld a patch at least 2 inches larger than the puncture.

Installing the strainer

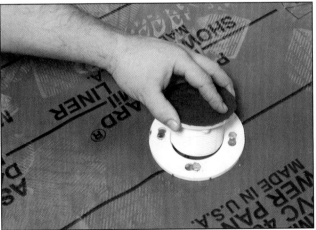

Wrap the threads of the strainer with four or five turns of plumber's tape and screw the strainer into the flange. To protect the strainer and drain from stray mortar and thinset, apply two layers of crisscrossed masking tape. Overlap the tape and cut it flush around the edge of the strainer.

D. Installing the mortared floor

1 If any of the walls are outside walls, insulate them with fiberglass batts. Then cut sheets of 4-mil polyethylene waterproofing membrane long enough to hang from the top of the walls down to 3 or 4 inches below the top edge of the pan membrane. Use only four or five staples on each stud to attach the poly, the minimum necessary to keep it in place. Make sure you don't put staples through the pan membrane lower than 1 inch from the top.

2 Clean off any grit with a damp cloth. As added protection you can cover the liner with a drop cloth to prevent a backerboard corner from puncturing it. Cut backerboard to fit the walls and set it on ½-inch shims. Fasten the backerboard to the studs with backerboard screws *(page 194);* keep the screws within the top 1 inch of the pan membrane. Remove the shims and caulk the space at the bottom with silicone. Tape and mud the seams with modified thinset.

Sloping the floor

1 Using a torpedo level or 2-foot level (the longest size that will fit the enclosure), transfer the plane of the bottom of the strainer to the walls and the curb. Mark the plane on the backerboard with a felt-tip pen.

2 The floor of the pan must slope ¼ inch for every linear foot. Compute the amount of slope based on the dimensions of the enclosure and mark this point on the backerboard.

3 Mark the slope on the walls. Protect the weep holes from clogging and mix up another batch of dry mortar. Spread the mortar about halfway to your marks, keeping the slope at about one-third of a bubble on a level. Lay metal lath over the first course, then pack and level a top layer, starting at the wall, even with the marks. Work in sections, sloping the floor toward the drain. Bend lath to fit the curb and pack it also, slanting the top inward.

E. Laying the floor tile

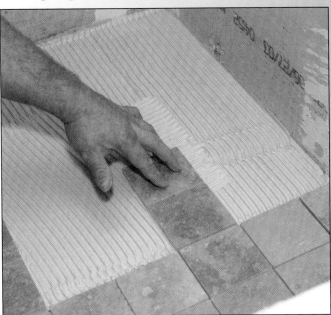

When the floor has dried, scrape off any remaining imperfections with a steel trowel, then spread and comb latex-modified thinset. Press the tiles firmly into the mortar to make sure they conform to the slope of the floor. Line up all the edges with a 2-foot straightedge and let the mortar cure overnight. Grout the tiles with latex-modified grout, cleaning off the excess and wiping off the grout haze.

PROTECT THE WEEP HOLES

Weep holes allow moisture trapped in the mortar bed to escape down the drain. If the moisture can't go down, it will go up—into your grout, causing mold and mildew. To keep the weep holes from clogging with mortar, put a few spacers or pieces of gravel around them.

STANLEY PRO TIP

Prebend the lath

Metal lath is sharp, especially its cut edges, and can easily put holes in the membrane that covers the curb. To avoid puncturing the membrane when fitting the lath, prebend the lath over the 2×4s before installing the membrane. Make the bends slightly oversize so you can put the lath section down over the curb without tearing the membrane.

WHAT IF...
You puncture the membrane?

If you do happen to puncture the liner, it doesn't mean you have to take the whole thing up and start over. Clean the punctured area thoroughly and cut a patch at least 2 inches wider than the puncture. Apply the appropriate solvent to both the membrane and the patch. Roll the patch flat and let the repair dry.

Don't forget the tile
Don't mortar right to the top of the drain. Leave room for the tile so it comes out level with the top of the drain.

INSTALLING A WHIRLPOOL TUB

Some whirlpool tubs (also called spas) have a finished side or two, so framing for the side panel and tiling are not required. Rectangular models install much like a standard tub *(pages 186–188)*, except that a GFCI electrical receptacle is required. Triangular whirlpools fit into a corner.

The drop-in model shown on these pages fits into a frame. No special supply lines are needed; the whirlpool circulates water after it's filled by a standard spout. Some models have heaters to keep the water hot without replenishing. Other models have their own spouts; follow the manufacturer's instructions for running supply lines.

Large whirlpools are very heavy when filled with water, so you may need to strengthen the floor by adding joists. Check the manufacturer's instructions and local codes.

Ideally it's best to lay flooring after the tub is framed and installed but before tiling.

PRESTART CHECKLIST

☐ **TIME**
Two or three days to frame, install, and tile a whirlpool tub

☐ **TOOLS**
Carpentry tools, groove-joint pliers, PVC saw, wiring tools, tiling tools, putty knife, screwdriver, adjustable wrench

☐ **SKILLS**
Connecting PVC pipe, basic carpentry, basic wiring, installing tiles

☐ **PREP**
Measure the space carefully, taking into account the framing, backerboard, and tile thickness

☐ **MATERIALS**
Whirlpool tub, waste-and-overflow unit, lumber and screws for framing, GFCI receptacle, cable, breaker, cement backerboard with screws, mortar mix, tile, mastic, grout, caulk, spacers, pipe-thread tape, rag, wheelbarrow

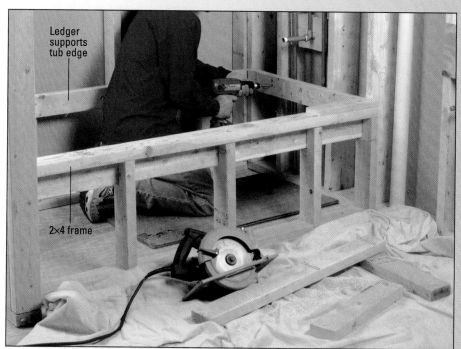

Ledger supports tub edge

2×4 frame

1 Build a frame following the manufacturer's directions. It's especially important to get the height right. You may snug the whirlpool up against one, two, or three walls. Where you snug the tub against the wall, attach a 2×4 ledger as you would for a standard tub *(page 186)*. Where you will install tiles, plan the framing carefully, taking into account the thickness of the backerboard and tile (Steps 2 and 11). Most whirlpools require access to the plumbing at one end and the pump motor at the other end; check the manufacturer's directions.

WHIRLPOOL TUB INSTALLATION

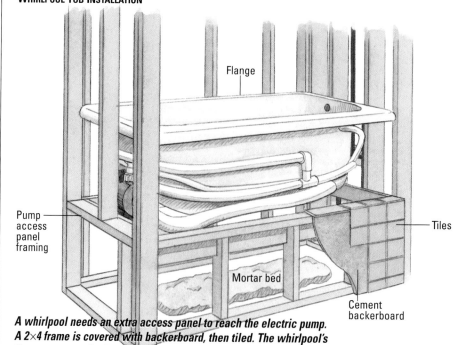

Flange

Pump access panel framing

Tiles

Mortar bed

Cement backerboard

A whirlpool needs an extra access panel to reach the electric pump. A 2×4 frame is covered with backerboard, then tiled. The whirlpool's flange rests on tile, but its weight must be supported by a mortar bed.

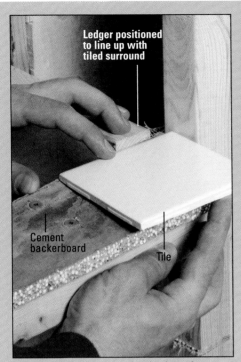

Ledger positioned to line up with tiled surround

Cement backerboard

Tile

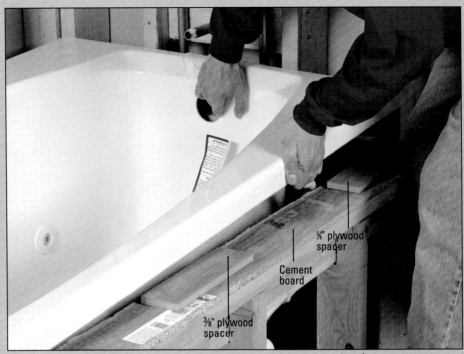

⅜" plywood spacer

Cement board

⅜" plywood spacer

2 Cut strips of cement backerboard to fit where needed on top of the framing. Backerboard pieces should overhang the framing by ½ inch. You can also cut the side backerboard pieces, but don't install them yet. Attach the backerboard using special backerboard screws.

3 Cut several spacers ⅛ inch thicker than the tiles you will install. (For ¼-inch-thick tiles, cut pieces of ⅜-inch plywood.) Set the spacers on top of the backerboard wherever there will be tile.

Set the whirlpool in place and see that it fits. Be sure the bottom of the tub is at the correct depth so it will rest on the mortar bed (Steps 7 and 8).

Installing a GFCI receptacle

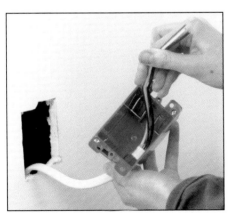

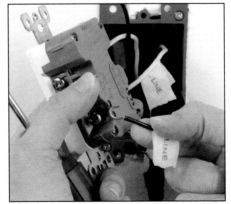

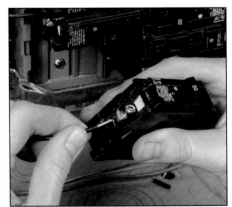

Most whirlpools plug into a GFCI receptacle, though some are hardwired into an electrical box. For most models you will need a 15-amp circuit that supplies only the whirlpool. Check the manufacturer's instructions. Consult with an electrician if you are not sure how to run cable and install a new circuit. Use cable that meets

local codes—either NM cable, armored cable, or conduit with wires running through it. Run cable from the service panel to the whirlpool. Strip the cable and clamp it to an electrical box (left).

Wire a GFCI receptacle (center), wrap the connections, secure the receptacle in the box, and attach a cover plate.

Shut off power to the service panel. Strip the cable and connect the hot wire to a new electrical breaker (above). Connect the neutral and ground wires to the neutral and/or ground bus bar, and snap the breaker into place. Restore power and test.

INSTALLING A WHIRLPOOL TUB *(continued)*

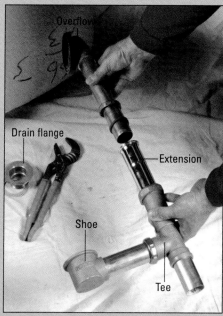

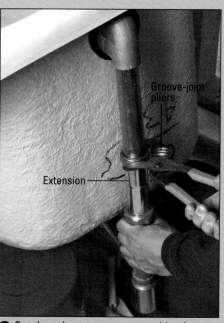

4 Check to make sure the drain trap is positioned at the correct height so that the whirlpool waste-and-overflow unit will slide into it (Step 9). Plan how you will make this connection, either from the basement or crawlspace below or through the access panel *(pages 178–181)*.

5 Assemble the waste-and-overflow unit. Some whirlpools come with a waste-and-overflow; if not you'll have to purchase a standard unit and add an extension (shown). Insert the shoe (cut to length if necessary) into the tee fitting.

6 Set the tub on two overturned buckets. Install the overflow by slipping in the plunger assembly, tightening the screws on the cover plate, and screwing the drain flange into the shoe *(page 187)*. Tighten the nuts on the drain extension.

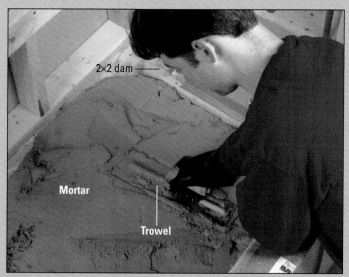

7 Test-fit the whirlpool to see that the waste-and-overflow unit will slip into the drain trap. Remove the whirlpool. Screw 2×2s to the floor around the drain hole to keep mortar out of the hole. In a bucket or wheelbarrow, mix water with dry mortar mix. The mortar should be just wet enough to be poured. Smooth enough mortar onto the floor to support the bottom of the whirlpool.

8 Place spacers (Step 3) on the backerboard atop the side-panel frame. With a helper gently set the tub in place. Guide the waste-and-overflow into the drain trap but do not tighten the connection. Push down on the tub until the lip rests on the spacers, but do not press hard. Allow the mortar to harden overnight.

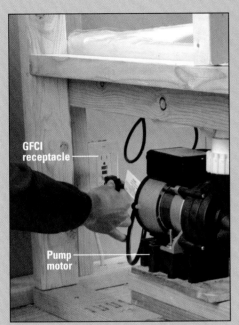

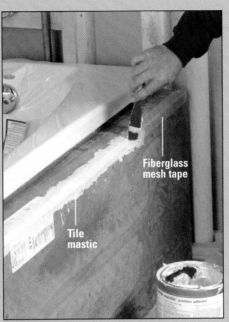

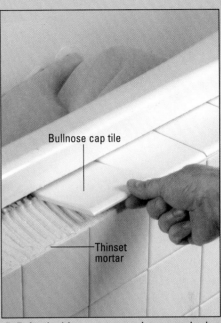

9 Connect the waste-and-overflow to the drain and tighten the fittings *(page 188).* Support the pump motor with pieces of lumber and attach it in place with screws. Plug the cord into the GFCI receptacle. Follow the manufacturer's instructions for testing the whirlpool.

10 Install cement backerboard on all exposed sides. Drive backerboard screws every 6 inches or so. Wrap corners with fiberglass mesh tape.

11 Apply thinset mortar using a notched trowel and set standard tiles on the side. When tiling the top edge, use bullnose caps for the outside corner for a finished look. After the thinset has dried, apply grout and clean the joints. Caulk the joint where the whirlpool rests on the tiles.

Adding the tub hardware

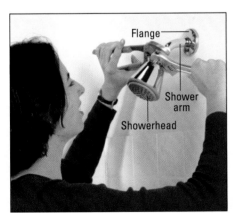

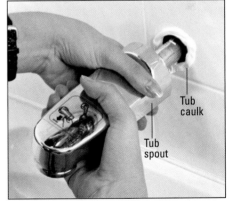

1 Once the wall is finished, wrap pipe-thread tape around the ends of the shower arm and screw it into place. Slip on the flange. Twist on the showerhead, then tighten with an adjustable wrench and groove-joint pliers. Protect the chrome with tape.

2 Following the manufacturer's instructions, slide the escutcheon over the faucet and screw it into place. It should seal against the tiles with a rubber gasket. Attach the faucet handle.

3 Apply caulk around the spout hole. Choose a nipple of proper length for the spout and wrap pipe-thread tape around the threads of both ends. Twist the spout on by hand. Finish by wrapping the spout with a rag and tightening it against the wall with groove-joint pliers.

HOOKING UP A SHOWER OR TUB FAUCET

This plan calls for separate ¾-inch lines to supply the shower. This ensures good water pressure and protects anyone in the shower from a sudden change of temperature when a faucet is turned on or the toilet tank refills. Tap into the house's cold and hot water lines as near to the water heater as possible.

Choose the tub or shower faucet before you start installing pipes. Read the manufacturer's directions carefully so you know exactly where the pipes should go.

If your faucet does not have integrated shutoff valves (see *page 211*), install reachable shutoff valves on the lines leading to the shower so you can easily turn off the water if repairs are needed.

Assuming an 18-inch-tall tub, position the faucet about 28 inches above the floor for a tub, about 48 inches for a shower. You may want to compromise and position it about 38 inches above the floor.

PRESTART CHECKLIST

☐ **TIME**
About half a day to run supply lines and install a tub/shower faucet

☐ **TOOLS**
Drill, propane torch, tubing cutter, multiuse wire brush, flame guard, damp rag, groove-joint pliers, flux brush

☐ **SKILLS**
Accurate measuring and drilling, working with copper pipe

☐ **PREP**
Tap into the hot and cold water lines and run ¾-inch pipe up into the room; if needed, move a stud to make room for the plumbing behind the tub

☐ **MATERIALS**
Tub/shower faucet, copper pipe and fittings, flux, solder, pipe-thread tape

Crossbrace

1× scrap stands for ½" backerboard plus ¼" tile

1 Most faucets come with a plastic cover that protects the faucet and serves as a guide for the depth at which it must be set. To determine where to place the braces, consider the total thickness of the finished wall—often ½-inch-thick backerboard plus ¼-inch-thick tiles.

2×6 crossbrace

2 Determine how high you want to locate the spout (make sure it will clear the tub), the faucet handles, and the showerhead. Install a 2×6 brace for each. Anchor the braces with screws rather than nails so you can move them more easily if they need adjustment.

TUB/SHOWER INSTALLATION

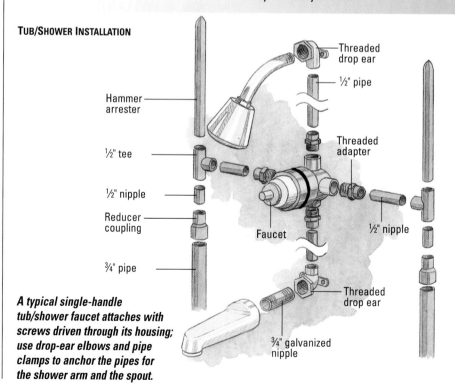

Threaded drop ear

½" pipe

Hammer arrester

Threaded adapter

½" tee

½" nipple

½" nipple

Reducer coupling

Faucet

¾" pipe

Threaded drop ear

¾" galvanized nipple

A typical single-handle tub/shower faucet attaches with screws driven through its housing; use drop-ear elbows and pipe clamps to anchor the pipes for the shower arm and the spout.

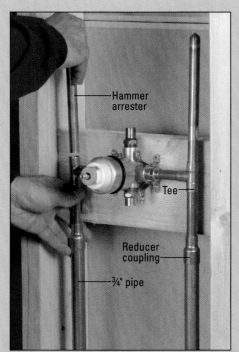

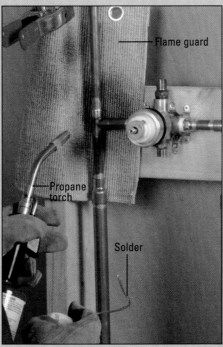

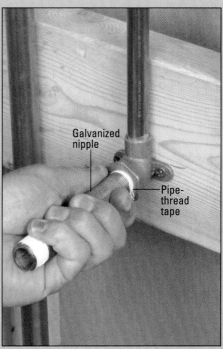

3 Assemble all the pipes in a dry run. Install ¾-inch pipe up to the height of the faucet, add reducer couplings or elbows, and run short lengths of ½-inch pipe to the threaded adapters on the faucet. Add hammer arresters. Anchor the faucet according to the manufacturer's directions.

4 Once you are sure of the connections, sweat all the fittings *(pages 140–141)*. Start at the faucet, then move on to the shower arm and spout connections. Run ½-inch pipe up to the shower arm and down to the spout; attach drop-ear elbows at both spots.

5 Finger-tighten a threaded nipple—either brass or galvanized—into both drop-ear elbows. Once the wallcovering is in place, remove them and install the shower arm and the tub spout.

STANLEY PRO TIP

Add reinforcement to shower-arm drop ears

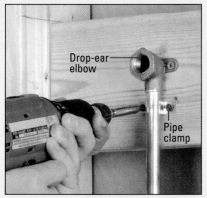

Whacking the showerhead with your elbow can bend or crack a drop-ear elbow. As an extra safeguard, screw a pipe clamp just below the drop ear.

WHAT IF...
You have other faucet setups?

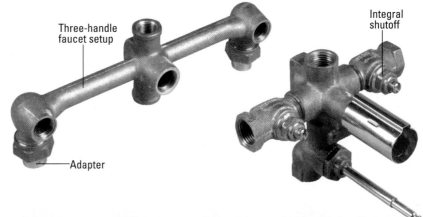

A three-handle faucet may require that supply pipes be spread farther apart than for a single-handle faucet. Threaded adapters screw in for the supplies, spout, or shower arm.

A faucet with integral shutoffs comes with a large escutcheon (cover plate), so you can more easily reach the shutoff valves.

INSTALLING A TOILET

Installing a toilet is one of the last things you will accomplish in your bathroom remodeling project. Before the toilet is installed, complete the rough plumbing, run electrical lines, and install the lights, switches, receptacles, and a ceiling fan. Lay the finish flooring if you haven't already done so. Install cement backerboard on the walls that surround the tub/shower *(pages 192–195)* and moisture-resistant drywall (also called greenboard) on the other walls. Tile or apply prefab sheets to the tub/shower surround. Tape, prime, and paint the walls and the ceiling. You may want to install baseboard and trim, but often it's best to wait until the sink and toilet are installed to avoid bumps and nicks on the trim.

To install a stop valve for the toilet, follow the instructions on *pages 150–151.* Measure the length of the supply tube needed and confirm the connection dimensions.

PRESTART CHECKLIST

☐ **TIME**
Half a day to install a toilet

☐ **TOOLS**
Adjustable wrench, groove-joint pliers, torpedo level, screwdriver, drill

☐ **SKILLS**
Assembling plumbing parts, cementing PVC fittings

☐ **PREP**
Finish all the wiring, carpentry, and wall preparation; remove the drop cloth from the floor

☐ **MATERIALS**
Toilet, wax ring, toilet flange with bolts, supply tubes and decorative flanges, toilet, plumber's putty, silicone sealant, caulk, PVC primer and glue

Installing a toilet

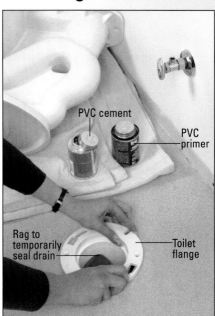

1 Install finish flooring to within an inch of the drain hole. The toilet flange can rest on top of the finished floor or on top of the subflooring. Test-fit the flange, then prime and glue it so that you will be able to place the hold-down bolts on either side of the opening (Step 2). Remove the rag.

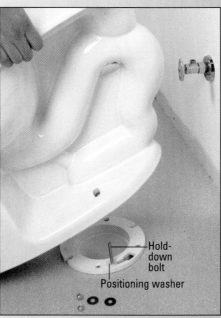

2 Press a wax ring onto the bottom of the toilet. Place the hold-down bolts in the flange and slip plastic positioning washers over them. Lower the bowl, threading the bolts through the holes in the bowl. Press down to seat the bowl firmly. Slip on washers and nuts and gently tighten.

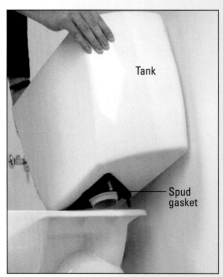

3 Assemble the tank and the bowl of a new toilet following the manufacturer's instructions. A large spud gasket seals the opening below the flush-valve seat. Place a rubber washer under the head of each mounting bolt. Don't overtighten the nuts.

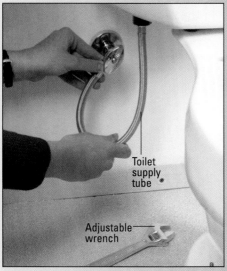

4 Attach a toilet supply tube by hand-tightening the nuts at the underside of the tank and the stop valve. Tighten a half turn or more with a wrench and open the stop valve. You may need to tighten the connection a bit farther.

Installing a pressure-assist toilet

Tighten nut on flange bolt   Supply tube

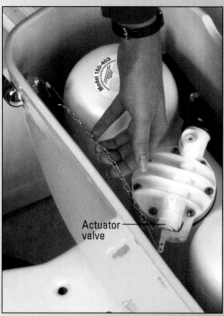

Actuator valve

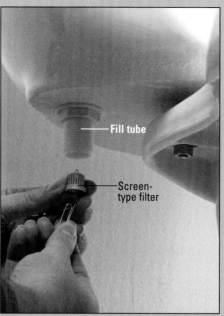

Fill tube

Screen-type filter

1 Many people want more flushing power than modern 1.6-gallon toilets provide. A pressure-assist toilet delivers a more forceful flush. It installs the same way as a standard toilet.

2 Some manufacturers use a chain to link the flush handle to the actuator valve. Check that the chain is nearly taut; too loose a chain won't fully open the actuator valve and will interrupt the flush.

3 A screen-type filter at the base of the fill tube catches bits of rust and minerals. Check it periodically by turning off the supply valve and detaching the supply tube. Pry out the filter with a bent paper clip and flush it with hot water. Reassemble and attach the tube.

UPFLUSH TOILET INSTALLATION

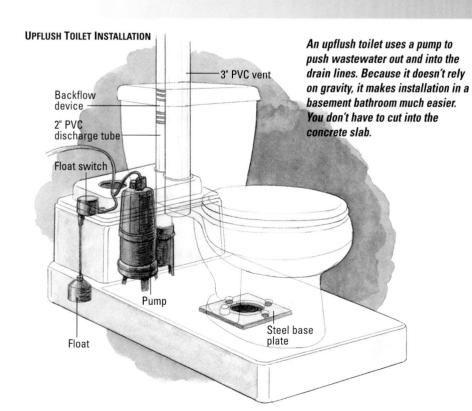

3" PVC vent

Backflow device

2" PVC discharge tube

Float switch

Pump

Float

Steel base plate

An upflush toilet uses a pump to push wastewater out and into the drain lines. Because it doesn't rely on gravity, it makes installation in a basement bathroom much easier. You don't have to cut into the concrete slab.

How much will you save?

Old toilets use from 3 to 5 gallons per flush. That adds up to serious water usage, so current federal regulations require that toilets use no more than 1.6 gallons per flush.

The first low-use toilets were no different from their older counterparts, except they allowed less water into the tank. As a result people often had to flush two or more times to clear the bowl, sending water savings down the drain!

Newer 1.6-gallon toilets are better designed, so water flows more smoothly and waste is more effectively flushed away. For maximum efficiency buy a power-assist toilet such as the one shown on this page.

If you have an older toilet and want to decrease water consumption, put a brick or two into the tank to displace water.

INSTALLING A PEDESTAL SINK

A pedestal sink saves space in a bathroom but requires strong support from the wall, which often means adding extra framing.

Installing the framing and patching the wall will take more time than the plumbing. The project will probably require several days. On the first day, install the framing and patch the wall. On the second day, finish the patching and paint the wall. Install the sink on the third day. (If you have a tiled wall, consider installing the framing by cutting into the wall in the room behind the sink location.)

An inexpensive pedestal sink may actually rest on the pedestal—an arrangement that makes the plumbing installation difficult and future repairs nearly impossible. Buy a sink that mounts on a bracket; the pedestal is for looks only.

If your supply lines are close together, you may be able to hide them behind the pedestal. Otherwise let the plumbing show.

PRESTART CHECKLIST

☐ **TIME**
About five hours of work spread over a period of three days (see above)

☐ **TOOLS**
Drill, hammer, drywall saw, taping knife, sanding block, paintbrush, screwdriver, adjustable wrench, groove-joint pliers

☐ **SKILLS**
Installing a bathroom faucet with pop-up drain, connecting a trap, cutting drywall

☐ **PREP**
Locate studs behind the wall near the plumbing

☐ **MATERIALS**
Pedestal sink, bathroom faucet, supply tubes that fit the stop valves, plumber's putty, 2×6 or 2×8 piece, screws, drywall, joint compound, drywall tape, paint

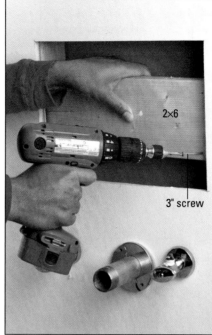

1 Measure and mark the bracket height. To support the bracket, cut a hole in the wall that spans two studs. Cut a piece of 2×6 or 2×8 to fit between the studs and attach it with screws. Drive the screws at an angle through the brace and into the studs.

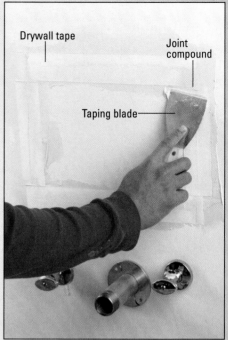

2 Cut a piece of drywall to fit and attach it to the brace with screws. Smooth pieces of drywall tape around the edges. Use a taping blade to cover the tape with joint compound. Allow the compound to dry, then sand until the patch is smooth. Paint the patch.

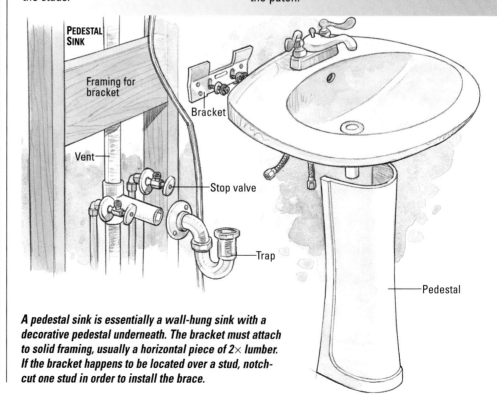

A pedestal sink is essentially a wall-hung sink with a decorative pedestal underneath. The bracket must attach to solid framing, usually a horizontal piece of 2× lumber. If the bracket happens to be located over a stud, notch-cut one stud in order to install the brace.

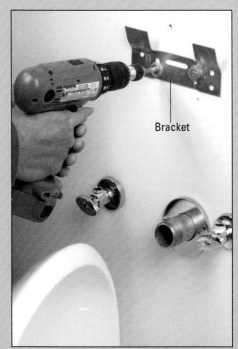

3 Set the sink on top of the pedestal and against the wall. Hold the bracket in place and mark the position of the bracket. Install the bracket by driving screws through the wall into the 2× brace.

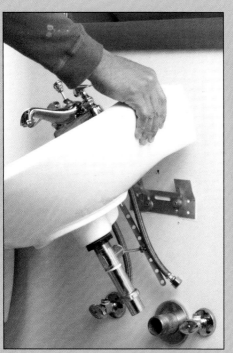

4 Install the faucet and the drain body on the sink *(pages 210–211)*. Lower the sink onto the bracket. Slide the pedestal in place to make sure the bracket is at the right height and adjust it, if necessary. Hook the supply tubes to the stop valves and attach the drain.

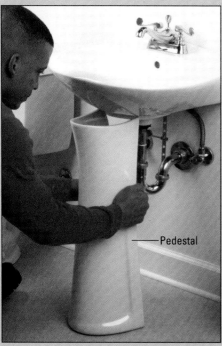

5 Slide the pedestal under the sink. Stand back to determine if the pedestal looks level and sits squarely on the floor. Adjust it as needed. You may caulk the bottom of the pedestal or leave it uncaulked so it can be removed for cleaning.

WHAT IF...
You want a freestanding bowl sink?

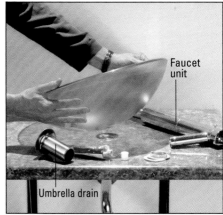

1 Drill two holes in the countertop, one for the drain and one for the faucet. There is no overflow, so use an umbrella drain (shown), which covers the drain but does not close it. Apply silicone sealant and anchor by tightening the nut from below.

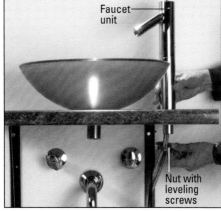

2 The faucet unit comes with flexible supply tubes already attached. Apply silicone sealant to the bottom of the faucet and drop the lines through the hole in the countertop. Anchor the faucet from below by tightening the nut and leveling screws.

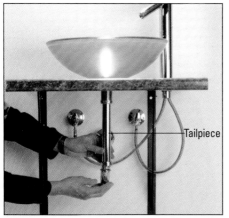

3 Wrap the threads of the stop valves with pipe-thread tape and attach the supply tubes. Make a tailpiece from a section of trap and attach it with a rubber washer and trap nut.

INSTALLING A SINK FAUCET

Like a kitchen sink, a bathroom sink typically has three holes, but they are spaced closer together. Installation is similar to a kitchen faucet, with the added complication of a pop-up stopper assembly.

Unless you have a wall-hung sink with no cabinet or pedestal below, the work space under a bathroom sink can be cramped. If you have a pedestal sink, check to see whether the bowl is securely attached to a wall bracket. If so you can remove the pedestal while you work *(pages 214–215)*. If you have a vanity sink with a cabinet below, it may be easier to detach the trap, remove the sink, and install the faucet with the sink on top of sawhorses.

If there are no stop valves under the sink, install them before putting in the new sink *(pages 150–151)*.

Whether you reuse the old supply tubes or buy new ones, make sure they are long enough to reach the stop valves. Purchase fittings (either ⅜ or ½ inch) that will fit your stop valves.

PRESTART CHECKLIST

☐ **TIME**
About two hours to install a bathroom faucet with a pop-up drain assembly

☐ **TOOLS**
Screwdriver, adjustable wrench, putty knife, groove-joint pliers, basin wrench

☐ **SKILLS**
Shutting off water, working under a sink, attaching plumbing parts

☐ **PREP**
Shut off the water to the old faucet; if the drain trap is in the way, you may have to remove it

☐ **MATERIALS**
New faucet, new pop-up drain (usually comes with the faucet), plumber's putty, perhaps supply tubes

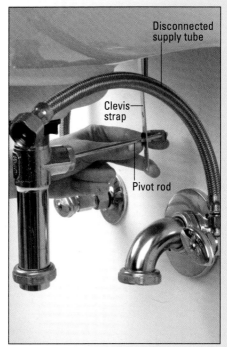

1 **Shut off the water.** From below disconnect the supply tubes and the mounting nuts from the stop valves. Loosen the setscrew that holds the clevis strap to the lifter rod, pinch the spring clip, and slide the clevis strap off the pivot rod.

2 Pull out the old faucet and clean the sink deck. You may be able to connect the supply tubes to the faucet using two wrenches. If no rubber gasket is provided, press a rope of putty to the sink deck or to the underside of the faucet body. Lower the faucet into place.

TWO TYPES OF BATHROOM FAUCETS

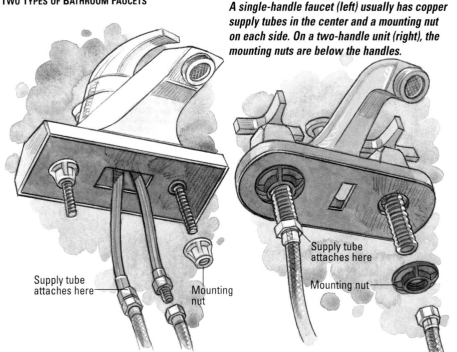

A single-handle faucet (left) usually has copper supply tubes in the center and a mounting nut on each side. On a two-handle unit (right), the mounting nuts are below the handles.

Supply tube attaches here

Mounting nut

Supply tube attaches here

Mounting nut

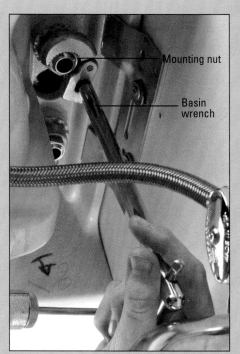

3 Have a helper hold the faucet straight while you tighten mounting nuts from below. If the faucet is not solidly attached after hand-tightening, use a basin wrench to tighten the nuts farther.

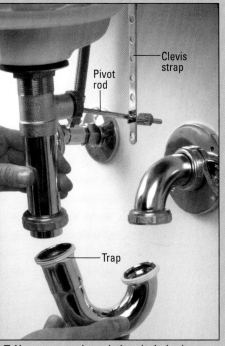

4 You can use the existing drain body or install a new drain body. With the stopper closed all the way, slide the clevis strap onto the lift rod and the pivot rod, using the spring clip to hold it in place. Tighten the setscrew that holds the strap to the lift rod. Install the trap.

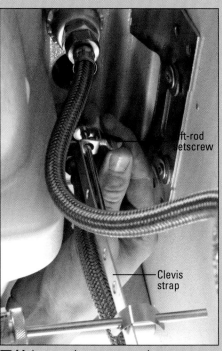

5 Make sure the stopper seals water when the lift rod is pulled up and that it opens fully when the rod is pushed down. To adjust, loosen the setscrew and move the clevis strap up or down.

Install a new drain body

1 Loosen the slip nut to disconnect the drain body from the trap. Remove the locknut under the sink and slide out the old drain body. Clean away caked-on putty. Place a new rope of putty around the hole, slip the new drain flange through the hole, and press it into place.

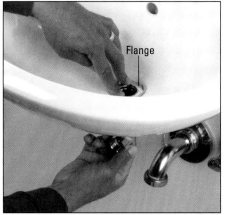

2 Twist the locknut onto the drain body, and slip on the friction washer and the rubber gasket. Hold the flange with one hand while you hand-tighten the drain body into it. Tighten the locknut with groove-joint pliers, taking care that the drain body faces rear.

3 Install the pivot rod and the clevis strap (see Step 4 above). Apply pipe-thread tape to the threaded end of the tailpiece and screw it onto the drain body. Install the trap.

INSTALLING GRAB BARS

Grab bars, once considered a luxury, or simply a requirement for accessible bathrooms, are more and more considered "standard" for any bathroom. Installed at locations that contribute to falls, they greatly increase the safety of any bathroom.

As their use has become increasingly prevalent, grab bars are also beginning to make a design statement. You'll find them in an assortment of colors, shapes, and sizes.

The most comfortable style will be one with a 1¼- to 1½-inch diameter installed at the same distance from the wall. Make sure the anchors you use can support at least 250 pounds.

If you're installing them in a new bathroom, plan their location and back them up with blocking. If you're retrofitting them into an existing bath, it's best to anchor them in the studs.

PRESTART CHECKLIST

☐ **TIME**
About 20–30 minutes for each bar

☐ **TOOLS**
Tape measure, pencil, stud finder, level, cordless drill, masonry bit, screwdriver bits, screwdriver, cold steel punch

☐ **SKILLS**
Using a stud finder, measuring, drilling in tile, fastening with cordless drill

☐ **PREP**
Install blocking in new walls

☐ **MATERIALS**
Wall anchors, mounting screws, grab bars, masking tape, hollow wall anchors, silicone caulk, china marker

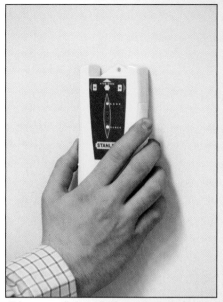

1 In a retrofit installation, use a stud finder to locate the studs and mark their location on the wall. Use a china marker on tile. Stud finders may not "see" through a tiled surface, so try to locate the studs in an area above the tile. If you can't find the studs, you'll have to use heavy-duty hollow wall anchors.

2 At both ends of the bar location, mark the fastener holes. Depending on the pattern of the holes, try to get at least two of them on the stud. Mark one side first, then use a level to mark the other side. As an alternative, mount one fastener in one flange and use a level on the bar to position the other side.

LOCATING GRAB BARS

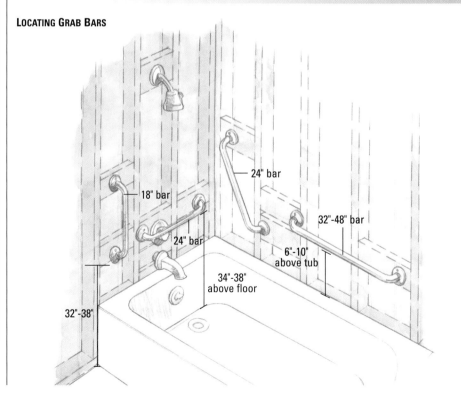

24" bar

18" bar

24" bar

32"-48" bar

6"-10" above tub

34"-38" above floor

32"-38"

3 Use the point of a cold steel punch to chip the surface of the tile. Without this small hole in the surface, the drill will not penetrate the tile. Cover the tile with masking tape to minimize chipping. Drill a ⅛-inch hole first with a masonry bit, then drill again with a fastener or anchor-size bit.

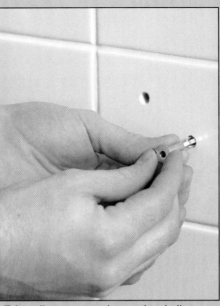

4 Install masonry or heavy-duty hollow wall anchors if the holes don't hit a stud. Follow the manufacturer's installation instructions and push the anchor in flush with the surface of the tile.

5 Apply a bead of silicone caulk around the edge of the flange. Insert the fastener in the flange and then in the anchor hole. That will keep the flange from sliding. Tighten all fasteners until the bar does not move when you apply force.

LOCATING GRAB BARS

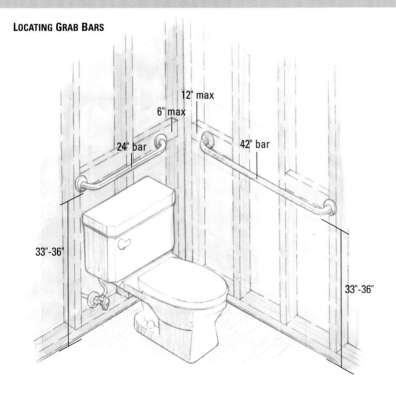

12" max
6" max
24" bar
42" bar
33"-36"
33"-36"

WHAT IF…
A fastener falls between the studs?

If you hit the studs with two out of the three fasteners, anchor the bar in the remaining hole with toggle bolts. Make sure to snug, but not overtighten, the bolt screw.

VANITIES & CABINETS

A vanity and cabinets can make a major contribution to both the design and comfort of your bathroom. Because of their size, and the fact that much of the activity of the bath takes place around them, they occupy center stage in a bathroom design.

Installing your own cabinetry requires only a moderate familiarity with basic carpentry skills, and a few hand and small power tools—many of which you probably have in your toolbox. Certain tasks call for one or two power tools stocked by most rental centers. If power-tool use seems over your head, make arrangements with a local jobber or lumber supplier to do the work for a small fee.

Completing the job yourself will save you a considerable amount of money— from a third to half the amount you would pay a professional. That savings might mean the difference between new storage space or none at all.

Bathroom design

In many ways designing cabinets for a bath is easier than planning for any other room, largely because bathrooms are usually the smallest room in the house.

Although size may limit your options, approach cabinet planning in your bathroom with the same care as you would any other room. For example, make sure that the vanity you're planning has sufficient room to open its doors and drawers without interference, and the storage area is large enough for your needs. You won't have much control over sizes if you order a stock vanity. Just be sure it fits comfortably in the space.

Don't overlook the medicine cabinet.

It can contribute as much to convenience and style as any other element. You have almost as many options with medicine cabinet doors as with other cabinets.

Doors come with hinges or are made as sliding units. Some cabinets solve space problems by mounting in a corner. Hinged three-panel mirrors can create a view covering almost 180 degrees. Choose a frame material that matches the construction of the vanity and be sure the cabinet size is proportional to the vanity. If it's too big, it will overwhelm the vanity and the room. If it's too small, the room will feel out of balance.

Before you commit your plans to paper, take a trip through your home center. If you haven't looked at bathroom fixtures and cabinets in a while, you'll find a wealth of ideas for do-it-yourself design.

Plan the installation of your vanity with care. In addition to a work surface, it's the centerpiece of your bathroom design.

CHAPTER PREVIEW

Installing a new vanity countertop base
page 222

Installing a vanity and sink
page 224

Tiling a vanity
page 226

Laminating a vanity
page 228

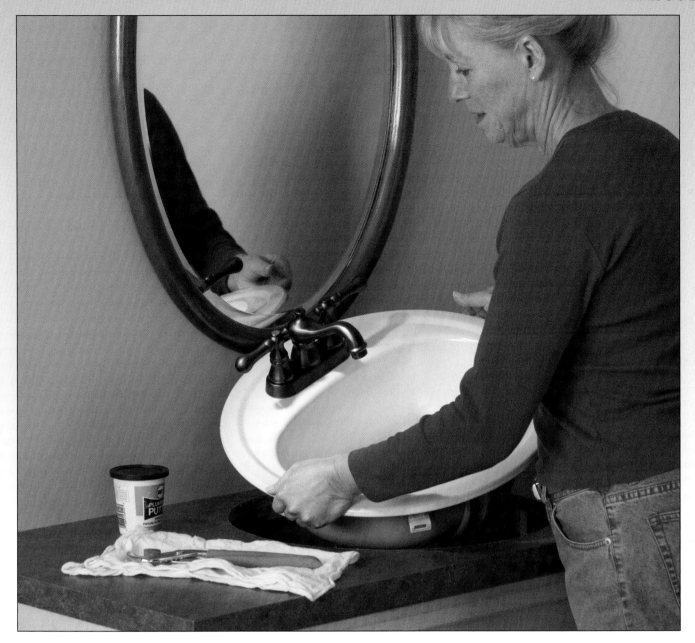

Constructing a corner linen cabinet
page 230

Built-in cabinet
page 238

INSTALLING A NEW VANITY COUNTERTOP BASE

Ceramic tile requires a rigid base—far more sturdy than provided by a typical vanity. If you like the style of your vanity and want to keep it, you can tile the top, but only if you build a new base.

Start the base by shoring up the edges—screw 1× cleats into the front and back frame and attach 1×3 braces. Add bracing under any joints—for example where the sheets will meet in an L-shape.

Use ¾-inch exterior-grade plywood. This grade is constructed with moisture-resistant glues. Most vanity tops can be cut from a standard 4×8-foot sheet. Cut the plywood to the depth you want plus a ½- to ¾-inch overhang. If the back wall is not perfectly flat, cut the sheet wide enough so you can contour it to the wall.

PRESTART CHECKLIST

☐ **TIME**
About 30 minutes to measure and cut countertop base; one to two hours to install it, depending on its size and configuration

☐ **TOOLS**
Carpenter's level, tablesaw, hammer, cordless drill and bit, jigsaw and plywood-cutting blade, hole saw

☐ **SKILLS**
Measuring and leveling, driving fasteners, sawing with jigsaw and tablesaw (optional)

☐ **PREP**
Remove old countertop

☐ **MATERIALS**
Wood shims, ¾-inch exterior-grade plywood, 2-inch coated screws, sink and faucet template or stiff cardboard for making template

Checking the frame for level

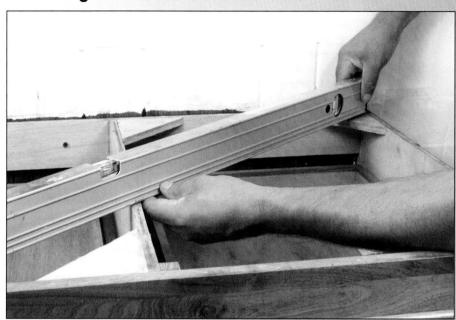

Although an out-of-level countertop will not affect the actual installation of the tile, it will create unattractive tapered edges at the backsplash. Before installing a new countertop on an old frame, make sure the frame is level. Set a 4-foot carpenter's level along the rear edge. Raise the carpenter's level, if necessary, and mark the wall for level. Check the sides of the frame, then both sides of an L-shape counter. If you are installing a new vanity, you can level it by placing shims under the frame. If not, leave the cabinets in place and level the countertop base.

COUNTERTOP BASE
Use shims to correct an out-of-level cabinet

Shims

If the results of your checking indicate the vanity frame is not level, you can add shims to correct the problem instead of removing the vanity and leveling it.

Cut the countertop base to the correct dimensions and set it in place on the vanity. Do not anchor it yet. Set a 4-foot level against the rear of the plywood at the wall and insert shims under the countertop base at locations that will level it. Mark the wall at the locations of the shims. Repeat the process for the sides and the front of the cabinet, being careful not to dislodge the shims already in place. Recheck the countertop for level. Install the new base as noted on *page 223*, driving the screws through the plywood and the shims.

Building a new base

Measure the exterior of the vanity and cut ¾-inch exterior-grade plywood wide enough to overhang the front by ½ to ¾ inch. Set the plywood on the cabinet and fasten it to the cleats with 2-inch coated screws. Install a waterproofing membrane and backerboard after cutting the sink hole.

Cutting the sink hole

Starter hole

1 If available use the manufacturer's template to mark the sink cutout. Otherwise set the sink upside down on the plywood base and trace its outline. Remove the sink and draw parallel lines about 1 inch (or equal to the width of the lip of the sink) inside the outline.

2 Drill a starter hole and cut the interior line with a jigsaw. Keep the base plate of the saw flat on the plywood base and push the saw into the wood slowly. As you cut the final turn, have a helper carefully support the cutout from below to keep the saw blade from binding.

Cutting faucet holes

Some sinks, especially decorator models, require faucets mounted in the countertop (deck-mounted faucets).

If the faucet manufacturer has provided a template for marking the faucet holes, position the template at the appropriate location to the sink hole and use a center punch (a nail or nail set will work also) to mark the points at which to drill.

If a template is not available, you can make one from stiff cardboard, punching out holes and tracing the outline of the faucet plate.

If the faucets have individual spouts, mark the countertop base for each faucet, spacing them at the appropriate location and at an equal distance from the center of the sink basin hole.

Use a hole saw with a diameter equal to the faucet mounts to drill the faucet holes.

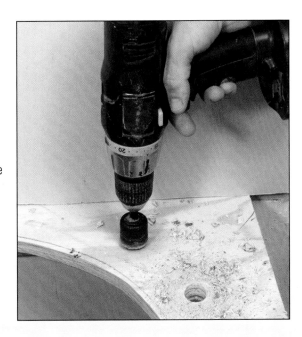

Backing up the surface

Not all vanity countertop materials will require a ¾-inch exterior-grade plywood base. Ceramic and stone tile will need the plywood backup, and so will solid-surface materials. Solid stone requires the continuous support that a solid base provides. Cultured marble or other preformed acrylic tops with an integral sink are self-supporting, and a postformed laminate top comes with its own base. If you're laminating your own top *(pages 228–229)*, you'll need to install the plywood.

INSTALLING A VANITY AND SINK

Installing a bathroom sink in a vanity is easier than other installations because the supply lines and the drain are all hidden within a cabinet. If the cabinet has no back, attach it to the wall and it will hide the plumbing. However, if the cabinet has a back, measure and cut three holes for the two supply lines and the drain.

Choosing a cabinet and top

A high-quality vanity cabinet is made of hardwood to resist water damage. A less expensive cabinet made of laminated particleboard will quickly disintegrate if it gets wet.

A vanity top typically is a single piece comprised of the bowl, countertop, and backsplash. Acrylic or plastic vanity tops are inexpensive, but they scratch and stain more easily than other materials.

PRESTART CHECKLIST

☐ **TIME**
Two to three hours to install a basic cabinet and vanity top with faucet

☐ **TOOLS**
Drill, hammer, screwdriver, level, adjustable wrench, groove-joint pliers, basin wrench

☐ **SKILLS**
Installing a faucet, attaching a P trap, connecting supply tubes, simple carpentry

☐ **PREP**
Shut off the water and remove the old sink

☐ **MATERIALS**
Vanity cabinet and top, faucet, P trap, supply tubes that fit the stop valves, plumber's putty, wood shims, screws

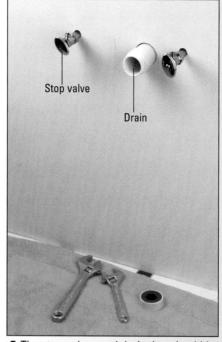

Stop valve

Drain

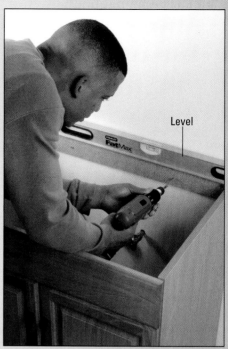

Level

1 The stop valves and drainpipe should be in place and close enough together to be enclosed by the cabinet. If your vanity cabinet has a back (many do not), remove the handles from the stop valves. Then measure and cut holes for the drain and the two supply pipes.

2 Slide the cabinet into place and check it for level in both directions. If necessary slip shims under the bottom or behind the back of the cabinet. Drive screws through the cabinet framing into wall studs to secure the cabinet.

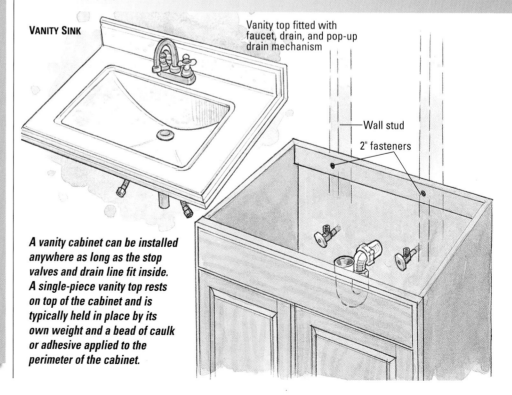

VANITY SINK

Vanity top fitted with faucet, drain, and pop-up drain mechanism

Wall stud

2" fasteners

A vanity cabinet can be installed anywhere as long as the stop valves and drain line fit inside. A single-piece vanity top rests on top of the cabinet and is typically held in place by its own weight and a bead of caulk or adhesive applied to the perimeter of the cabinet.

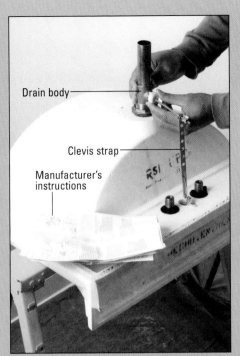

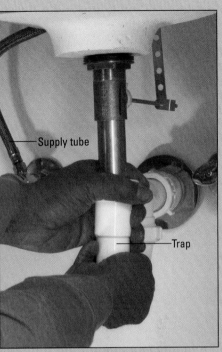

Drain body

Clevis strap

Manufacturer's instructions

Supply tube

Trap

3 Set the vanity top upside down on a pair of sawhorses and install the plumbing. See *pages 216–217* for installing the faucet, drain body, and pop-up assembly. Check the manufacturer's instructions for details.

4 Set the top onto the cabinet and check that it is centered. Remove it, apply caulk or adhesive along the top edge of the vanity, and reinstall the top.

5 Connect the supply tubes to the stop valves. Connect the trap *(pages 216–217)*.

Installing a drop-in sink

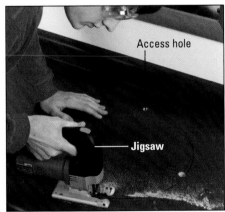

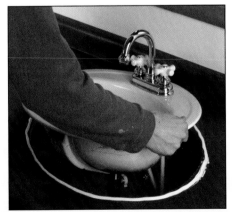

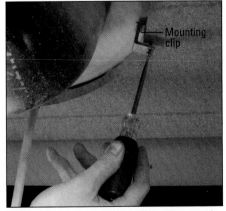

Access hole

Jigsaw

Mounting clip

1 To install a drop-in, self-rimming sink, first install a laminate countertop, or for a tile countertop, plywood and concrete backerboard. Use the template if provided, or turn the sink upside down on the counter and trace its outline. Draw a line ¾ inch inside the first line. Cut this second line with a jigsaw.

2 Plumb the sink (Step 3 above). Apply a bead of bathtub caulk or a rope of plumber's putty around the hole and set the sink. If the sink doesn't have mounting clips, apply a bead of silicone caulk instead of putty. Set the sink in, wipe away the excess caulk, and wait several hours before attaching the plumbing.

3 If your sink has mounting clips, slip several of them in place and turn them sideways so they grab the underside of the counter. Tighten the screws. Attach the supply lines and the drain trap.

TILING A VANITY

A tiled vanity gives your bathroom a designer look without completely redesigning the whole room. If you plan to tile a bathroom wall, tiling the vanity will make the vanity and sink an integral part of the space.

Even if your existing base cabinet is in good condition, you'll have to build up the top. Commercial vanity countertops are made to handle less weight. Remove the top and add bracing, a ¾-inch plywood base, and a polyethylene waterproofing membrane *(pages 222–223)*.

Buy the tile for all the surfaces you'll be tiling—vanity tile, wall tile, and bullnose trim. That way you can be more certain of getting tiles of a consistent color throughout the entire project. Make sure the cartons have the same lot number.

Select the right tile to use on your vanity. Use glazed tile ⅜ to ½ inch thick. Purchase a sink whose texture matches the glaze—vitreous china and enameled cast iron are good choices. Self-rimming sinks are easy to install, and the rim will cover the rough edges of the cut tile.

PRESTART CHECKLIST

☐ **TIME**
Eight to nine hours to build the substrate and lay the tiles; an hour more the next day to grout them

☐ **TOOLS**
Circular saw, cordless drill, jigsaw, level, stapler, notched trowel, beater block, straightedge, caulking gun, grout float

☐ **SKILLS**
Basic carpentry skills, setting tile, cutting tile, grouting

☐ **PREP**
Remove existing vanity top or install a new prefab or custom unit

☐ **MATERIALS**
Drywall screws, ¾-inch exterior-grade plywood, cement backerboard, backerboard screws, tile, thinset mortar, 4-mil polyethylene or 15-pound felt, grout

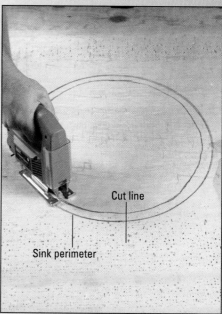

Backerboard   Membrane

¾" plywood   Bracing

Sink perimeter   Cut line

1 Build your own base or modify a commercial unit. Glue and screw bracing inside the cabinet, then install ¾-inch exterior-grade plywood with a 1-inch overhang, according to your design. Staple waterproofing membrane to the plywood and install ½-inch backerboard *(page 115)*.

2 Mark the outline and cut line of the sink using the manufacturer's template. If a template isn't available, center the sink upside down on the surface and mark its shape. Draw a second line 1 inch inside the first line and drill a starter hole. Cut the second line with a jigsaw.

Removing a flush-mounted or recessed sink

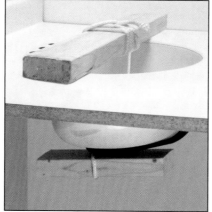

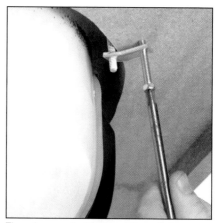

Most flush-mounted and recessed sinks are supported with clips under the cabinet. If you remove the clips without some sort of bracing, the sink will fall into the cabinet.

First unhook the plumbing, then support the sink with 2×4 braces tied with nylon rope.

Thread one end of the rope through the drain and tie it to the bottom brace. Soak any rusted clips with penetrating oil, then remove them. Lift the sink or let it down with the braces.

3 Lay out the tiles in a dry run using spacers. Try to minimize cutting as much as possible. Mark the edges of your dry run and snap chalk lines to guide the installation. Then comb thinset onto the backerboard.

4 Set the tiles in place and level them *(page 122)*. Cut tiles don't have to fit exactly to the edge of the sink hole but must not extend beyond the edge. Keep the tiles in line using a metal straightedge. Let the mortar cure, then grout the tiles.

5 When the grout has cured, run a bead of silicone caulk around the edge of the hole and set in the sink. To avoid pinched fingers, ask a helper to support the bottom of the sink. Install and tighten any mounting clips and hook up the plumbing lines. Run another bead of caulk around the edge of the sink.

WHAT IF...
You're tiling an alcove?

If you plan to tile a sink enclosed in an alcove, design the layout carefully. First decide whether you want the grout joints on the wall to line up with those on the vanity. Draw a scaled plan to avoid ending up with small slivers of tile at the edges—you'll want the same-size tile on both ends of the installation.

Tile the walls first, then the countertop, then the ledge. Finish with V-cap edging.

Other sink installations

Both flush-mounted and underhung sinks make for easier cleaning, but they require special countertop treatments.

Install a flush-mounted sink with its rim resting on plywood substrate. Install concrete backerboard around the sink and top it with tiles that partially rest on top of the sink flange.

Install and plumb an underhung sink after the substrate is installed. Then install tiles, as shown, with thin vertical pieces around the perimeter and bullnose trim overlapping them.

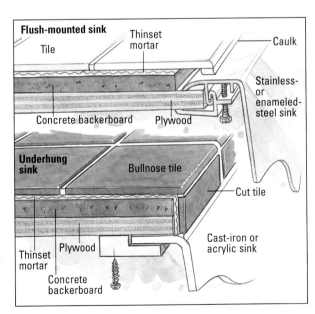

Laminating a Vanity

Laminating a vanity countertop requires some careful planning. Your primary weapon against mistakes is cutting the laminate slightly oversize to provide a little margin of error.

You can laminate over an existing laminated countertop or apply laminate to a new base as shown here (see *pages 222–223* for information about building a new base). Laminate will stick securely to an existing laminate countertop as long as it is clean and in good repair.

Preparation steps
Bring the laminate into the room at least 48 hours before you work with it so it can acclimate to the conditions.

Make sure the countertop surface is clean of anything that would hinder the adhesive bond—grease, cooking residues, or dust. Cut the sink hole in the base *(page 223)* before you laminate the top. You will cut out the sink area in the laminate as the final step.

Prestart Checklist

☐ **Time**
Between 8 to 10 hours to build the base and cut and install the laminate

☐ **Tools**
Metal straightedge, laminate scribing tool, tablesaw with laminate cutting guide (optional), router or laminate trimmer with flush-cutting bit, brushes for adhesive application (in lieu of spray application), 3-inch rubber roller, venetian blind slats or dowels, fine-toothed file, cordless drill

☐ **Skills**
Measuring and marking, gluing, cutting and trimming laminate

☐ **Prep**
Prepare clean, smooth, and level surface

☐ **Materials**
Exterior plywood, laminate, adhesive

1 Mark the sheet for the top an inch larger than the base. Mark the edge laminate ¼ to ½ inch wider than the thickness of the plywood. Lay the sheet face up on a work surface and clamp a straightedge on the line. Score the line in several passes with a laminate scribing tool. Lift one side of the sheet to snap it along the line.

2 Two pieces that butt together must have perfectly straight edges. Clamp two pieces between 1× guides, overlapping them about an inch. Make sure the sheets are square with each other. Trim the pieces using a router with a flush-cutting bit.

STANLEY Pro Tip

Cut laminate

You can cut laminate sheets with a variety of tools. One of the easiest and least expensive is the laminate scriber shown on these pages. Used correctly and with a little patience, it will produce clean straight cuts.

If you own a tablesaw equipped with a wide table, you can cut laminate faster. Cut the sheet with its good side up to prevent chipping the surface. You'll have to have a zero tolerance rip fence or a laminate cutting guide to keep the laminate edge from creeping under it as you saw. A variety of hand and electric shears are also available, some from rental outlets.

Getting the right adhesive

Once a canned or bottled product only, contact adhesive for laminates now comes in spray cans or as solvent- or water-based liquids applied with a brush. Use natural bristles for solvent-based products. Synthetic bristles are fine for water-based brands. Plan on throwing the brushes away.

You may find water-based adhesives easier to apply, and they change color as they cure, a feature which lets you know when the pieces are ready to install.

If you choose a spray-on product, take a couple of test sprays on scrap to get the hang of applying it evenly. Once you start spraying the adhesive, don't stop until the surface is covered completely. Setting the spray can down in the middle of the job can cause the spray head to clog.

3 Spray or brush contact adhesive on both the edge of the base and the back of the laminate edgestrip. Let the adhesive set up. Tack one end of the strip and, coiling it in one hand, work your way down to the other end. Keep an even amount of overhang on top and bottom.

4 Use a laminate trimmer or a router with a flush-cutting bit to trim the laminate even with the top and bottom of the plywood base. To save time you can trim one piece while the adhesive on another edge is setting up, working your way around the top until all edges are trimmed.

5 Lay the top sheet upside down on the countertop or other work surface. Spray or brush on the adhesive. Make sure to cover 100 percent of the surface (even if the manufacturer recommends only 80 percent). Remove the sheet and set it aside to dry. Apply adhesive to the plywood base.

6 To keep the sheet from bonding, lay venetian blind strips on the base and carefully set the laminate on them. Start at one end and pull out the spacers, pressing down on the sheet as you go. Roll the surface with a 3-inch rubber roller and trim the overhangs.

7 When the adhesive has cured, file the outside corners of the trimmed edges, holding a fine file almost flat. File with a forward motion only. Then file the top edges, filing forward and down. Use light pressure.

8 Go under the countertop and drill a starter hole at the corner of the sink outline. Working from above, trim the laminate to the opening using a router with a flush-cutting bit.

CONSTRUCTING A CORNER LINEN CABINET

Corner cupboards put often unused space to work. This compact closet is designed to hold linens or towels. It's small enough to tuck into a hallway by the bathroom, the bathroom itself, or a corner of a bedroom. Don't be put off by those handsome doors; there's no fancy joinery involved in building them.

Materials and finishing

The face frame and doors of this cabinet are made of birch plywood and solid poplar that looks great when painted. You might choose to make these parts of oak and matching plywood or of another hardwood with a clear finish. The sides and shelves, which won't be visible with the doors closed, are made of lauan plywood, which doesn't take paint quite as smoothly as birch but still looks fine and is a bit less expensive.

PRESTART CHECKLIST

☐ **TIME**
About 16 hours to construct, plus finishing time

☐ **TOOLS**
Hammer, nail set, combination square, bar clamps, tape measure, chisel, stepladder, tablesaw, circular saw with ripping guide, power drill/driver with #6 adjustable counterbore bit and 1/16-inch bit (for predrilling nail holes), router with 1/2-inch piloted rabbeting bit, doweling jig, pocket-hole jig, straightedge

☐ **SKILLS**
Accurate measuring, sawing, routing, drilling

☐ **PREP**
Assemble tools and materials, prepare a large work area, prepare installation site

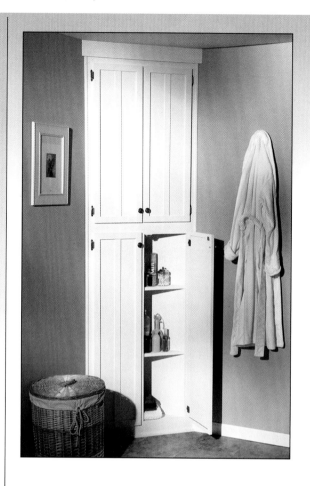

MATERIALS NEEDED

Part	Finished size T	W	L	Mat.	Qty.	Part	Finished size T	W	L	Mat.	Qty.
CABINET						**UPPER DOORS**					
A side	3/4"	19 7/16"	94"	LP	1	J rails	3/4"	1 1/2"	12 3/4"	PL	4
B side	3/4"	18 5/8"	94"	LP	1	K stiles	3/4"	1 1/2"	34 1/2"	PL	4
C shelf blanks	3/4"	12 5/8"	25 3/8"	LP	7	L panels	1/4"	10 3/4"	35 1/2"	BP	2
D side cleats	3/4"	3/4"	6"	Pine	14	M center stile	1/4"	1 1/2"	34 1/2"	PL	2
FACE FRAME						**LOWER DOORS**					
E side stiles	3/4"	2 1/2"	87"	PL	2	N rails	3/4"	1 1/2"	12 3/4"	PL	4
F upper center stile	3/4"	1 1/2"	36 1/2"	PL	1	O stiles	3/4"	1 1/2"	45"	PL	4
G lower center stile	3/4"	1 1/2"	47"	PL	1	P panels	1/4"	10 3/4"	46"	BP	2
H rails	3/4"	3 1/2"	30"	PL	2	Q center stile	1/4"	1 1/2"	45"	PL	2
I center rail	3/4"	3 1/2"	25"	PL	1	**TRIM**					
						R top trim	1/4"	3 1/2"	31 1/2"	PL	1
						S shoe molding	3/4"	3/4"	31 1/2"	Pine	1

Material key: LP—lauan plywood, BP—birch plywood, PL—poplar
Hardware: Eight semiconcealed hinges, four magnetic catches, four handles or knobs, 1 1/4-inch coarse-thread drywall screws, 1 1/2-inch coarse-thread drywall screws, 4d finishing nails, 1 1/2-inch brads, pocket-hole screws
Supplies: Edge-banding veneer, glue, 80-grit sandpaper, paint, 1/4-inch dowels

CORNER LINEN CABINET

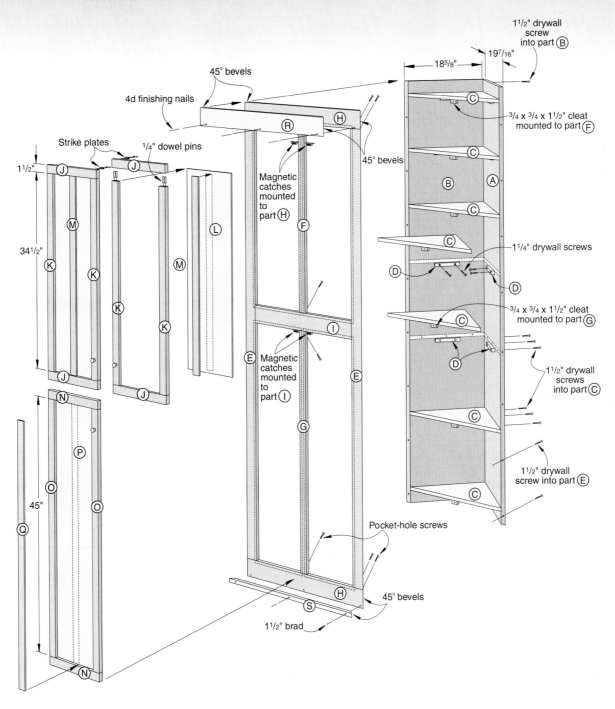

1½" drywall screw into part Ⓑ

18⅝"

19⁷⁄₁₆"

45° bevels

4d finishing nails

Ⓒ

¾ x ¾ x 1½" cleat mounted to part Ⓕ

Ⓒ

45° bevels

Strike plates

¼" dowel pins

Ⓗ

Magnetic catches mounted to part Ⓗ

Ⓑ   Ⓐ

1½"

Ⓙ   Ⓙ

Ⓡ

Ⓒ

34½"

Ⓜ

Ⓕ

Ⓛ

Ⓒ

1¼" drywall screws

Ⓚ   Ⓚ

Ⓜ

Ⓓ

Ⓓ

Ⓚ

¾ x ¾ x 1½" cleat mounted to part Ⓖ

Ⓒ

Ⓙ   Ⓚ

Ⓘ

Magnetic catches mounted to part Ⓘ

Ⓓ

Ⓙ

Ⓔ

1½" drywall screws into part Ⓒ

Ⓝ

Ⓔ

Ⓒ

Ⓟ

Ⓖ

1½" drywall screw into part Ⓔ

Ⓞ

45"

Ⓞ

Ⓒ

Ⓠ

Pocket-hole screws

Ⓗ

45° bevels

Ⓢ

1½" brad

Ⓝ

A. Make the cabinet

1 Set the rip guide on the circular saw to cut 2 inches wide, including the kerf—the wood cut away by the blade. Cut off one end of a sheet of ¾-inch lauan plywood, leaving a 94-inch sheet for the sides (A and B).

2 Set your tablesaw fence to 19⁷⁄₁₆ inches and tilt the blade 45 degrees. With someone to help support the plywood, rip the sheet to make side A. You could make the cut with a circular saw set to 45 degrees and guided by a straightedge.

3 Set the blade to 90 degrees and set the fence to 18⅝ inches. Put the beveled side of the remaining piece against the fence with the bevel's point on top, then rip side B. With a circular saw and straightedge, it's better to leave the factory edge square and recut the beveled side.

CUTTING DIAGRAM

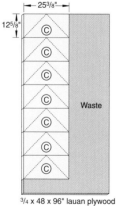

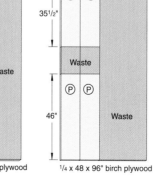

¾ x 48 x 96" lauan plywood · ¾ x 48 x 96" lauan plywood · ¼ x 48 x 96" birch plywood

BEVEL'S POINT ON TOP
Avoid dangerous kickback

Whenever you rip with a beveled edge against the fence, make sure the bevel's point is the top of the board. If the point were at the bottom, it could get wedged under the rip fence, ruining the cut and possibly causing dangerous kickback.

4 Have a helper hold side B upright while you stand on a stepladder to apply glue to the long square edge. Put side A in place and make sure its edge is flush with the back of B as you join the pieces with 1½-inch drywall screws spaced about 12 inches apart.

5 Check the inside dimensions of the cabinet. Because plywood thickness can vary, you might have to slightly adjust the shelf dimensions (below right). Rip a sheet of ¾-inch lauan plywood to 25⅜ inches for the shelf blanks (C). Then set the fence to 12⅝ inches to rip the blanks to width.

6 Lay out the triangular shelves on the blanks as shown in the drawing below. Set the miter gauge on your tablesaw to the 45-degree mark to the left of 90 degrees. Put the gauge in the slot to the right of the blade and make one cut on each blank.

WHAT IF...
You have tall ceilings?

This cabinet is 94 inches tall so you can easily maneuver it into place under an 8-foot ceiling. (A trim board covers the gap.) If your ceiling is taller, you can purchase a 10-foot-long panel of hardwood plywood for sides A and B. Depending on species of wood, you may have to order the panels at a lumberyard. Be prepared to wait until the yard's next delivery from the supplier.

RIP THE BLANKS TO WIDTH
Start with smaller pieces

It's dangerous and awkward to make a narrow cut across a full-length plywood panel. Instead do a little math and rough-cut the panel near the middle first with a circular saw. In this case four shelf blanks need 50½ inches plus ½ inch for four kerfs. If you cut the sheet at 51½ inches to be safe, that leaves 44½ inches, plenty for the remaining three panels.

TRIANGULAR SHELF

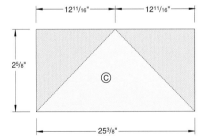

A. Make the cabinet *(continued)*

7 Reset your miter gauge to the 45-degree mark on the right side of 90 degrees. Put the gauge in the slot to the left of the blade and make the second cut to complete the shelf triangles.

8 Cover the front edges of the shelves with self-stick edge-banding veneer. Lay out the positions of the shelves on the sides as shown in the drawing (below left). Extend the lines around the outside of the cabinet to help locate screws later when you install the shelves.

9 Rip and crosscut side cleats (D) to the dimensions listed. Predrill and countersink two holes in each cleat. With glue and 1¼-inch drywall screws, attach a side cleat under each shelf location, 6 inches from the back of the cabinet.

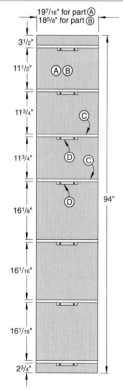

SHELF POSITION

19⁷/₁₆" for part Ⓐ
18⁵/₈" for part Ⓑ

3½"
11½" — Ⓐ Ⓑ
11¾" — Ⓒ
11¾" — Ⓓ Ⓒ
16⅛" — Ⓓ
16¹/₁₆"
16¹/₁₆"
2¾"
94"

STANLEY PRO TIP: **Label parts with sticky notes**

You should always label parts as you cut them. You can mark the parts in pencil, but the marks can be hard to find and you'll have to sand them off for finishing. Use sticky notes instead to label the parts. They come off easily and don't leave adhesive residue on the wood.

B. Assemble the face frame

10 Apply glue to the top of a pair of cleats and install a shelf. Drive three 1½-inch drywall screws through each cabinet side into the shelf. Install the remaining shelves the same way.

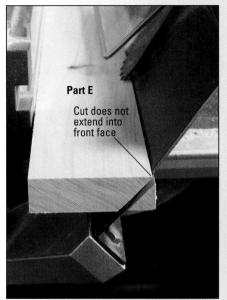

Part E
Cut does not extend into front face

1 Rip and crosscut poplar to make the face frame parts E through I. Set the tablesaw blade to 45 degrees and bevel one back edge of each side stile (E) and the ends of the rails (H). Be careful not to reduce the front face dimensions of the pieces.

2 Use glue and pocket-hole joinery to join the parts. Use two pocket-hole screws for each joint to attach the rails (H and I) to stiles and one screw at each joint to attach the center stiles (F and G) to rails.

The right bit makes the job simple and neat

The #6 adjustable counterbore bit shown is the size you'll need to predrill and countersink drywall screws. Loosen the setscrew to set the bit 1 inch from the countersink depth to drive 1¼-inch screws flush to the surface.

3 Lay the frame face down. Apply glue to the edges of the cabinet sides, top, bottom, and middle shelf. With someone to help, place the cabinet on the face frame. Make sure the stiles extend equally past both cabinet sides. Drive 1¼-inch screws every 12 inches straight into countersunk holes through the back and into the stiles.

4 Turn the cabinet on one side. Add a pocket-hole screw through the bottom of each shelf into the center stile. Drive screws into the middle of the rail for the top, bottom, and middle shelf.

C. Make the doors

1 Rip and crosscut poplar to make the door rails and stiles (J, K, M, N, O, and Q). Use glue and two ¼-inch-diameter dowels at each joint to join the stiles to the rails. Clamp the joints with bar clamps.

3 Rip and crosscut ¼-inch birch plywood to make four door panels (L and P). Apply glue in the rabbets and press the panels in place. Turn the doors over and wipe off any glue squeeze-out.

2 Put a ½-inch piloted rabbeting bit in the router and set the depth to ¼ inch. Rout clockwise around the inside of all the rails and stiles. Square the rounded corners of the rabbets with a chisel.

4 When the glue has cured, mark each rail at the center of the door panel. Mark center points on the ends of the ¼-inch-thick center stiles (M and Q). Align the marks and glue the stiles to the panels.

D. Install the doors

1 To locate the hinges on the doors, lay out lines across the back of each left stile 2 inches from each end. Position semiconcealed hinges on the lines and screw them to the backs of the doors.

2 The doors will overlap the face frame by ½ inch on all sides. To locate the doors, set a combination square to ½ inch and draw guidelines around the opening, ½ inch from it. Have someone help align the door on the lines while you predrill hinge holes in the stiles.

E. Finish and install

1 Remove the hinges from the doors to paint the cabinet. Rip stock for the top trim (R) but leave it long for now. Smooth all the solid wood parts with 80-grit sandpaper, slightly rounding the edges. Prepaint the top trim along with about 3 feet of shoe molding.

2 If there is baseboard in the corner, carefully remove it. Put the cabinet in place. Cut the baseboard at 45 degrees to butt into the cabinet, then reinstall it.

3 Measure across the top of the cabinet and cut 45-degree angles on the top trim to fit. Remember, your measurement is for the back of the miters—the front will be 1½ inches longer. Cut the shoe molding to fit the same way.

What If…
There are gaps on the sides?

4 Put the trim piece against the ceiling. Predrill holes and attach the trim piece to the face frame with 4d finishing nails. Attach the shoe molding with 1½-inch brads. Replace the doors and touch up the paint.

5 You can use any door pulls or knobs that suit your taste and decor. Center them across and along the stiles. Screw magnetic catches under the top for the top doors and under the shelf below the middle shelf for the bottom doors. Attach the mating metal plates to the inside of the doors.

Walls often aren't plumb or perfectly flat, so there may be small gaps on the sides. Cover them with a thin flexible molding—¾-inch cove molding works well.

BUILT-IN CABINET

Built-in cabinets can lend a vintage authenticity to your bathroom design scheme. Even if your home is brand new, you can add style and value by building the cabinet yourself.

A little detective work is required to find a bay in the wall that is free of plumbing, wiring, cold air returns, and heating or air-conditioning ducts. If you can get into the attic and basement of your house, look for pipes, wires, and ductwork going into the stud bay you're considering *(page 59)*.

If you're installing the cabinet in a new bathroom wall, the job is easier.

The cabinet construction is straightforward—nothing more complicated than butt joints assembled with glue and screws. There's no fancy fitting for the back either. The frame for the front can be butt-jointed or mitered to coordinate with the window and door casings in your home.

PRESTART CHECKLIST

☐ **TIME**
Approximately 4 hours, plus time for the finish to dry

☐ **TOOLS**
Tape measure, stud finder, 2-foot level and torpedo level, drywall saw, combination square, mitersaw, tablesaw, hammer, drill with bits, nail set

☐ **SKILLS**
Driving nails and screws, drilling, using tablesaw and mitersaw

☐ **PREP**
Wall surface should be painted; apply finish to all components of the cabinet

☐ **MATERIALS**
2×4 lumber for blocking, #6×2-inch flathead screws, quartersawn white oak or other lumber for box and optional shelves, shelf pins, masking tape, ¾- and 1¼-inch brads, stain and finish, construction adhesive and caulking gun, woodworking glue and applicator brush, colored putty, 6d finishing nails

1 After selecting the cabinet location, find the studs with a stud finder and mark their edges with masking tape. With a 2-foot level, mark the top and bottom of the opening. Cut the opening using a drywall saw.

2 Cut a piece of 2×4 blocking at the bottom of the opening. Drive a screw to use as a handle while you anchor the blocking. Drive screws through the drywall to secure the blocking in a level position, then toe-nail it to the studs. To avoid interference with the cabinet, countersink the screwheads.

CABINET ASSEMBLY

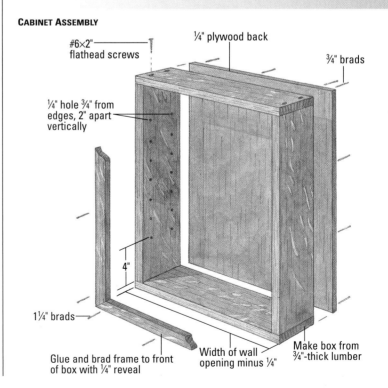

#6×2" flathead screws

¼" plywood back

¾" brads

¼" hole ¾" from edges, 2" apart vertically

4"

1¼" brads

Glue and brad frame to front of box with ¼" reveal

Width of wall opening minus ¼"

Make box from ¾"-thick lumber

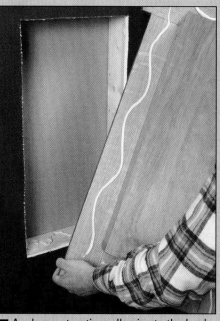

3 Referring to the drawing *(page 238)*, cut the sides, top, and bottom of the cabinet. Drill ¼-inch holes for adjustable shelves, with the lowest holes 4 inches from the bottom and the top holes 4 inches from the top. Screw and glue the box together; square the frame and attach the back.

4 Make a 1× face frame for the cabinet, with a ¼-inch reveal and mitered corners. Attach the face frame to the cabinet with glue and predrilled 6d finishing nails.

5 Apply construction adhesive to the back edges of the face frame and to the lower blocking. Slide the cabinet assembly into the recess. Drive predrilled 6d finishing nails through the stiles of the face frame into the studs. Fill all holes with colored putty that matches the final color of your finish.

Prefabricated niche

A prefabricated niche allows you to skip the work of shaping the insert. In addition you'll find that manufacturers produce these products in flowing and ornate forms that would require an expert carver to duplicate. Plastic and fiberglass are two common materials, but the products have convincing wood texture and appearance.

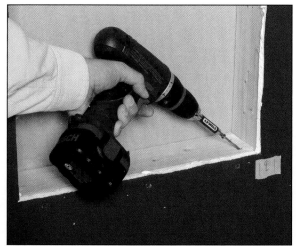

With some niches you cut out a template that's printed on the shipping box and trace around it between studs at the installation site. Install blocking (see Step 2, opposite) if the directions for your niche require it.

Some niches require that you use a special adhesive, while others recommend ordinary construction adhesive around the perimeter. For extra security drive finishing nails or trim-head screws, then patch the holes.

LIGHTS & FANS

No matter how old your electrical system, it is always possible—and usually easy—to remove an old wall light or ceiling light fixture and install a new one. New lighting—whether replacing old lights or newly installed—can dramatically contribute to the beauty of your new bathroom. Small vent fans can also increase the comfort of your bathroom. They require only basic wiring; it's the installation of the fan and ducts or vents that requires the most time.

Lighting hardware

If your home was built after World War II, attaching a new fixture will be easy. Mounting hardware has changed little, and the new fixture should come with all the parts you need. Simply attach a strap to the ceiling box, and perhaps a center stud as well. Splice the wires, screw the fixture to the strap or the stud, and you are done.

If you have an older home, the old fastening hardware may not line up with the new fixture. Fortunately home centers carry adapters to solve this problem.

If the new canopy (the part that snugs up to the ceiling) is smaller than the old one, a medallion can hide the problem and save you from painting.

Wiring a light or fan

Shut off power before removing an existing fixture. Test the box for power after removing the fixture.

Wiring a light or fan is straightforward: Splice white lead to white wire, black to black, and connect the grounds. Installing a new fixture where there was none before is more involved and best left to a professional electrician or someone with experience running new cable. Running cable through walls is a time-consuming and complicated task.

Choosing the right fan

When you shop for a bathroom fan, you'll see many sizes and styles. Fans are sold by the volume of air they move, and most fan packaging will make it easy for you to determine which size fan to install for your room. If you're in doubt, do a little Internet research. Or ask your home center staff. If you have a fan and the bathroom stays steamy even with it on, poorly designed or blocked ductwork may be the culprit. Inspect the ductwork before investing in a new fan, unless the current one is annoyingly noisy.

Make your bathroom more attractive and comfortable with new lighting and a vent fan.

CHAPTER PREVIEW

Recessed cans
page 242

Wall-mounted lighting
page 246

Installing flush-mounted lights
page 248

Installing track lights
page 250

A wall fixture such as this one should be mounted between wall studs. A hole is cut into the wall to house the electrical box. After the wires are connected they are pushed into the electrical box and the mounting plate and fixture are attached. The power is turned off during this process and is not turned back on until the fixture and light bulb are fully installed.

Installing a bath vent fan
page 252

Installing electric heaters
page 256

RECESSED CANS

The most inconspicuous way to illuminate your new bathroom is with a series of recessed canister lights, also called "cans" or "pot lights." Install them in pairs about 6 feet apart and centered on the ceiling. Use eyeball-type can lights to highlight wall features, task lights to brighten a vanity, and a watertight recessed fixture above a tub or shower.

Remodel can lights are easy to install in finished walls. Even running cable is not too difficult, because cans are usually spaced only two or three joists apart. Using a fishing drill bit *(page 171),* you may need to cut only a few holes in the ceiling.

See *page 245* for trim styles. Most inexpensive recessed cans are rated to use only 60-watt bulbs.

PRESTART CHECKLIST

☐ **TIME**
About a day to cut holes, run cable, and install six to eight lights with a switch

☐ **TOOLS**
Voltage tester, drill, spade bit or fishing drill bit, stud finder, ladder, drywall saw, level, hammer, fish tape, screwdriver, wire stripper, long-nose pliers, lineman's pliers

☐ **SKILLS**
Precision cutting of drywall or plaster; stripping, splicing, and connecting wires to terminals; installing boxes; running cable through walls and ceilings

☐ **PREP**
Find power source and make sure the new lights will not overload the circuit; clear the room of all obstructions and lay a drop cloth on the floor

☐ **MATERIALS**
Recessed canister lights, cable, switch box and clamps, wire nuts, electrician's tape

A. Rough-in the wiring

Mark center of fixture

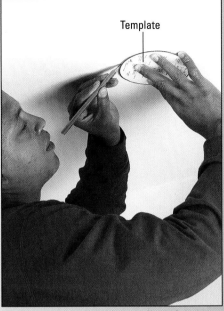
Template

1 Plan the locations for the lights and draw lines marking the center of each. Use a stud finder or a bent wire *(page 243)* to see if a joist is in the way. You can move the light several inches to avoid a joist—the inconsistency won't be noticeable.

2 Center the hole in the cardboard template over your location mark. Holding the template in place, mark your cut line.

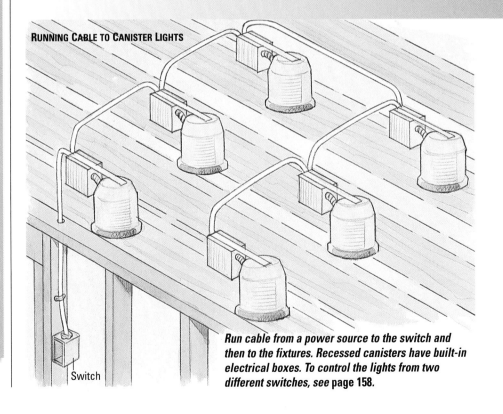

RUNNING CABLE TO CANISTER LIGHTS

Switch

Run cable from a power source to the switch and then to the fixtures. Recessed canisters have built-in electrical boxes. To control the lights from two different switches, see **page 158.**

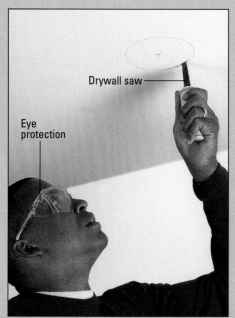

Eye protection

Drywall saw

3 Cut the hole with a drywall saw. Wear safety glasses because drywall dust stings terribly if it gets into the eyes. Cut precisely—the canister trim is narrow and leaves little room for error.

¾-inch spade bit

4 Drill holes for the cable as far up the joist as possible so drywall nails cannot reach the cable. See *page 170* for tips on running cable through walls and ceilings.

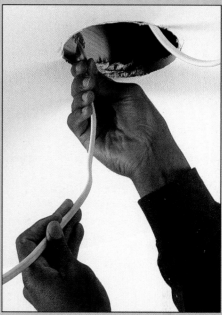

5 Run cable up from the power source to the switch box, then run cable to each fixture hole (see illustration *page 242*). Allow at least 16 inches of cable to hang down from each hole.

STANLEY PRO TIP

Bent wire test

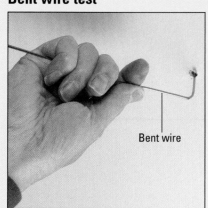

Bent wire

To make sure the fixture will not bump into a joist, use a stud finder. Or drill a ¼-inch hole, insert a bent wire, and spin the wire around to see whether you encounter an obstruction.

WHAT IF...
The ceiling framing is exposed?

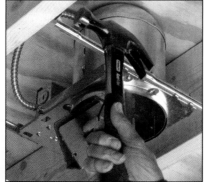

If the ceiling joists are not covered with drywall or plaster, install a new-work can light. Adjust the light to accommodate the thickness of the drywall that will be put up later. Slide the mounting bars out and hammer each tab into a joist. Slide the light to position it precisely.

Mapping can lights

With a standard flood bulb, a recessed light will illuminate an area about as wide as the ceiling is high. Make a scale drawing of your room and map a grid of lights that are at least fairly consistent in their spacing.

■ If your ceiling is 8 feet high, a typical recessed light will shine on a floor area with a diameter of 8 feet (a radius of 4 feet). To light the room, install a grid of lights spaced no more than 8 feet apart. The perimeter lights should be no more than 4 feet from the walls. Lights placed closer together—perhaps 6 or 7 feet apart and only 2–3 feet from the walls—will more fully light the room.

■ If you have a 10-foot ceiling, lights can be 7–10 feet apart and as much as 5 feet from the walls.

B. Install the lights

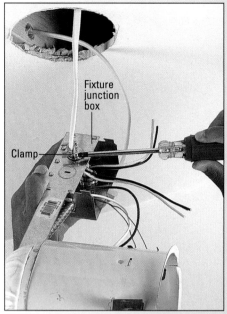

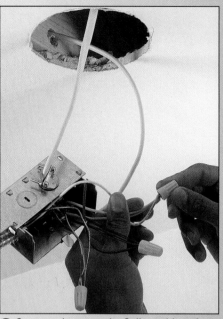

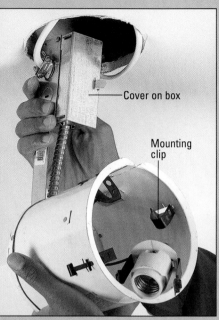

1 Strip about 6 inches of sheathing from the cable. Remove the cover from the fixture junction box and twist off a knockout for each cable. Slide the cable in and clamp the cable.

2 Connect the grounds. Splice white wires with white leads and black wires with black leads. Fold the wires into the junction box and replace the cover.

3 Pull the mounting clips inside the can so they will not be in the way when you push the canister into the hole. Without tangling the cables, guide the junction box through the hole and push in the canister.

STANLEY PRO TIP

"IC" light near insulation

If insulation will come within 3 inches of a recessed light, be sure to install a fixture rated "IC" (insulation compatible). A non-IC light will overheat dangerously.

WHAT IF...
Ceiling space is sloped or tight?

If the ceiling is sloped, buy special canisters that are adjustable so the light can point straight down.

If the vertical space above the ceiling is less than 8 inches, buy a low-clearance fixture. Some are small enough to fit into a space only 4 inches high.

Compact low-voltage halogen can lights are expensive, but they present new style options and produce an intense light.

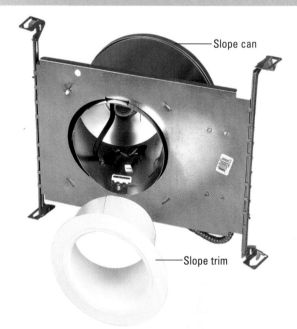

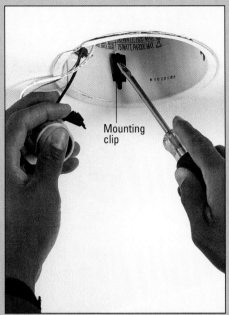

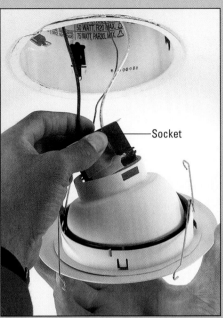

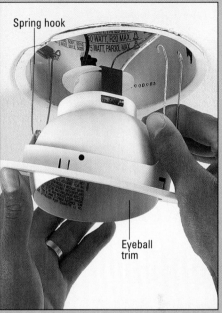

4 Push the canister so its flange is tight to the ceiling. With a slot screwdriver, push up each mounting clip until it clicks into place, clamping the canister to the drywall or plaster.

5 Many canisters have sockets that attach to the trim with two spring clips. Slip one clip into the notch provided and rock the socket so the clip engages.

6 If the trim has two spring hooks, squeeze and guide their ends into the slots provided, then push up the trim until it snaps into place. Twist an eyeball trim to face in the desired direction.

WHAT IF...
The canister has a spring hook?

To mount trim that uses coil springs (shown), hold the trim in place up against the ceiling. Insert a pencil tip into the looped end of each spring and guide it up into the hole provided.

Trim options

Baffle trim (either white or black) diffuses the light, while reflector trim increases the brightness of a bulb. With open trim the flood bulb protrudes slightly downward. For above a tub or shower, choose a watertight lens. An eyeball (or fish-eye) trim rotates to point where you want it; a wallwasher highlights the texture of a brick or stone wall.

Baffle trim

Reflector trim

Open trim

Flush watertight lens

Wallwasher trim

Eyeball trim

Extended watertight lens

WALL-MOUNTED LIGHTING

Wall sconces can provide indirect or soft lighting that's ideal for bathrooms and at the sides of mirrors. Place them just above eye level.

Use a standard ceiling box and wire just as you would a ceiling light. Most sconces mount with a center stud so you can adjust the fixture for level even if the box is not level. To control sconces from two locations, use three-way switches.

A strip of lights over a bathroom mirror or medicine chest calls for a similar installation method. Such fixtures use several low-wattage bulbs to reduce glare while providing plenty of light.

PRESTART CHECKLIST

☐ **TIME**
About three hours to run cable and install a switch and two sconces (not including cutting a pathway for the cable and patching walls)

☐ **TOOLS**
Voltage tester, drill, saw, hammer, fish tape, screwdriver, wire stripper, long-nose pliers, lineman's pliers

☐ **SKILLS**
Stripping, splicing, and connecting wires to terminals; installing boxes; running cable through walls and ceilings

☐ **PREP**
Find power source and make sure the new lights will not overload the circuit; spread a drop cloth on the floor below

☐ **MATERIALS**
Sconce(s), ceiling boxes and a switch box with clamps, cable, switch, wire nuts, electrician's tape

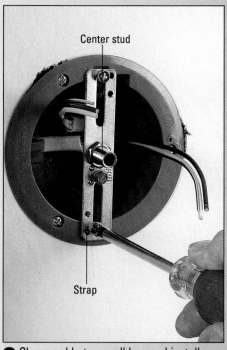

1 **Shut off power to the circuit.** Cut holes for the sconce boxes and the switch. Run cable from the power source to the switch, then to the sconces *(page 242)*.

2 Clamp cable to a wall box and install the box. Most sconces come with all the necessary hardware—usually a strap with a center stud. If the strap is provided, use it; it helps carry away heat from the fixture.

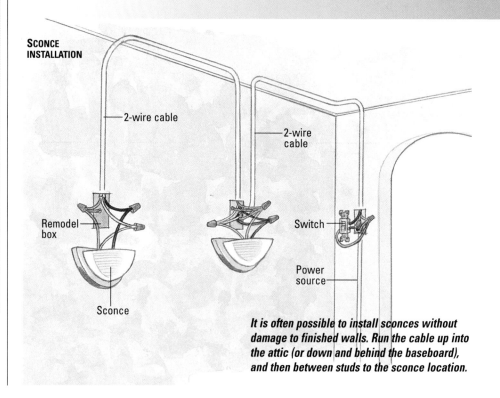

SCONCE INSTALLATION

It is often possible to install sconces without damage to finished walls. Run the cable up into the attic (or down and behind the baseboard), and then between studs to the sconce location.

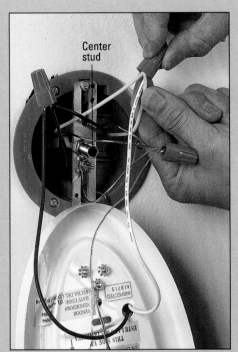

3 To wire a sconce, connect the grounds. Splice the white fixture lead to the white wire(s), and the black lead to the black wire(s).

4 Slip the sconce over the center stud and start to tighten the nut. Stand back and check that the base is plumb, and then tighten the base.

5 Install the lightbulb, making sure it does not exceed the manufacturer's recommended wattage. Clip the lens into place. Wire the switch *(page 173)*.

Lights mounted on a mirror

To install a bathroom strip light, center the box over the mirror or medicine chest. Attach the fixture over the box, wire the fixture, and attach the cover.

To install a light fixture directly on a mirror, have a glass supplier cut three holes to match the fixture—a large hole for the electrical box and two smaller holes for mounting screws. Wire the fixture. Apply a thin bead of clear silicone caulk to its back to act as an adhesive. Attach with mounting screws, but don't overtighten them— you might break the mirror.

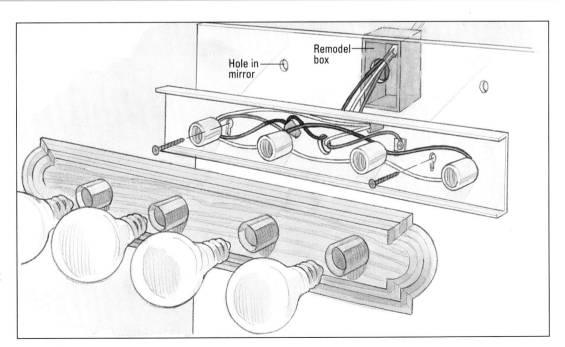

INSTALLING FLUSH-MOUNTED LIGHTS

Installing a flush-mounted ceiling fixture is an easy job. The hardware that held the old fixture typically can be reused to attach the new. If not, a new fixture most often comes with all the hardware needed to install it.

When buying a fixture, make sure it is designed to provide the amount of light you want in the bathroom. Compare its wattage with the old fixture. Don't install bulbs that exceed recommendations, or you will dangerously overheat the fixture and its box. Choose a fixture with a canopy large enough to cover any imperfections in the ceiling, or use a medallion *(page 249)*.

If possible, ground the new fixture. If it is being installed in a metal box, connect the fixture ground lead to the box and to the house ground wire. Check local codes.

PRESTART CHECKLIST

☐ **TIME**
About half an hour to remove a fixture and install a replacement, as long as there are no problems with the hardware

☐ **TOOLS**
Screwdriver, wire stripper, side cutters, voltage tester, ladder

☐ **SKILLS**
Stripping wire, splicing stranded wire to solid wire

☐ **PREP**
Spread a drop cloth on the floor below; set up a stable, nonconductive ladder

☐ **MATERIALS**
Replacement fixture, wire nuts (the ones that come with the fixture may be too small), electrician's tape

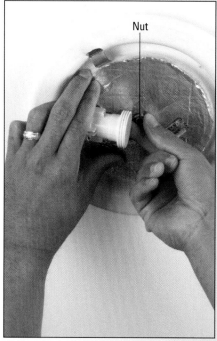

Nut

1 If replacing an existing fixture, **shut off power to the circuit.** Open the fixture. Remove the nut or screws holding the fixture to the box and pull the fixture down. Remove the wire nuts and **check for power in the box.** Pull the leads off the house wires and remove the fixture.

New strap

Grounding screw

2 If replacing a fixture and the existing hardware will not fit the new fixture, or if it doesn't have a grounding screw, remove it and attach a new strap to the box. If adding a new fixture, run cable and install a ceiling box. Install the mounting strap that came with the fixture.

STANLEY PRO TIP: **Attach a fixture to an older box**

Hickey

An older "pancake" box like this may have a ⅜-inch pipe running through the middle. To install a center-mount or pendent fixture, use a hickey, which has two sets of threads, one for the pipe attached to the pancake box and the other for a center stud. A hickey is helpful for wiring chandeliers because it has an opening through which a cord can run.

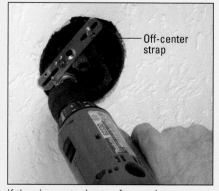

Off-center strap

If the pipe protrudes too far, purchase a mounting strap with a hole large enough to accommodate the pipe. Or attach the strap off center by drilling pilot holes in the box and driving sheet metal screws through the slots in the strap and into the box. However, make sure the fixture's canopy is large enough to cover the box.

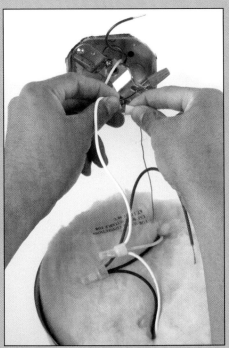

3 If the fixture is heavy, support it with a coat hanger wire while you work. Connect the ground wire. Splice white lead to white wire and black to black. Wrap the wire nuts with electrician's tape. The insulation may be difficult to work around, but don't remove it; it's a safety feature.

4 Fold the wires up into the box. Start one mounting screw, then the other, then tighten them. If the fixture has keyhole-shape screw holes, attach the screws to the box; slip the fixture over the large holes. Rotate the canopy so the screws fit into the smaller slots, then tighten the screws.

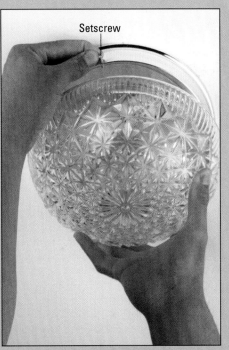

Setscrew

5 The setscrews that hold the globe may already be in the base or may have to be installed. Push the globe to raise the lip above all the setscrews, then hand-tighten all the setscrews evenly.

WHAT IF...
The new fixture's canopy doesn't cover the old hole?

If the new canopy is not large enough to cover up holes or unpainted portions of the ceiling—or simply to add a decorative touch—purchase a medallion. Hold it against the ceiling while you wire the fixture. Before tightening the canopy, see that the medallion is centered.

MOUNTING SCREWS
Installing a center-mounted fixture

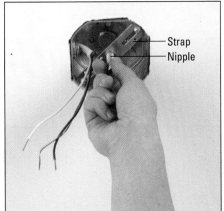

Strap
Nipple

1 Some fixtures mount with a nipple (short threaded pipe) and a nut in the center rather than two screws. Install a strap and screw in a nipple. If the nipple that comes with the fixture is too short or too long, purchase another one.

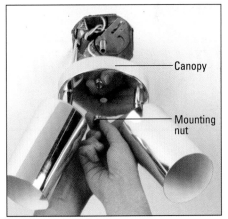

Canopy

Mounting nut

2 After wiring the fixture, slide the canopy up so the nipple pokes down through the center hole. Screw on and tighten the mounting nut.

INSTALLING TRACK LIGHTS

Track lighting offers plenty of options for style, layout, and design. You can install the track in a straight line, or form a T, L, or H shape. Choose from among a variety of lamp styles. Place them anywhere on the track and point them in any direction. You can even use two or more types of lights, some for general illumination and others to highlight small areas, such as an architectural accent in your bathroom design.

At some point the track must cross over a light fixture box to grab power via a mounting plate. Sketch your planned installation and show the drawing to a salesperson, who can help assemble all the parts required: track, mounting plate, lamps, and other fittings. Chances are a kit will supply everything needed.

PRESTART CHECKLIST

☐ **TIME**
About four hours to remove an old fixture and install about 8 feet of track with a turn or two, as well as several lamps

☐ **TOOLS**
Screwdriver, tape measure, wire stripper, drill, side cutters, voltage tester, lineman's pliers, stud finder, nonconducting ladder

☐ **SKILLS**
Measuring accurately, driving screws into joists, stripping wire, splicing stranded wire to solid wire

☐ **PREP**
Spread a drop cloth on the floor and set up one or two ladders; a helper will come in handy when installing long pieces of track

☐ **MATERIALS**
Parts for the track system (see illustration), plastic anchors, screws, wire nuts, electrician's tape

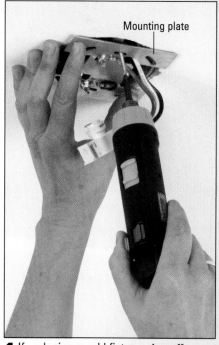

Mounting plate

1 If replacing an old fixture, **shut off the power** and remove the fixture. If installing a new system, run cable and install a ceiling box. Splice the new leads to the house wires, color to color. Fold the wires up into the box. Screw the mounting plate snugly to the box.

2 If necessary cut pieces of track to length. To cut a track, hold it firmly in place. If you use a vise, take care not to bend the metal. Cut with a hacksaw that has a metal-cutting blade. Support the waste side of the piece when nearing the end of a cut so it does not fall and bend the track.

TRACK LIGHTING SYSTEM

The mounting plate live-end connector supplies power to the track, which carries power to the lamps via two strips of wire.

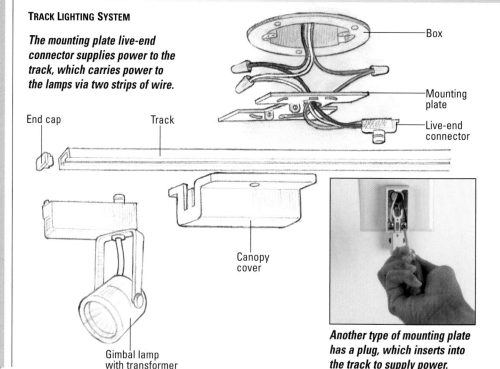

Box

Mounting plate

Live-end connector

End cap

Track

Canopy cover

Gimbal lamp with transformer

Another type of mounting plate has a plug, which inserts into the track to supply power.

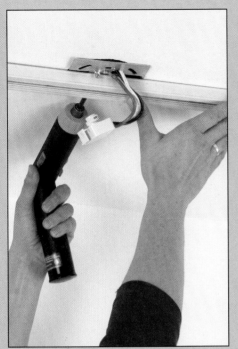

Track

3 With a helper holding one end of the track, push the track up against the mounting plate. Secure it by tightening the setscrews.

4 With a helper holding one end of the track, measure at two points along the track so it is parallel to the nearest wall. If the track configuration includes any 90-degree angles, use a framing square to mark a guideline.

5 Locate joists with a stud finder. Drive a screw into every joist the track crosses. If the track runs parallel to the joists, drill holes every 16 inches, tap in plastic anchors, and drive screws into the anchors.

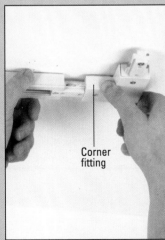

Corner fitting

Live-end connector

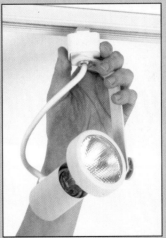

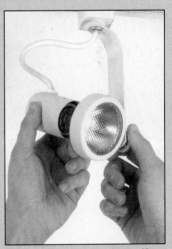

6 If the track has to turn a corner, slide a fitting onto the track piece just installed. Slide the next piece onto the connector, measure to see that it is parallel to the nearest wall, and anchor it to the ceiling.

7 Once all the pieces are installed, place end caps on all the track ends. Push the live-end connector plug into the track; twist it to make contact with both strips of metal in the track. Attach the canopy cover.

8 Insert the plug of a lamp into the track and twist to tighten. To move a lamp along the track, loosen it first—do not force it while it is still attached.

9 Restore power and test. If a lamp does not work, remove it and twist it back on again. Once it works, adjust the lamp to direct the light where needed.

INSTALLING A BATH VENT FAN

Many bathroom fans do little more than make noise, either because they are too weak or because their ductwork does not permit free movement of air. Usually venting is the culprit. Plan for a vent duct that is as short as possible and that makes as few turns as possible.

In addition to a vent fan, a bathroom unit may have a light, night-light, and/or heater unit. Because a heater uses much more power than a light and fan, it may need to be on its own circuit.

A fan-only unit or a light and fan that come on at the same time require only two-cable wiring. The more features you want to control separately, the more complicated the wiring becomes. To replace an existing fan, check the wiring; you may need to replace two-wire cable with three-wire cable or even two cables.

PRESTART CHECKLIST

☐ **TIME**
About seven hours to install ducting, a fan, and a switch (not including cutting a pathway for the cable and patching walls)

☐ **TOOLS**
Voltage tester, pry bar, drill, drywall saw, jigsaw, hammer, nonconductive ladder, fish tape, screwdriver, wire stripper, long-nose pliers, lineman's pliers

☐ **SKILLS**
Cutting through siding or roofing; stripping, splicing, and connecting wires; installing boxes; running cable

☐ **PREP**
Find the shortest path for the ductwork; find power source and make sure the new lights will not overload the circuit *(page 119);* spread a drop cloth on the floor below

☐ **MATERIALS**
Vent fan, switch, ductwork, duct tape, sheet metal screws, cable, clamps, switch box, wire nuts, electrician's tape

A. Install the vent fan housing

Pry bar
Old ceiling box

Fan housing

1 To replace an existing ceiling light with a fan/light, **shut off power to the circuit.** Remove the light and pry out the ceiling box. If you cannot work from above, cut carefully around the box before prying. You may need to cut through mounting nails.

2 Disassemble the new fixture and use the housing as a template to mark for the opening. The fan must be securely mounted; if there is no joist to attach it to, install blocking nailed to nearby joists.

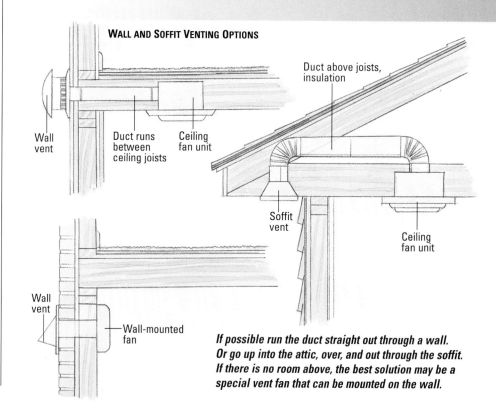

WALL AND SOFFIT VENTING OPTIONS

Wall vent

Duct runs between ceiling joists

Ceiling fan unit

Duct above joists, insulation

Soffit vent

Ceiling fan unit

Wall vent

Wall-mounted fan

If possible run the duct straight out through a wall. Or go up into the attic, over, and out through the soffit. If there is no room above, the best solution may be a special vent fan that can be mounted on the wall.

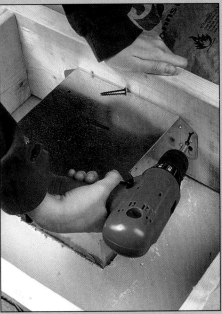

3 If necessary install blocking to keep the insulation away from the fan. Cut the hole with a drywall saw or reciprocating saw. If the ceiling is plaster, drill locator holes at the four corners and cut the opening from below.

4 If necessary run new cable from the switch to the box. (The fan shown in this project has separate controls for the fan and the light and requires one three-wire cable.) Screw the fan to a framing member.

5 For the wall vent, drill a locator hole from the inside through the outside wall. Outside, cut a hole for the duct.

WHAT IF...
You must work from below?

If there is no access to an attic space above, cut the hole next to a joist. If the duct can run parallel to a joist and the outside wall is not too far away, use a long bit to drill the locator hole.

STANLEY PRO TIP

Ducts should be short, wide, and smooth

The shorter, smoother, and wider the ductwork, the more freely air can move through it. Most ductwork for bathroom fans is 4 inches in diameter; don't use anything smaller. Solid ducting is the smoothest and most efficient, but it may be difficult to install in tight places. All-metal flexible duct is bendable and fairly smooth. Plastic-and-wire ducting is the easiest to install but is the least efficient.

At every joint use sheet metal screws or clamps to make tight connections; then cover the joint completely with professional-quality duct tape.

Venting through the roof

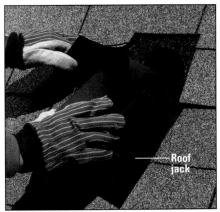

To install a roof jack *(page 183)*, follow the manufacturer's instructions exactly to ensure that the jack will not leak. First cut through the roof, then cut back shingles. Install the jack and cover its top half with shingles. Cover all nails with roofing cement *(page 183)*.

A. Install the vent fan housing *(continued)*

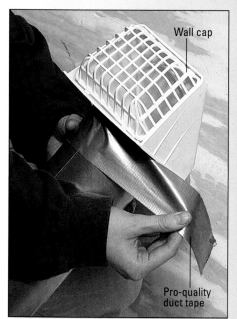

6 Measure from the outside to the fan. Attach a piece of solid duct to the wall cap so it is long enough to reach the fan or as close as possible. Fit the duct to the cap, drill pilot holes, and drive sheet metal screws to hold it in place. Then cover the joint with professional-quality duct tape.

7 Run a bead of caulk around the exterior hole. Slide the duct through the hole and fasten the wall cap to the wall with screws.

8 Fill any gap between duct and fan with another piece of solid duct or with flexible metal ducting. At each joint attach clamps and wrap with duct tape.

ROOF VENT

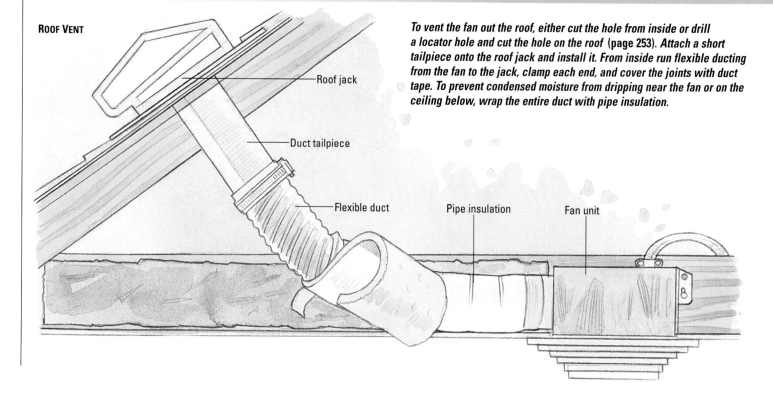

Roof jack

Duct tailpiece

Flexible duct

Pipe insulation

Fan unit

To vent the fan out the roof, either cut the hole from inside or drill a locator hole and cut the hole on the roof (page 253). Attach a short tailpiece onto the roof jack and install it. From inside run flexible ducting from the fan to the jack, clamp each end, and cover the joints with duct tape. To prevent condensed moisture from dripping near the fan or on the ceiling below, wrap the entire duct with pipe insulation.

B. Wire the fan

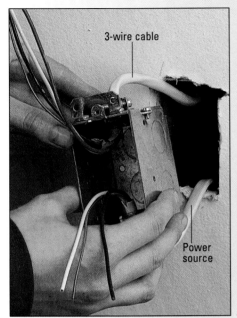

3-wire cable

Power source

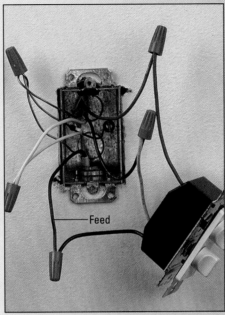

Feed

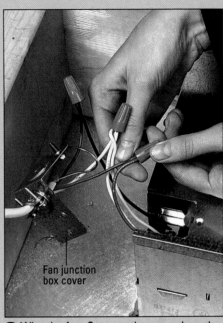

Fan junction box cover

1 If necessary run the correct cable or cables to the switch box. As shown above, power enters the switch box. If power enters the fan, consult the manufacturer's instructions.

2 To wire a fan/light switch, connect the grounds and splice the white wires. Connect the red and black wires from the fan to the fan and light terminals. Connect the feed wire to the remaining terminal.

3 Wire the fan. Connect the grounds and splice the white wires. Splice the black wire to the black fan lead and the red wire to the colored lead. Attach the junction box cover. In the bathroom install the light and the fixture canopy.

Timer switch for a fan with a heater

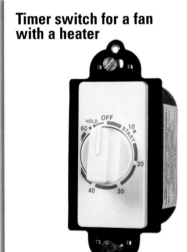

To avoid wasting energy and creating a hazardous situation by leaving on the fan heater, install a timer switch (above) along with a two-function switch for the fan and light. To do so, install a double-gang box.

WIRING A MULTIPURPOSE UNIT

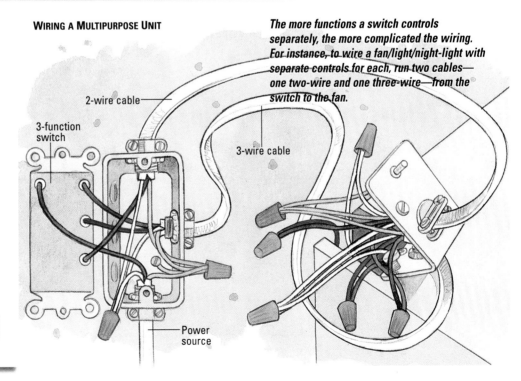

2-wire cable

3-function switch

3-wire cable

Power source

The more functions a switch controls separately, the more complicated the wiring. For instance, to wire a fan/light/night-light with separate controls for each, run two cables—one two-wire and one three-wire—from the switch to the fan.

INSTALLING ELECTRIC HEATERS

Even if your home is not heated by electricity, adding an electric baseboard or wall heater can be a cost-effective way to bring heat to a cold bathroom.

When planning assume 10 watts of heater capacity per square foot of room area. In other words a 10×10-foot room will need two 500-watt baseboard heaters. Check your local codes for circuit requirements; some municipalities require a dedicated circuit protected by a 20-amp double breaker. In some cases heaters can be added to existing 120-volt circuits—see *page 119* for how to calculate maximum permissible load. Confirm that the circuit voltage matches that of the unit—120-volt circuit for a 120-volt unit, 240-volt circuit for a 240-volt unit.

Place heaters on outside walls and below windows. Check manufacturer's specs for locating furniture and drapes. Never locate a heater beneath a receptacle. In general baseboard units are best for enhancing whole-room heat; blower-heaters are best for intense heat of short duration.

PRESTART CHECKLIST

☐ **TIME**

About three hours to run cable, install a baseboard heater and thermostat; about two and one-half hours to run cable and install a blower-heater

☐ **TOOLS**

Voltage tester, drill, ½-inch bit, drywall saw, fish tape, screwdriver, wire stripper, long-nose pliers, lineman's pliers

☐ **SKILLS**

Cutting into walls; stripping, splicing, and connecting wires to terminals; installing boxes; running cable into boxes

☐ **MATERIALS**

Heater, box for thermostat, 12/2 cable, electrician's tape, wire nuts, drywall screws

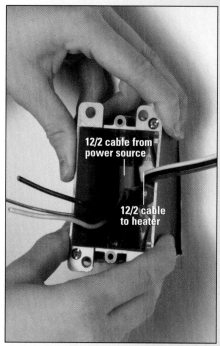

12/2 cable from power source

12/2 cable to heater

1 Cut an opening for a large-capacity remodel box. Run 12/2 cable to the location of the thermostat. **Do not connect the cable to its power source.** Run cable from the opening to the heater location. Strip cables and clamp in the box. Install the box *(page 171)*.

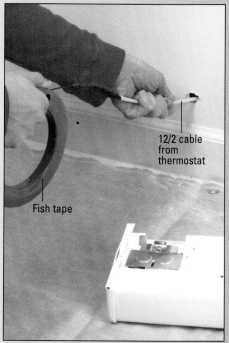

12/2 cable from thermostat

Fish tape

2 No junction box is required for the cable running to the heater—the box is built into the unit. Strip the incoming wires *(page 172)*. (You can also run the feeder line directly to the heater and then to the thermostat. Check the manufacturer's instructions.)

ASSEMBLING AND WIRING ELECTRIC HEATERS

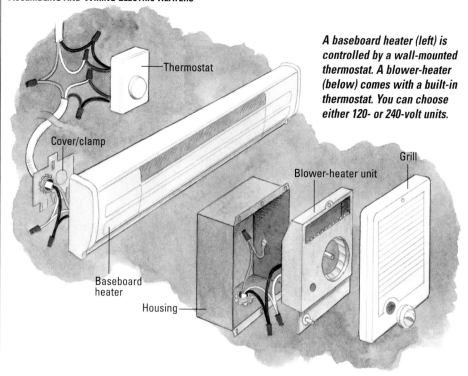

Thermostat

Cover/clamp

Baseboard heater

Housing

Blower-heater unit

Grill

A baseboard heater (left) is controlled by a wall-mounted thermostat. A blower-heater (below) comes with a built-in thermostat. You can choose either 120- or 240-volt units.

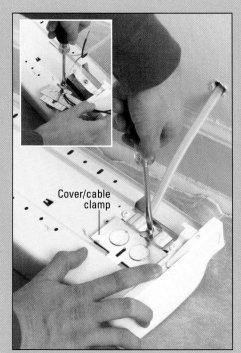

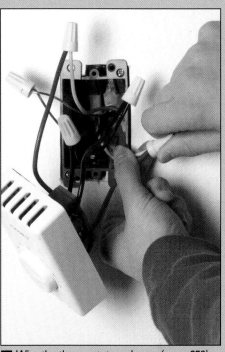

3 Place the heater face down on the floor and remove the cover/cable clamp. Attach the house ground line to the green screw on the heater (inset). Using wire nuts, connect incoming lines to the heater leads. Close and fasten the cover/clamp.

4 Locate and mark wall studs. Push the cable into the wall. Attach the unit with at least two 1½-inch drywall screws. Tighten, then back off a half turn to allow for the expansion and contraction of the metal housing when the unit is turned on and off.

5 Wire the thermostat as shown (page 256) using wire nuts and electrician's tape. Install the thermostat and snap on its cover. Connect to the power source or new circuit and test the unit.

WHAT IF…
You're installing a blower-heater?

A blower-heater unit fits between wall studs and is somewhat easier to wire because it has a self-contained thermostat. The unit shown runs on 240 volts. Check local codes for requirements.

A blower-heater must be a safe distance from nearby walls and furnishings. When choosing a location for the heater, maintain 12 inches from any adjacent walls. For safe and effective operation, locate the box 12 inches above the floor and keep the area clear 3 feet in front of the box. Check the manufacturer's recommendations before locating the unit.

Before cutting an opening for the unit, drill a finder hole and use a wire to check that the wall cavity is clear of pipes and wires (page 59). Use a drywall saw to cut the opening between studs. Run 12/2 cable to the opening.

1 Remove one of the knockouts in the housing. Insert a clamp and pull 10 inches of cable into the box. Clamp the cable and fasten the housing in place with 1-inch (longer if needed) drywall screws. Strip incoming wires (page 172).

2 Attach the incoming wires to the heater leads (page 256). Fasten the heater unit in the housing, being careful that the wires do not get caught between the motor and the housing. Attach the grill and thermostat knob. Connect to the power source.

GLOSSARY

Access panel: A removable panel in a wall or ceiling that permits repair or replacement.

Actual dimensions: The actual size of a tile as measured with a tape or ruler. *See also nominal size.*

Adapter: A plumbing fitting that makes it possible to go from male endings to female endings or vice versa.

Amp: Short for ampere, a measurement of the electrical current flowing through a wire or appliance.

Apron: The bottom piece of window casing that finishes the window frame beneath the sill (stool).

Back-butter: To apply mortar or adhesive to the rear face of a tile before setting it.

Backerboard: Any of several cement or gypsum-based sheets used as substrate for setting tile. *Also called cement board.*

Banding: Solid wood trim attached to plywood edges to conceal plies.

Baseboard: Trim running along the bottom of a wall to cover gaps between the wall and floor and to protect the bottom of the wall. *See also cap molding.*

Basin wrench: Special plumbing tool with a long shaft to reach into small spaces to loosen or tighten hold-down nuts.

Bearing wall: A wall that carries a portion of the weight of the building above it.

Biscuit joint: A joint that uses wooden wafers glued into slots cut in edges of mating pieces.

Bisque: The clay-and-liquid mixture that forms the body of the tile.

Blocking: Pieces of lumber that are nailed horizontally between wall studs to serve as anchor points for molding or cabinetry.

Buffalo box: A type of whole-house shutoff where the valve is in a plastic or concrete box set in the ground.

Bullnose tiles: Flat tile with at least one rounded edge. Used to trim the edges of a tiled installation. Also called caps.

Butt joint: A joint where ends of the two adjoining pieces are cut square and the pieces are simply placed against each other.

Cable: Two or more insulated wires wrapped in metal or plastic sheathing.

Cap molding: A molding made to be applied to the top edge of another material as a finishing treatment.

Cement-bodied tile: Tile whose bisque is formed of mortar as opposed to clay.

Circuit breaker: A protective device in a service panel that automatically shuts off power to its circuit when it senses a short or circuit overload.

Cleanout: A removable plug in a trap or a drainpipe that allows easier access to blockages inside.

Cleft: Describes process of forming stone paving pieces by splitting smaller pieces from larger rock.

Closet bend: The elbow-shape fitting beneath a toilet that carries waste to the main drain.

Continuity tester: A device that tells whether a circuit is capable of carrying electricity.

Corner bead: A plastic or metal molding that is attached to outside drywall corners to make them easier to finish and to protect them from damage.

Counterbore: A screw hole deep enough to accept a wooden plug after the screw is in place.

Countersink: A drilled hole that fits the shape of a woodscrew.

Coupling: A copper, galvanized steel, plastic, or brass fitting used to connect two lengths of pipe in a straight run.

Crosscut: A cut across the grain that reduces material to a desired length.

Dado (groove): A channel cut in wood that runs across the grain. A groove is a channel that runs with the grain.

Deadman: A T-shape brace used to help hold drywall in place against ceiling joists while drywall is fastened in place.

Dielectric fitting: This fitting joins pipes of dissimilar metals to insulate the pipes from an otherwise corrosive chemical reaction.

Dimension lumber: Lumber that is 2 to 5 inches in nominal thickness and up to 12 inches in nominal width.

Diverter: A valve on a faucet that changes the flow of water from a faucet spout to a hand sprayer or showerhead.

Dowel: A cylindrical piece of wood, often a joint reinforcement.

Drum trap: Found in older homes, this cylindrical trap is built into the floor and covered with a brass, chrome-plated, or expandable cap.

Dry-fit: Preliminary joining of wood or other materials without glue to check fit.

Elbow: A fitting used to change the direction of a water supply line. Also known as an ell.

Face frame: A four-piece wooden assembly attached to the front of a cabinet.

Fall: A word used to express the slope of drain lines.

Field tiles: Flat tiles with unrounded edges used within the edges of a tiled installation.

Fire stop: A piece of wood nailed across a stud bay to prevent the bay from acting as a chimney and conduit for fire.

Fitting: Any connector (except a valve) that lets you join pipes.

Flow restrictor: A device found in some showerheads to restrict the flow of water and thus reduce water use.

Flush: Having the same surface or plane as an adjoining surface.

Flux: A stiff jelly brushed or smeared on the surfaces of copper and brass pipes and fittings before joining them.

Green bisque: Clay that has not been fired (not a reference to its color).

Greenboard: A moisture-resistant drywall product made for wet installations, such as baths and showers. Greenboard is not waterproof.

Hammer arrester: A shock-absorbing device that provides a cushion of air to prevent water hammer—sudden surges in water pressure that sometimes result in noisy pipes.

I.D.: The abbreviation for inside diameter. All plumbing pipes are sized according to their inside diameter. *See also O.D.*

J-bead: A molding made to cover the edge of a drywall sheet so the raw edge does not show in the finished product.

Jig: A device that holds a workpiece or tool in a certain way to efficiently and accurately saw or shape wood.

Kerf: The slot left by a saw blade as it cuts through material.

Latex-modified thinset: Thinset mortar mixed with latex additive to increase its flexibility, resistance to water, and adhesion.

Middle-of-run: A receptacle located between the service panel and another receptacle.

Miter: An angle, often 45 degrees, cut across the grain on a piece of wood.

Molding: Shaped wood used as trim.

Mortar: Any mixture of masonry cement, sand, water, and other additives. Also describes the action of applying mortar to surfaces or joints.

Mortise: An opening cut in a piece of wood to accept a mating piece of wood (tenon).

Mud: Trade jargon for cement-based mortars.

Nipple: A 12-inch or shorter pipe with threads on both ends that is used to join fittings.

No-hub fitting: A neoprene gasket with a stainless-steel band that tightens to join PVC drain pipe to ABS or cast-iron pipe.

Nominal size: The designated dimension of a pipe or fitting or piece of lumber. It varies slightly from the actual size.

O.D.: The abbreviation for outside diameter. *See also I.D.*

Open time: The interval between application of adhesive and when it can no longer be worked; also called working time.

Organic mastic: One of several petroleum or latex-based adhesives for setting tiles. Exhibits less strength, flexibility, and resistance to water than thinset adhesives.

Packing: A plastic or metallic cord-like material used chiefly around faucet stems. When compressed it results in a watertight seal.

Partition wall: A wall whose only purpose is to divide a space—it does not contribute to supporting the weight of the building.

Pigtail: A short length of wire spliced with two or more wires in a box and connected to a terminal so that two or more wires will not be attached to a terminal.

Plumb: A surface that lies on a true vertical plane.

Plunge cut: Starting a saw in wood away from an edge.

Pocket-hole: A joining technique that employs screws driven into holes drilled at an angle.

Polymer-modified: A substance like grout or mortar to which an acrylic or latex solution has been added to increase its strength and workability.

Rabbet: A channel sawed or formed on the edge of a board or panel.

Radius trim: A trim tile whose edge turns down to form a smooth, glazed border.

Rail: One of the two horizontal pieces in a face frame.

Reducer: A fitting with different size openings at either end used to go from a larger to a smaller pipe.

Reveal: A narrow flat area on a molding or board left purposely uncovered for visual effect.

GLOSSARY *(continued)*

Revent: A pipe that connects a fixture drain pipe to a main or secondary vent stack.

Rip-cut: To reduce a wide board by sawing with the grain; a cut along the long dimension of a sheet or panel.

Riser: A pipe supplying water to a location or a supply tube running from a pipe to a sink or toilet.

Rough-in: The early stages of a plumbing project during which supply and drain-waste-vent lines are run to their destinations.

Rout: Shaping or cutting wood with a router and bit.

Run: Any length of pipe or pipes and fittings going in a straight line.

Saddle-tee valve: A fitting used to tap into a water line without having to cut the line apart. Some local codes prohibit its use.

Sanded grout: Grout containing sand, which increases the strength and decreases the contraction of the joint.

Sanitary fitting: Any of several connectors used to join drain-waste-vent lines. Their design helps direct waste downward.

Sanitary sewer: Underground drainage network that carries liquid and solid wastes to a treatment plant.

Self-rimming sink: Common type of kitchen or bathroom sink that includes a formed lip that rests on the countertop, holding the sink in place.

Semi-vitreous tile: Tile of moderate density that exhibits only a partial resistance to water and other liquids.

Septic tank: A reservoir that collects and separates liquid and solid wastes, then digests the organic material and passes the liquid waste onto a drainage field.

Service entrance: The point where power from the utility enters the house.

Service panel: A large electrical box containing either fuses or circuit breakers.

Slake: To allow a masonry mixture additional time after initial mixing. Allows the liquid to thoroughly penetrate the solids.

Soil stack: The main vertical drainpipe that carries waste toward the sewer drain.

Square: Surfaces exactly perpendicular or at 90 degrees to another. Also describes a hand tool used to determine square.

Stand pipe: A special pipe that connects a washing machine drain hose to the drain system.

Stile: One of the two vertical pieces in a face frame.

Straightedge: A metal or wood implement clamped to the workpiece to ensure a straight cut.

Stubout: A brass drop-ear elbow that has one threaded opening and two holes that can be screwed tightly against a wall. Some can be sweated; some have threaded ends.

Subfloor: A layer of wood sheet material, generally plywood, used to provide a stable foundation for other flooring materials.

Substrate: Any of several layers, including the subfloor, beneath a tile surface.

Tailpiece: That part of a fixture drain that runs from the drain outlet to the trap.

Tee: A T-shape fitting used to tap into a length of pipe at a 90-degree angle to begin a branch line.

Toe-kick: The wood part that is recessed beneath a cabinet base.

Trap: Part of a fixture drain required by code that creates a water seal to prevent sewer gases from penetrating a home's interior.

Union: A fitting used in runs of threaded pipe to facilitate disconnecting the line (without having to cut it).

V-cap: V-shape trim, often with a rounded upper corner, used to edge countertops.

Veneer: Thin sheets or strips of solid wood.

Vent: The vertical or sloping horizontal portion of a drain line that permits sewer gases to rise out of the house. Every fixture in a house must be vented.

Vent stack: The upper portion of a vertical drain line through which gases pass to the outside.

Vitreous tile: An extremely dense ceramic tile with a high resistance to water absorption.

Wet wall: A strategically placed cavity (usually a 2×6 wall) in which the main drain/vent stack and a cluster of supply and drain-waste-vent lines are housed.

Y: A Y-shape drainage fitting that serves as the starting point for a branch drain supplying one or more fixtures.

INDEX

METRIC CONVERSIONS

U.S. Units to Metric Equivalents			Metric Units to U.S. Equivalents		
To convert from	**Multiply by**	**To get**	**To convert from**	**Multiply by**	**To get**
Inches	25.4	Millimeters	Millimeters	0.0394	Inches
Inches	2.54	Centimeters	Centimeters	0.3937	Inches
Feet	30.48	Centimeters	Centimeters	0.0328	Feet
Feet	0.3048	Meters	Meters	3.2808	Feet
Yards	0.9144	Meters	Meters	1.0936	Yards
Square inches	6.4516	Square centimeters	Square centimeters	0.1550	Square inches
Square feet	0.0929	Square meters	Square meters	10.764	Square feet
Square yards	0.8361	Square meters	Square meters	1.1960	Square yards
Acres	0.4047	Hectares	Hectares	2.4711	Acres
Cubic inches	16.387	Cubic centimeters	Cubic centimeters	0.0610	Cubic inches
Cubic feet	0.0283	Cubic meters	Cubic meters	35.315	Cubic feet
Cubic feet	28.316	Liters	Liters	0.0353	Cubic feet
Cubic yards	0.7646	Cubic meters	Cubic meters	1.308	Cubic yards
Cubic yards	764.55	Liters	Liters	0.0013	Cubic yards

To convert from degrees Fahrenheit (F) to degrees Celsius (C), first subtract 32, then multiply by $\frac{5}{9}$.

To convert from degrees Celsius to degrees Fahrenheit, multiply by $\frac{9}{5}$, then add 32.

KNOWLEDGE IS
THE BEST TOOL

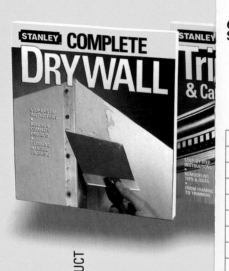

643.52
S

Stanley complete
baths.

DATE			

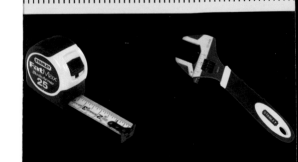

ENHANCE

MAINTAIN